KERNEL LESSONS

KERNEL LESSONS INTERMEDIATE

TEACHER'S BOOK

ROBERT O'NEILL
ROY KINGSBURY
TONY YEADON

EUROCENTRE

LONGMAN

LONGMAN GROUP LIMITED
London
Associated companies, branches and representatives throughout the world.

© **Eurozentren 1971**

All rights reserved. No part of this publication may be reproduced, stored in a retrieval system, or transmitted in any form or by any means, electronic, mechanical, photocopying, recording, or otherwise, without the prior permission of the Copyright owner.

First published 1971
New impression 1979
I S B N 0 582 52241 2

Printed in Hong Kong by
Commonwealth Printing Press Ltd

Eurocentre Research and Development Unit, Bournemouth.

Illustrated by James Val

ACKNOWLEDGEMENTS

Many people helped the authors at various times while this book was being written and it would be impossible to mention all of them. We wish, however, to give particular mention to:

Miss Jean McNiff, who did the original artwork for the first pilot editions and whose time, attention and criticism later was invaluable in producing the final version.

Miss D. King and Miss J. Croad, who did all the demanding typing involved in the pilot editions and in the final version.

The staffs of the Bournemouth Eurocentre, and the London Eurocentre, who gave a great deal of constructive criticism and comment based on their experience of using the material.

Robert O'Neill, Roy Kingsbury, Tony Yeadon.
June 1970.

Contents

Foreword
Introduction
The Tests and Entry Test
Students' Introduction

Unit 1 **Present simple and position of time adverbs**
2 **Present continuous**
3 **Simple past tense Regular and irregular verbs**
4 **Mass and unit**
5 **Some, any, a few, a little**
6 **Past tense with 'Ago' and questions with 'How long ago?'**
7 **Adjectives and adverbs**
8 **Comparison of adverbs**
9 **Going to do**
10 **Requests and offers and Take/get/bring/show someone something**
11 **Present perfect with 'For' and 'Since'**
12 **Have been doing/have just done/haven't done yet/had better do**
13 **Past continuous and past simple**
14 **Simple future used in requests, offers, and of 'Must' and 'Can'**
15 **Present perfect + 'Just' + preview of contrast with simple past**
16 **Present perfect and past simple**
17 **Frequent gerund constructions**
18 **Future simple with 'If' or 'When' and present simple clause**
19 **Common patterns with verb + him/her/etc. + infinitive with/without 'To'**
20 **Future in the past**
21 **Past perfect**
22 **Conditional sentences**
23 **Passive voice in present perfect and past**
24 **Reported speech**
25 **Past conditional**
Irregular verb list

Foreword

This book represents a further step in our efforts to provide the language-teacher with modern techniques and materials in areas not yet fully covered. Our first four publications were concerned with teaching method and were intended for the teacher. The fifth, *English in Situations,* was course material for the use of both teacher and student.

Kernel Lessons Intermediate is a new development in that it makes a clear-cut division between teacher and student material and contains a full programme of separate materials for the student. This programme, specially designed for the 'faux débutant' or post-elementary student, consists of written material (exercises and informational texts), pictures and tapes.

In the introduction to the Teacher's Book a description is given of how this material can be put to the best use. Both the techniques here described and the course-material itself were continuously utilised and revised in the English Eurocentres for over 2 years before publication.

We believe that with this book we are meeting a real need and that through it teachers and students at this particular level will find more interest and satisfaction in language-teaching and learning.

Erh. J. C. Waespi
Director of the Foundation for European Language and Educational Centres.

The Eurocentres are a group of language schools directed by the Foundation for European Language and Educational Centres, Zürich. The schools offer full-time courses for adult students all the year round, and each language is taught in the country where it is spoken.

Introduction *Very important*

Introductions like this are frequently written but seldom read. Please regard this book as no more than a tool and this introduction as no more and no less than the instructions you get whenever you buy a new tool. This general introduction contains the absolute minimum of essential information. The rest of the introduction gives precise suggestions about how to use the book.

1. This is the Teacher's Book and it contains all the material in the Students' Book as well as special teacher's material.
2. The book has 25 units. There are six pages in each unit in the Students' Book. Your book has ten pages in each unit.
3. Except for the very first two pages of each unit, there is always one teacher's page for each student's page. On the teacher's page the unit is always given in a black box whereas in the Students' Book the unit number is always given in a white box. This happens on every page.
4. The teacher's material is on one page; the students' material is on the opposite page.
5. The first two pages of each unit in your book are almost exactly what the student sees in his. The difference is only that the pictures on the very first page have been reduced in size. What the student does not have on his page are the main teaching points and extra points and activities directly under the pictures.
6. These first two pages are called the Presentation Pages. In the first presentation the student will look only at the pictures on the left hand page and will cover the right hand page with a special mask we have provided. This right hand page contains the texts that explain each picture or situation on the left hand page.
7. The Students' Book has five main components:
   (a) Presentation material (2 pages)
   (b) Formation and Manipulation (1 page)
   (c) Episode (1 page)
   (d) Further Practice (1 page)
   (e) Summary and Exercises for Homework (1 page)

See page ix–xii of this introduction for a further description. The purpose of each page is explained to the student in his book (see page xviii–xix).

8. The Presentation situations, the Episode, and the Conversation on the Further Practice page have been recorded. The teacher can use either the tape or the printed page or both. The recording of the Episode never deviates from the text but it does use sound effects and other elements which add to the dramatic value of the text.
9. The Students' Book also has an introduction. We strongly recommend that you should go through this introduction with the class. At first at the beginning of the term, you can summarise the introduction in the language of the class if that class is monolingual. Later, either in the middle or at the end of the term, it might be very useful to go through the introduction again. If the class is not monolingual ask them to read it at home with the use of a dictionary if necessary. The introduction should not be too difficult however to be read entirely in English by the class.
10. Please look at the following pages of the introduction now to see how the material can best be used.

To the Teacher

1. *Who is the course for?*
   It is for these two types.
   (a) Intermediate students who are fresh from an *intensive* beginners' course.
   (b) What the French call 'faux débutants'.

Students who belong to the second category have studied English before and probably have been spoiled by it. They have not mastered what was presented to them, frequently because it was not presented to them correctly. They may have been hurried through a series of exercises on various things which gave them no real control of them at all. They may have been taught a few rules but were never given enough practice to master what the rules describe. They are a very special problem. We suspect that this type is far more common than many teachers realise. We also suspect that they are far more common in the world today than real beginners.

Both types of intermediate student have certain common problems. They both need practice in certain very basic things, but no teacher can afford simply to treat them like beginners who have failed. They have to be motivated either to revise or to learn properly some of the fundamentals of English. This means that when these fundamentals are reintroduced, the contexts and vocabulary must be challenging and different from what would be used with beginners. The material used for them must also contain a certain amount of 'Problem-Setting.' 'Problem-Setting' does not mean one sets deliberate traps for them to fall into. This is emphatically not what is meant. 'Problem-Setting' means simply that students should be given natural situations in which they have to use a pattern quickly and without prior warning.

2. *Upon what principles was the course designed?*

These were our design-criteria:

(i) The material must make possible the maximum amount of oral participation from the class.

(ii) Teachers must be able to adapt it to their teaching-styles rather than have to adapt their teaching-styles to it. The only provision is that teachers using this course must be willing to engage in active oral teaching and try to engage the class in as much response as possible.

(iii) Some of the material must be inessential. That is: teachers can use it if they wish, or use their own material instead.

(iv) The material must be written with its use in class firmly in mind. The writers must ask themselves whether the material is to be used (a) by the teacher with class (b) by the student alone, or (c) by the teacher with the class and then by the student alone.

An illustration of why this is necessary is the substitution table. Substitution Tables are often difficult to use in class because there seems really very little for the teacher to do except tell the class to look at the table. Substitution tables are really designed to be used individually by students alone, who generate sentences by combining all the elements in the table. In other words, substitution tables are meant to be used at home, and so have their rightful place in that part of the book which is supposed simply to be looked at and worked with at home. The teacher needs something else. This something else is provided here by substitution drills, so designed that the teacher can fire individual prompts at individual students. Precisely what is meant here can be seen by looking at the formation and manipulation page of any unit. What is meant for teacher and class use appears on the right-hand page. Student use material is on the left. Compare the two types of material.

(v) The material must allow for very intensive and less intensive kinds of learning. Students need a rest from intensive phases of activity, but even in the less intensive phases, their attention and interest still have to be engaged.

(vi) The materials must make it possible for the teacher to phase lessons. That is, lessons or sessions must be phased to allow for different kinds of activity. We are not thinking now only of active and less active phases, but of complete changes in the nature of activity and the combination of physical-senses used. 'A change is as good as a rest' has been quoted before as a good maxim for language-teachers.

Detailed description with suggested mode of use for each component—

 PRESENTATION PAGES

Physical Description

Always the first two pages of each unit in both Teacher's and Students' Books. Left-hand page has pictures which depict texts of situations on right-hand page. There are always between four to six situations and accompanying pictures in each unit.
Example: See Unit 1, part a, pages 2 and 3.

Mode of Use

The teacher presents each situation orally. The class looks only at pictures in this phase. They cover right-hand page with mask provided in their book. Thus, their attention is directed solely to the picture and the teacher's oral presentation. No interference from written text or tendency to 'read ahead of teacher'.

After oral presentation and intensive question and answer work, the teacher can give his class a short break by telling them to uncover right-hand page, read texts and ask any questions about things not understood. Stress to class that they will have chance to ask such questions but should not worry during oral presentation about occasional word they have not understood. First, they should try and get idea of complete situation. They can worry about details later.

In oral presentation, the teacher should use questions printed in book as stage *after* 'Closed Question Practice'. The teacher first asks a number of lower memory-load questions. For example, in presenting situation 1, Unit 1, the teacher might ask first questions like these:

> Does Julia Frost work in a factory?
> Does she usually get there on time?
> Is she late or early this morning?
> Does the manager know she often comes late?

This is a less complicated type of question than those printed with the situation. Such questions help establish all the details of the situation if asked before questions in book. Another device is the 'Correct these statements' technique. The teacher says something that is grammatically but not factually correct about the situation, like this (again, about situation 1, Unit 1):

> Julia Frost works in a small office
> (Class: No, she works in a large office)
> She never gets there late
> (Class: No, she often gets there late)

Observe that on the left-hand page, next to each picture, there are a number of 'prompts'. These suggest questions that the class can ask in 'paired practice'. After the teacher has made sure that the class has grasped the pattern and its use, and can handle questions with it, he can ask the class to pair off into groups of two or three and ask and answer the questions suggested by those prompts. If you do this, tell the class to talk quietly and not to shout. Then move among them, listening to their work. This should come at the *end* of the intensive question and answer phase, that is, after you have asked closed questions and gone on to those in the book.

Rationale and Aim

To give students a clear idea of one main type of situation in which to use the pattern. In other words, an idea of when to use the pattern in this meaning. To do this in such a way that the student can form his own conclusions inductively. The teacher may or may not decide to offer a verbal rule. However, whether or not rules are used, they are not enough in themselves. The teacher must also have some safeguard against mere verbal learning; students often learn only the words of the rule and nothing else.

Level of Activity

Very intensive throughout, except for brief pauses.

 FORMATION AND MANIPULATION

Physical Description

Always on the second page of each unit. In the teacher's book, of course, two pages.

Consists of special comments on stress and

pronunciation, and above all, material that points out basic features of the construction of each pattern, such as substitution tables and 'generative matrixes'.

Mode of Use

The material on the students' page is designed to be looked at and worked from. The generative matrixes will help the class to make their own examples. The substitution tables will give them more fluency practice. This page can often be started in class and finished at home. The teacher may find it useful to create short pauses with this material after intensive oral work. Simply direct the class to look at the page or some item on it for a minute. Then ask questions. With unit 1, questions and exercises might be:

Make these sentences into questions now!
1. He works in a factory.
2. Julia lives in a large house. etc.

Often, such exercises are written out on the page. When this is so, use them orally. After the class has seen them, ask them to turn the book face down and go through the exercises quickly, and orally.

There is also special fluency practice material on the teacher's page. A glance at unit 1 will demonstrate this. This is optional, to be used at the discretion of the teacher. Much of the material here will suggest or adapt itself to language-laboratory work.

Rationale and Aim

After the class has seen the pattern under study in the context of the presentation situations, they also need a chance to focus attention on particular features of the pattern. This is a more analytical phase than the previous one. It can also be, as already mentioned, a break and a variation from the first phase. Above all, this material helps students to make analogies and comparisons, and to note particular points.

Level of Activity

Less intensive than the presentation pages.

 THE EPISODE

Physical Description

Again, one leaf. Always third part of each unit. Each Student Page an episode. Together, all the episodes form a continuous story. The Teacher Page consists of suggested explanations, questions and answers, suggestions for further exercises and activities.

Use and Rationale

The vocabulary load here is much heavier than in the situations in the presentation phase. This is deliberate. First, the vocabulary is often taught for recognition rather than for production, i.e. the class is not expected to make full and automatic use of it. We believe that before truly active knowledge can be gained, the student must often be exposed to its elements repeatedly and over a certain period of time. In the presentation we make use, to a certain extent, of the students' previous passive knowledge; in the episode we replace some of this passive knowledge now activated.

The episodes have all been recorded. The recorded version rarely lasts more than four minutes and frequently less. The teacher can use either this version or the printed page. He may choose to use both. The recorder, if used, should always have a pause control, so that at any point the teacher can stop and ask questions.

The teacher should often encourage students to do two things whenever unfamiliar vocabulary occurs. These two things are:

(i) to guess at the meaning by examining the context
(ii) to ignore words if they do not appear to be essential.

In real life, students will often have to deal with English they have not yet learned. They will often have no chance to consult a dictionary. When watching television or listening to directions given in the street, for instance, you cannot look up words without losing the thread of what is being said.

The episode should provide some *controlled*

practice in coping without a dictionary. The two techniques already mentioned are essential if the student is not to confine his reading to simplified texts all the time. Above all, students should learn not to become anxious or focus their attention on the wrong things when they hear unfamiliar vocabulary. To focus on the wrong thing means, in this case, to focus on what is unfamiliar rather than all the other clues to the meaning found in what is familiar. Students tend to do the first rather than the second.

Aims

Although various kinds of intensive study can result from this material, and have even been indicated in the teacher's page, this phase is designed generally to lower intensity without lowering attentiveness and (we hope) interest-level as well. The class can and should participate actively, but that participation is not always as demanding as elsewhere.

 FURTHER PRACTICE

Physical Description

Again, one leaf. Consists of various kinds of exercise, of which all, a part, or none may be used. The exercises are:

(i) Practice Situations
(ii) Invention Exercises
(iii) Transformation Exercises
(iv) Conversations
(v) Very short reading passages

The first two are new in type.

Practice Situations do not call for transformation of the structure or a filling in of the blank. They consist of usually no more than two sentences which describe a situation. The situation calls for the use of a particular pattern.

Invention Exercises are simply single-word prompts that suggest whole sentences. They force the student to supply all the lexical content of his response himself. For instance, if the pattern under study is:

'Tom was reading a paper when I saw him', the word *lunch* produces 'Tom was eating lunch when I saw him.'

Use, Rationale and Aims

The Conversations need a special note. Their purpose is to introduce socially useful phrases like 'Don't mention it' and 'I wonder if I could . . .?', and also to show the pattern under study in further, conventional contexts.

The tape-recorder, although not essential, is particularly valuable here. The teacher should ask the class to listen to, and *not* to look at the conversation first. This is why the conversations have all been recorded.

The teacher can play the conversations several times. We strongly recommend that the class should get practice in listening to this material without the aid of the text. Intonation patterns and other things, all described on the teacher's page, can be practised.

The material, after it has been thoroughly practised, should then be read by the class. Any reading aloud by the class should come only after the class has had a good chance to listen to and practise pronunciation and intonation. As a relaxation, the class can often be asked to play the parts in the conversation themselves.

The Reading Passages, which are scattered throughout the book, are designed to introduce students to the sort of English encountered in newspapers, instructions, etc.

 THE SUMMARY

Physical Description

Always one leaf. Summary and additional exercises.

Use, Rationale and Aims

The summary simply states what the student has already learned. It gives a verbal rounding-off to

The Tests

the knowledge the student should have gained. It can be ignored by the teacher, or read in class briefly.

The additional Exercises provide conventional forms of homework exercise with the main structure taught in the Unit.

Special composition material has also been included. At first, it is usually 'guided' or 'controlled' material, and the purpose and reasons for using this sort of material should be explained to the class carefully. The teacher may refer the class to the notes in the Students' Book about this.

Later, the composition material becomes much freer. Throughout the book, this material will lend itself to very useful work by the student, involving him in the writing of letters, telling short stories, writing similar situations to those on the presentation page, news items, etc.

The tests which have been constructed to accompany this book are intended to help the teacher answer the important questions about his students. The questions are:
(i) How ready are my students to begin learning from this particualr course book? Or, put another way: how much of the prerequisite knowledge necessary to use the book have my students got, and how much do they need to revise before they start using the book?
(ii) How much have my students learnt after 5, 10, 15, 20 or 25 Units?
(iii) How much have my students learnt now that they have finished the course, i.e. now that they have finished the book?

To help the teacher answer these questions, we have constructed a series of tests which consists of an Entry Test, five Progress Tests, and an Exit Test.

The Entry Test, of which there is a copy on the next few pages, is a 50-item multiple choice Test, designed to be administered in 25 minutes. It tests students' knowledge of a number of grammatical patterns and structures which are taught in the majority of beginners' courses and which are assumed known at the beginning of this book. This Test can be used not only to give an indication of the students' proficiency on entering the course, but also diagnostically. This means that a teacher can quickly see which points the class ought to revise before they start to use the book.

The Progress Tests are designed as formal achievement test to be administered to a class at the end of each group of five Units. Each Test is specifically designed to test students' knowledge of the preceding five Units, and each uses a variety of testing techniques to achieve this aim. Multiple choice is only one of the techniques employed: other techniques mirror some of the types of exercises which the student will have become used to whilst learning from the book. In the main, the Progress Tests are production tests, in which answers must be written, and not simply indicated with a cross or a tick, as is the case with the Entry Test. We are certain that most teachers will also use these Progress Tests diagnostically, revising,

Entry Test

reviewing or if necessary re-teaching those particular points which students do not seem to have mastered.

The Exit Test is an achievement test based on the whole of the book. Naturally it cannot hope to test *everything* which the book sets out to teach—even the Progress Tests do not test *everthing*. But it does test a large sample of the English which the students should have acquired while learning from the book. As with the Entry Test, we have given a suggested grading scheme which the teacher can use when assessing students' individual achievement on the whole course.

The Tests. A copy of the Entry Test, together with relevant information regarding the assumed knowledge of students about to use the course, and a copy of the Marking Key follows on the next few pages, and is provided for the teacher's information. It does *not* appear in the Students' book. The full series of tests, comprising the Entry Test, five Progress Tests, and the Exit Test, is available as a separate publication. There is also an accompanying Teacher's Book which contains the Keys to all the tests, together with other relevant information. Full details of both may be obtained from Longman Group Ltd., Longman House, Burnt Mill, Harlow, Essex.

The Entry Test, of which there is a copy in the next few pages and about which there is more information in the separate Test Book publication, is designed to measure students' control of those structures in English which are taken as prerequisites for study from this book. If a student is going to gain the maximum use and benefit from the book, we assume that he or she has an active knowledge of certain basic structures in the language, together with a passive or recognition knowledge of other structures. Some of the latter will in fact be activated in the book. The Entry Test tests at least recognition of some of the following:

(i) *this / that / these / those – the / a / an*
(ii) personal pronouns – *I / me / my / mine* etc.
(iii) *there is / it is*
(iv) the verbs *be* and *have* in the Present, all persons, statements, questions and negatives
(v) use of the Simple Present in statements, questions and negatives; and with frequency adverbs such as *often / never / always* etc.
(vi) use of Present Continuous in statements, questions and negatives
(vii) *want to do* and *want someone to do*
(viii) partative use of *of,* as in 'a piece *of* cheese'
(ix) concepts of Mass and Unit with *much / many / a lot of / a few / a little*
(x) use of future *going to do* in statements, questions and negatives
(xi) prepositions of (a) place – *in / at / on* etc.
    (b) time – *at 6 / on Friday / in 1963*
    (c) movement – *over / across / under / into* etc.
    (d) with certain verbs, e.g. *listen to*
(xii) Past tense (+ past pointer words *yesterday, last week,* etc.) with *be* (*was / were*) *have* (*had*) and other regular and irregular verbs in statements, questions and negatives
(xiii) question words *Who / Where / What / Why / When / How*; and the distinction between *why* and *because*
(xiv) adjectives; comparisons with *older than, more beautiful than* and *as old as*; superlatives – *biggest* and *most important*
(xv) adverbs with *-ly* or *-illy* – e.g. *carefully*

(xvi) *give / take someone something*
(xvii) *can / should / ought to / have to* in statements, questions and negatives

It should be stressed that the Entry Test cannot possibly test each of the items in the list above; it only samples knowledge of those items listed.

The Test is completely objective, consists of 50 multiple choice (A, B, C) items, and can be administered within 30 minutes. The time given to the students for actually doing the test is 25 minutes and this should be strictly adhered to. The marking of the test for a group of, let us say, 18 students should not take much longer than 10 minutes, although the interpretation of the results and decisions upon what action to take with the group or with individuals will naturally vary according to the situation. Although the main purpose of the test is to show how ready students are to begin working from the book, it can also be used as a diagnostic instrument. Fuller information about this and about scoring and grading are given in the Teacher's Book to accompany the Kernel Lessons Test Book. Here, we have only given the Marking Key (see below).

We sincerely hope that this Entry Test will help teachers in all situations to see whether the students they are teaching or are about to teach are really ready to use the book, or if they are not, what revision needs to be done before turning to Unit 1.

ENTRY TEST MARKING KEY

S.1	1. A	S.4	16. B	S.6	36. C
	2. B		17. C		37. A
	3. C		18. A		38. A
	4. B		19. C		39. B
	5. C		20. A		40. A
			21. C		
			22. B		
S.2	6. B		23. C	S.7	41. B
	7. B		24. C		42. C
	8. C		25. A		43. B
	9. A				44. C
	10. B				45. C
		S.5	26. B		
			27. A		
S.3	11. C		28. A	S.8	46. C
	12. C		29. B		47. A
	13. C		30. C		48. A
	14. A		31. B		49. A
	15. B		32. A		50. B
			33. C		
			34. C		
			35. B		

Entry Test

KERNEL LESSONS INTERMEDIATE
ENTRY TEST

Time: 25 minutes

To the student

DO NOT BEGIN UNTIL YOU ARE TOLD TO DO SO.

This test will help you to see how ready you are to begin learning English from this book, and what you should perhaps revise before you start Unit 1.

The test consists of 8 Sections, 50 items altogether.

Read each of the items carefully and work as quickly as possible. Do not guess.

If you do not know the answer to one item, go on to the next. You only have 25 minutes to complete the test.

There is only one correct answer to each item.

Examples are given to show you how to answer the questions.

DO NOT WRITE ANYTHING IN THIS BOOKLET. Write all your answers on a separate sheet of paper which your teacher will give you.

Instructions: Choose the word or phrase (A, B or C) which is correct in the sentence.

EXAMPLE I: 52 { A. am / B. is / C. are } tired today.

Only 'A' is correct, so you write 52A on your answer sheet.

EXAMPLE II: 78 When you want fruit you go to { A. the chemist's / B. the butcher's / C. the greengrocer's }

Only 'C' is correct, so you write 78C on your answer sheet.

Section 1

1. { A. These / B. This / C. That } oranges are very good.

2. Are { A. that / B. those / C. there } people very nice?

3. { A. It has / B. It is / C. There is } a dog in the garden.

4. What's that? { A. They / B. It / C. There } is my new car.

5. { A. Their / B. They're / C. There } is a good film at the Odeon.

Section 2

6. I { A. has / B. have / C. had } to go to town tomorrow.

7. You ought { A. stay / B. to stay / C. staying } at home.

8. He { A. knows / B. knows to / C. can } speak English.

9. He should { A. write / B. to write / C. writing } a letter.

10. Do you want { A. see / B. to see / C. seeing } the film?

xv

Section 3

11. I hope John's got { A. a / B. any / C. some } money.

12. He is { A. engineer / B. one engineer / C. an engineer }

13. I'd like { A. any / B. an / C. some } eggs, please.

14. We've got { A. a few / B. a little / C. a number } eggs left.

15. There aren't { A. a lot / B. many / C. much } people here today.

Section 4

16. { A. Is / B. Does / C. Has } she get up early every day?

17. Were you in London last week? No, I { A. didn't / B. weren't / C. wasn't }

18. She often { A. has / B. have / C. is having } a bath in the morning.

19. He { A. loses / B. has lost / C. lost } his hat last week.

20. They { A. caught / B. catch / C. catches } the 7.30 bus yesterday.

21. Mary is here, but her parents { A. isn't / B. wasn't / C. aren't }

22. He { A. hurries / B. hurried / C. hurry } because he was late.

23. { A. Doesn't / B. Does / C. Isn't } she going to do anything today?

24. They { A. watch / B. is watching / C. are watching } television at the moment

25. { A. Did you do / B. Do you do / C. Did you } much work yesterday?

Section 5 (Note: '–' means 'nothing', 'no word or words'.)

26. Who is she looking { A. on / B. at / C. to } ?

27. This is a nice piece { A. of / B. off / C. – } cheese.

28. Our holidays are { A. in / B. at / C. on } June.

29. They're listening { A. at / B. to / C. – } the news.

30. We came here { A. on / B. at / C. in } 1965.

31. What's the matter { A. by / B. with / C. from } him?

32. Your glasses are { A. in / B. of / C. into } the bathroom.

33. Stop him! He's going to jump { A. on / B. onto / C. into } the river!

xvi

34. No large ships can go { A. over / B. across / C. under } that bridge.

35. It's time for coffee. All the students are coming { A. off / B. out of / C. out } their lessons.

Section 6

36. This book is { A. my / B. me / C. mine }

37. She would like to meet { A. you / B. your / C. to you }

38. Give the money { A. to them / B. them / C. theirs } !

39. Whose is that big house? It's { A. her / B. hers / C. to her }

40. We're going to { A. our / B. us / C. ours } favourite shop.

Section 7

41. It is much { A. warm / B. warmer / C. more warm } here.

42. She is not as old { A. that / B. than / C. as } I am.

43. He's { A. very / B. more / C. plus } intelligent than I am.

44. He drives { A. more careful / B. very careful / C. very carefully }

45. Yesterday was the { A. very hot / B. most hot / C. hottest } day so far this year.

Section 8

46. { A. Where / B. Why / C. Who } wrote that letter?

47. She went home early { A. because / B. while / C. without } she had finished her work.

48. { A. Where / B. Who / C. When } did you put it?

49. { A. How / B. Why / C. Where } is Bill?' 'Very well, thanks.'

50. I'm going home to change first. { A. Than / B. Then / C. Therefore } I'm going out for a meal.

Introduction *To the Student*

Who is this book for?

This book has been specially written for Intermediate Students.

These are the special problems:

(i) You perhaps feel that you are no longer making very much progress. Somehow, it seems you are not learning as much as you did when you were a beginner.

(ii) Perhaps you realise that you need practice in some of the fundamentals of English. However, the type of practice you need is not the type of practice beginners need in these fundamentals.

(iii) There is a lot you have already studied but which you have not yet learned. In other words, there are many things which you can understand and have even practised, but which you still cannot use correctly, quickly, and as automatically as a native English-speaker does.

What exactly are the problems?

Problem (i) is probably the most important from the students' point of view. For teachers, problems (ii) and (iii) are the most important. These last two are really almost the same. Let us study each problem.

(i) The feeling that you are making little or no progress.

This is very common. It is partly true and partly an illusion. It is true because after you have passed the beginner's stage in anything, languages, mathematics, science, etc., you always reach a point where it is impossible to learn as much as you did before. This is because things are now more complicated, or seem to be.

It is partly an illusion because a great deal of the progress you make after the beginner's stage is not clear. At the beginner's stage, when you first learn a new thing, you can go away and say 'Today I learned this.' But, of course, you did not really learn it. You only saw it for the first time. But did you learn to use it automatically? Did you learn to use it without thinking about it? As an intermediate student you can make a great deal of progress in this direction: you can learn to use automatically many of the things you saw for the first time when you were a beginner. In many ways, it is the most important type of progress.

(ii) The need to practise certain fundamentals again but not in the same way as beginners do.

You already have a reasonable vocabulary. You have difficulty in using this vocabulary but not too much difficulty in understanding it. You need some more practice in the same things beginners need practice in, but you do not need the same type of practice. You can now practise constructions with a larger vocabulary and in a great variety of situations. This book will sometimes give you practice in some of the things beginners practise, but it will not be the same type of practice.

Remember always that all students, even the most advanced, need this practice. There are certain basic things in English that cannot be mastered without a great deal of practice. You must have this practice over a long period.

(iii) The need to learn some of the things you have already studied.

Learning a language is, in some ways, like learning how to fly or play the piano. There are important differences, but there is a very important similarity. It is this: learning how to do such things needs lots of practice. It is never enough simply to 'know' something. You must be able to 'do' things with what you know. For example, it is not enough simply to read a book on how to fly an aeroplane. A book can give you lots of information about how to fly, but if you only read a book and then try to fly without a great deal of practice first, you will crash and kill yourself. The same is true of playing the piano. Do you think it is enough simply to read a book about it? Can you play the piano without having lots of practice first?

Many language-students think it is enough simply to 'know' a grammar rule or the meaning of a word. They do not understand that there is a difference between such things and the actual capacity to make correct sentences and to use words correctly. You cannot say you know something unless you can

(a) understand it when it is spoken quickly, at normal speed

(b) use and understand it without asking yourself first what it means in your own language

(c) use it quickly and without pausing to think about it.

You must practise speaking and hearing English a great deal before you can have a good command of it. In this course, you will often have to practise things you already understand. Never think it is enough simply to understand something. There are many things you already 'know' which you cannot really use. In this course you will learn to use many of the things you already 'know'.

What must students realise in order to learn more?
The world is full of ex-students of English who stopped at the point you are now at. They stopped learning because they did not realise there is a difference between 'knowing' English and being able to use it. They lost interest because they think they cannot learn. 'I know that but I always make mistakes when I try to use it. I must be stupid!' they say. They are not stupid. They can learn English. What they need is more practice in interesting situations. They need more practice in listening to and using English.

In some ways, the point you are at now in learning English is more important than the beginner's stage. You must go on learning from here, or what you have already learned will be wasted. This course is for such students. You will, then, learn two types of things.

(a) Things which you perhaps have seen before but which you have not really learned to use.
(b) Entirely new things. Things which you have never seen before.

How will you use this book?
The book has 25 Units. It will probably take you between 2 and 3 lessons for each unit. Some groups will take more. A few will take less. Each unit has 6 pages, and these are divided into 5 parts.

PART A (2 pages) The pictures on the left help explain the texts or 'situations' on the right hand page. The situations are typical examples of when we use the new construction you are studying.

In class, first cover the 'situations' and look only at the pictures. Remember these things:

1. Individual words are not so important. Whole situations are very important. Try to understand whole situations even if you do not understand individual words.
2. You can learn to write words later. First learn to use and to pronounce words correctly.
3. Take an active part in the intensive question and answer work here. Do not be afraid to make mistakes. Everybody makes mistakes.
4. After you have done question and answer work with the teacher, use the words next to the picture to ask someone else, perhaps the student next to you, questions about the situation.
5. After this, you can read the situations quietly for a minute in class. Now you can ask any questions you have about words, etc.

PART B (1 page) This is the 'Formation and Manipulation' page. It directs your attention to important facts about the pronunciation and formation (or construction) of what you have done. There is a lot of opportunity here, too, for oral practice in class and written practice at home.

PART C (1 page) This is a simple detective story. It is not very serious but it is very useful. Each Unit has one part or 'episode' of this story. It goes on to the end of the book. In it, you can learn a lot of new words. You can get practice in reading and then talking about it. Sometimes there are examples of things you will learn in the next Unit, too. You can read this at home or quickly in class.

PART D (1 page) We call this 'Further Practice'. It has different special exercises and always a conversation. The conversation teaches you things we say in everyday life, and special things like the words you use when someone apologises to you, or how to say 'pardon' politely. You can listen to these conversations on tape. After you have listened to the tape or to the teacher, you can take parts yourself.

PART E This has a summary (or short version of what you have just learned) and special exercises for homework. The exercises are not the only homework you can do. They are only the minimum. There is also a 'Guided Composition'. This helps you to write a composition about something you have just learned. The compositions become 'freer' or 'less controlled' as you go along. There is also always a 'transfer exercise'. This is more help in using what you have learned in your own examples.

Unit 1
a
Present simple and position of time adverbs

1

(a) Where/Julia?
(b) When/begin?
(c) the manager?

2

(a) Where/work?
(b) start every morning?
(c) get there?
(d) time now?
(e) his wife/always/ to work?

3

(a) What/Tom want?
(b) father's question?
(c) Tom's answer?

4

(a) What/do?
(b) What kind of man?
(c) often watch?
(d) children and dogs

5

(a) What/do?
(b) house?
(c) car?
(d) How much money?
(e) Who/girl?

6

(a) life?
(b) When/up?
(c) always/ breakfast in bed?
(d) maid's question?
(e) answer?

Main Teaching-Points
1. Use of Present Simple and three pronunciations of *s* ending, as in
   a) 'lives'   b) 'works'   c) 'watches'.
2. Position of Frequency Adverbs (*often* etc.) before main verb.
3. Formation of Questions in Present Simple.
4. Meaning of 'What does he do?' in sense of 'What's his job?'.

Extra Points and Activities
1. Weak stress on *Do* and *Does* in questions.
2. Meaning of *really* as in 'Do you really love her?' and 'He's really a kind man'.
3. Telling the time using *past* and *to*.
4. Genitive *s* as in 'Susan's father'.
5. Weak stress on and use of prepositions *at* and *to*.

| He/She They etc. | never often always | DOES DO | (something) | at 12 on Thursday |

Unit 1 a

1

Julia Frost works in a large office. Work starts at 9 but she often gets there late. She is five minutes late today. It is 5 past 9 (9.05). Two typists are talking about her.

"Does the manager know she often comes late?"

"No, he doesn't. He often comes late too!"

1. Ask where Julia works!
2. What does she often do?
3. Why doesn't the manager know she often comes late?

2

Frank Martin does not work in an office. He works in a factory and he never comes late. Work starts at 7 but he always gets there early. He is five minutes early today. It is 5 to 7 (6.55). His wife always drives him to work.

1. Make sentences about Frank with these words:
   a) in an office   b) factory
   c) late   d) early
2. Ask when work starts!
3. What does his wife always do?

3

Tom Atkins wants to marry Frank's daughter, Susan.

"What do you do?" Frank wants to know.

"I'm a teacher. I teach languages."

"Do you really love my daughter?"

"Yes, I do. I love her and she loves me. We want to get married!"

1. What is Frank's first question and what is Tom's answer?
2. Make sentences about Tom
   a) a teacher   b) languages
3. Make sentences about Tom and Susan.
4. Ask what they want to do!

4

Charles Kay is a famous actor. He acts in horror films like "Frankenstein's Brother." He never watches horror films. He does not like them. He is really a kind man. He likes children and animals and they like him. He lives in a small house in the country.

1. Ask what Charles does!
2. Make sentences about him
   a) in horror films   b) watches
   c) doesn't like   d) a kind man
   e) children and animals f) house

5

Arthur and Deborah Tigers do not live in a small house. They live in a very large one. Arthur is a businessman. He earns a lot of money. His wife is very young. They are very happy.

1. Ask *questions* with these words:
   a) a small house?
   b) Arthur/an actor?
   c) a lot of money?
   d) wife/very old?
   e) happy?

6

Deborah leads a very easy life. She never gets up before 9 and always has breakfast in bed.

"Do you want your breakfast now?" her maid wants to know.

"Yes, please," is Deborah's answer.

1. Ask questions:
   a) a very hard life?
   b) when/up?
   c) where/breakfast?
2. What is her maid's question and what is her answer?

Unit 1 b

FORMATION AND MANIPULATION

1 a) Notice the *s*

He	work		in a factory
She	live	s	in a large house
	earn		a lot of money

Make sentences about your father, mother or teacher.

b) Notice how the question is formed

Does	he	work in a factory	?
	she	live in a large house	
		earn a lot of money	

Ask someone else questions about his or her father, mother, etc.

2 a) Notice there is no *s* with *I, You, We,* and *They*

I	work here
You	live in London
We	earn £30 a week
They	

Make sentences about yourself, the people in the class, etc.

b) Notice how the question is formed

Do	you	work here	?
	I	live there	
	they	earn a lot	
	we		

Turn the sentences you made in 2a) into questions.

3 Notice how *negative* sentences are formed

Julia	doesn't	work in a factory
Tom	(does not)	

You	don't	live in that house
I	(do not)	get to work before 6
We		earn £5,000 a year
They		

Make true sentences about yourself and other people with *doesn't/don't*

4 a) Notice the position of *often, always* and *never*

1	2	3
She	never	comes late
We	often	come early
	always	

What are some of the things you often do? Also make sentences with *never* and *always*.

b) Notice how the *first word* of a question is always repeated in the answer

Question	Answer
Do you live here?	Yes, I *do*/ No, I *don't*
Does he know?	Yes, he *does*/ No, he *doesn't*
Is he a teacher?	Yes, he *is*/ No, he *isn't*

Think of questions to ask the person next to you. Tell that person to give you a *short* answer.

FORMATION AND MANIPULATION

Unit 1 b

Pronunciation, Stress and Intonation

1. Point out that the *s* at the end of the verb can be pronounced in three ways. There are examples of all three in situation 4.
   i) 'He act*s* (unvoiced *s*) in horror films.'
   ii) 'He live*s* (voiced *z*) in a small house in the country.'
   iii) 'He never watch*es* ([iz]) them.'

2. Give the class practice in pronouncing *in, is, are, does, do, at* and *to* with weak stresses. The vowel in all these is weakened to the neutral [ə]. Do this in sentences from the situations. Make the class repeat them after you. This will help them stress sentences naturally, as well.

3. Point out and give practice in the rising tune of 'closed Yes/No questions.'

Fluency Practice

DEBORAH LEADS AN EASY LIFE
1. They
2. have
3. He
4. a lot of money
5. I
6. want
7. She
8. a large house
9. We
10. live in

DOES ARTHUR EARN A LOT OF MONEY?
1. you
2. want
3. a large house
4. live in
5. the maid
6. work
7. Julia
8. in an office

CHARLES DOESN'T LIKE HORROR FILMS
1. We
2. this book
3. She
4. understand
5. him
6. love
7. I
8. her
9. know
10. They

JULIA OFTEN COMES LATE
1. You
2. always
3. early
4. Frank
5. gets up
6. I
7. They
8. never
9. Deborah
10. has breakfast

Other Activities

1. Individual members of class produce sentences about themselves using pattern 'I always get up at . . ./never . . ./always eat at . . ./' etc.

2. Paired Practice using pattern 'When do you get up/have breakfast/get to work/come home/?' etc.'

3. Practise 'It's a quarter past, half past, a quarter to . . .' and 'five to, ten past . . .' etc. by putting figures on the board like '8.35', '10.20', '3.27' and asking the class to say them aloud. This is also a good way to practise numbers.

4. Practise additional points from situation texts such as (a) 'Arthur's a businessman' (use of *a/an*). (b) 'Work starts at 9' (use of *at* with clock times).

EXPLOITATION OF THE EPISODE

The purpose of the episode is explained in the introduction. It is important here to note these things:—
a) Each episode is divided into three clearly numbered sections. Line numbers are also given for ease of reference.
b) It is wise to read the episode only section by section, particularly at first.
c) The teacher may find it useful to explain and practise the pronunciation of some of the things in the episode before the class reads it.
d) Silent reading by the class of a particular section has been found a good and useful technique. The teacher briefly outlines what the section is about, points out a few questions the class should look for answers to, and then tells them to read the section silently. Afterwards the teacher asks a few general questions and a few detailed ones. Examples are given.
e) Silent reading should be varied with chorus reading (the class repeat in low voices after the teacher, sometimes looking at the section and sometimes not). We feel that reading aloud by individual students should be generally discouraged, unless there is a student in the class who reads very well indeed.

Key Patterns and Vocabulary	*Suggested Explanation*
a) 'used to be an army officer' (line 1)	'He was an army officer once but he isn't one now'
b) 'prison' (line 1)	'If you rob a bank or steal a car or kill someone and the police catch you, they send you to prison'
c) 'lasts an hour' (7)	'If lunch starts at twelve and ends at one o'clock, it lasts an hour'
d) 'Coke *usually* goes to . . .' (8)	'He often does this but he does not always do it'
e) 'He reads *until* 9.30' (9)	'He reads and then he stops at 9.30'
f) 'That is *all* he knows about him' (15)	'That is the only thing (or things) he knows about him'

Section 1
1. Sample general questions
a) Do you think Coke has an easy life? Why not?
b) Tell me some of the things that happen every morning!
2. Sample detailed questions
a) When does he get up?
b) Where do some of the men work and where does Coke work?
3. Ask the class to compare what happens in the prison every morning with
a) what they think Julia does every morning (or Deborah).
b) what they themselves do every morning.

Section 2
1. General and detailed questions.
2. Optional fluency practice of *lasts* LUNCH LASTS AN HOUR
a) Every lesson
b) All the lessons
c) 45 minutes
d) The programme
e) two hours
f) The film
3. Ask individual students to tell you what they do from lunch until the time they go to bed.
4. Point out use of *does* in 'Coke does' (line 13). Give other examples like: 'A lot of people like English food. I do.', etc. Then ask the class to make similar examples.

Section 3
1. After general and detailed questions ask the class why they think Coke wants to find Masters and Hugo.

THE MAN WHO ESCAPED
Episode 1

Unit 1

C

1   Edward Coke used to be an army officer, but he is in prison now. Every day is exactly the same for him.

  It is winter now and Coke and all the other men get up at six, when it is still cold and dark. They have breakfast at six thirty. Work begins at seven thirty. Some of the men work in the prison factory, where they make mail-bags, but Coke often works in the fields outside.

2   The men have lunch at twelve. Lunch lasts an hour and then the men go back to work again. Dinner is at six. Coke usually goes to the prison library after dinner and reads until 9.30. The lights go out at ten.

  The day is long, hard, and boring and every man has a lot of time to think. They usually think about why they are there. Coke does. He always thinks about two men.

3   One of the men is called Eric Masters. He used to be an army officer, just like Coke. Coke knows that Masters has a lot of money now. The second man's name is Hugo. That is all Coke knows about him. Masters knows where and who Hugo is, but Coke doesn't.

  Every night Coke lies in bed and thinks about Eric Masters and Hugo. There is another thing he thinks about, too. Escaping. He wants to escape and find Masters, and then the other man. Coke is in prison for something he did not do.

FURTHER PRACTICE

1. Invention Exercise

MODEL:

| He
She | often
never
always | does that |

PROMPT: football on Saturdays
RESPONSE: He always plays football on Saturdays
or: He never watches football on Saturdays

Prompts:

a) the theatre at week-ends
b) jazz
c) tea without sugar
d) to work by bus
e) French magazines
f) to the seaside in winter
g) brown bread
h) detective stories
i) coffee with cream
j) Turkish cigarettes

2. Conversation

Tom Atkins teaches languages at a Technical College. It is the teabreak. He is in the staff-room. There is another teacher there, too. His name is Ken Grimes, a friend of Tom's. Tom is smoking.

KEN: (sniffing) Phew! Is that a French cigarette?
TOM: Pardon?
KEN: Is that a French cigarette you're smoking?
TOM: Yes, that's right. Why? What's the matter?
KEN: I don't understand how you can smoke French cigarettes. They make a terrible smell.
TOM: I like them very much. I prefer them to English cigarettes.
KEN: Have you got a lot of them?
TOM: Yes, about 200, why?
KEN: Well ... er ... could I buy some from you?
TOM: Buy some from me? But ... you don't like French cigarettes!
KEN: No, I don't. But my wife does. I can't understand it.

Questions

1. What does Tom say when he doesn't understand Ken's question?
2. Why doesn't Ken like French cigarettes?
3. What does Ken want to do when he hears Tom has 200 French cigarettes?
4. Ask and answer why he wants to do this!

Practice

1. Repeat after the teacher or tape recorder Tom's intonation of 'Pardon!'
2. Make some sentences of your own with "Could I . . . . ?"
3. Observe the word order
       1   2   3
   "I like them very much"
   Think of some things you like very much. Use the same word order.

FURTHER PRACTICE

Unit 1
d

1. Invention Exercise

a) Let the class look at all the prompts and give them time to think of sentences. Then ask them to close the book and go around the class in random order, asking for responses to prompts you give orally.

b) Vary this sometimes by firing out a prompt and *not* indicating anyone in particular to answer it. Let anyone respond.

c) A short writing phase of perhaps a minute can be given for the students to record their responses.

d) Show, through a model conversation, how the prompts can be used in questions with *often*, *always*, or *ever* (introduced as a new item, and explained as 'at any time').

Example: jazz = A: Do you ever listen to jazz?
B: Yes, I do. Quite often.

Write the example on the board and then ask the class what other possible answers can be given to the other prompts. After variations like 'No, I don't. Never' and 'Yes, I do. Sometimes' etc. have been taught, pair the class.

2. Conversation

Key Points
1. Intonation of *Pardon?*
2. Meaning and intonation of 'What's the matter?'
3. Structure of 'prefer something to something'
4. Preview of 'is doing' in 'Is that a French cigarette you're smoking?'
5. Use of 'Could I . . . ?' in requests
6. Structure of phrase

      1   2   3
   like something very much

Presentation Notes
1. If possible, the class should listen to this conversation several times with the books closed! This is particularly possible if you are using the tapes. The class should read the conversation only after oral practice, as a kind of pause and transition to the next phase of the lesson.
2. After the class has listened to the conversation, do the questions and practice given below the conversation on the student's page.
3. Give the class some short, improvised fluency practice with any structures they are having difficulty with. For instance, if the class tends to put 'very much' before *them* in 'She likes them very much', give a few prompts like 'French coffee', 'I', 'Do you', 'England', 'this book', 'they' etc.
4. Go back to the intonation of *Pardon?* again. Make the class use it in natural situations. You might say things to them unclearly, so that they have to respond with the correct intonation.
5. If you are using the tape, test whether the class has grasped the correct intonation of various items in the conversation by asking them to say the sentences they remember with these words. Books should be closed.
   Example: matter = WHAT'S THE MATTER?
   a) French cigarette   d) terrible smell
   b) right   e) could
   c) don't understand how   f) from me?

Unit 1
e/f

e Summary

1
Do not try to teach the Present Continuous yet. Tell the class this will be the next thing to be done.

Another way of explaining the rule for the Present Simple is to say it is the 'no time' tense. We use it when there is no past, future or continuous colouring at all in our statement. Notice that even in statements like 'I always go to church on Sunday', no definite Sunday is meant. In other words, we use the tense when we are thinking of general time, and of the *general idea* of an action.

3
Draw the attention of the class once more to what happens to the *s* in 'live*s*' etc. when the statement is turned into a question. A simple diagram on the blackboard may be very useful, like this:

He work[s] in a factory

Do[es] he work in a factory?

In other words, it must be pointed out that the *s* goes to the *do* and is dropped from the verb itself.

4
Pair off the class and ask them to practise 'What do you do?' and the correct answer. Find out what the jobs of most of the people in the class are first. Make sure they put an *a* or *an* between *I'm*, and the name of the job they do (*mechanic, student,* etc.) This is also a good time to give the class the name of some of the main jobs and professions.

f Exercises for homework

1
A few of these can be done orally and quickly in class first simply to make sure the class know what they have to do.

2
This technique of guided composition may be new to your class. Explain that the idea is to give controlled practice in which as few mistakes as possible are made. The principle is that although one can learn from one's mistakes, one learns even more from not making them at all, particularly at this stage. As the course progresses, *freer* compositions will be given.

Unit 1
e/f

e Summary

Focal points in this Unit

1. Sentences like "He works in a factory", "She often comes late" and "They live in a large house" are all in the *Present Simple Tense*.

   Notice that in the situations the tense does *not* tell you what the people are doing at the moment. For instance, in situation 2, Tom says, "I teach foreign languages". That is *not* what he is doing at the moment.

   One of the main uses of this tense is to talk about what people often, always, never, or usually do. That is why we must use it when we want to say what Edward Coke does every day.

2. Remember that 'always', 'often', 'never', and 'usually' (Adverbs of Frequency) always go in front of the main verb.

       1   2   3
   "He always does that!"

3. Remember how we ask questions ("Does he work in a factory?") and how we make negative sentences ("They don't live in a small house"). Look at the Formation and Manipulation page for this.

4. The question "What do you do?" or "What does he do?" is often used to ask what a person's *job* is. It is *never* used to ask about someone's actions at the moment! For this, we use the question, "What is he doing?" and "What are you doing?" (See Unit 2)

f Exercises for homework

1. Make these sentences into questions and then into negatives like this:—
   Harry works in an office.
   Does Harry work in an office?
   No, Harry doesn't work in an office.
   a) Julia works in a factory.
   b) Arthur and Deborah live in a small house.
   c) Deborah is old.
   d) Arthur and Deborah are poor.
   e) People in prison lead an easy life.
   f) Charles acts in cowboy films.
   g) Tom and Susan want to get married next year.

2. **Guided Composition**

   Read lines 4 to 9 of the Episode again carefully and then, using the same sentence patterns, write about this person:

   Julia/breakfast/8.15//work/9//often late// lunch/12.30//lunch/an hour and a half// work/ finish/5.30//dinner/6.30//usually/ television/after dinner//often read/10.45// never/to bed before 11//

3. **Transfer Exercise**

   Write true sentences (at least 4) about yourself, friends and family. Use the pattern, "I/we . . . never/always . . . ."

Unit 2
a Present continuous

1

(a) What time?
(b) What/Deborah?
(c) What/maid?
(d) Where/Frank?
(e) the men/breakfast?
(f) What/talking about?

2

(a) What/Deborah/friends?
(b) they/lunch?
(c) What/one of them/wearing?
(d) Where/Frank?
(e) Frank/always/there?
(f) What/a lot of men?
(g) waiting for?

3

(a) Where/Arthur and Deborah?
(b) What/Deborah?
(c) Why/Arthur/the man?
(d) What/Frank?
(e) What/wife?
(f) What/Susan?
(g) Frank/a film?

4

(a) Who/Susan/to?
(b) Where/Tom/from?
(c) Susan's questions?
(d) What/Frank and his wife?
(e) Susan upstairs?
(f) Where/she?

Main Teaching-Points
1. Use of Present Continuous describing actions one can still see going on.
2. Formation of the Present Continuous in Statements, Negatives and Questions with 'am/is/are + ... ing'.
3. Concentration on the short forms 'I'm/you're/he's/she's/we're/they're' in Statements, and 'I'm not/you aren't/he isn't/etc.' in Negatives.

Extra Points and Activities
1. Strong stress on 'Are you/they' and 'Is he' in questions.
2. Use of *have* in 'She's having breakfast/lunch/morning coffee.'
3. Difference between *carry* and *wear*.
4. Questions like 'What is he waiting for?' and 'Who is she whispering to?'
5. 'listen to the radio' vs 'watch television'.

He/She	IS		**Unit 2**
They	ARE	DOING	**a**

1

It is half past nine (9.30). Deborah is having breakfast and listening to some music on the radio. The maid is carrying a tray with some more coffee on it.

Frank is in the factory. The men there are not having breakfast. It is their tea-break. They are talking about a football match this evening.

1. Ask questions with these words:
   a) What/Deborah   b) the maid
   c) Where/Frank   d) the men/breakfast
   e) talking about
2. Make some sentences with "isn't" and "aren't" (Frank/the radio, etc.)

2

It is half past eleven. Deborah and her friends are not having lunch. They are having 'morning coffee'. They are talking about their husbands. One of them is wearing a very strange hat.

Frank is eating in the factory canteen. He always eats there. A lot of men are standing in a queue. They are waiting for their lunch. It is raining outside.

1. Ask and answer these questions about Deborah and her friends:
   a) lunch   b) What
   c) football   d) Deborah/a strange hat
2. Ask these questions about Frank and the other men here:
   a) morning coffee   b) Frank/always
3. What are the men behind him doing and what are they waiting for?

3

It is 9 o'clock in the evening. Arthur and Deborah are at the opera. Deborah is whispering something to Arthur and he is looking at the man next to her. The man is disturbing her because he is snoring.

Frank is watching television but his wife and Susan are not. Susan is reading and her mother is writing. Frank is watching a football match.

1. Ask and answer questions about Arthur and Deborah:
   a) a football match   b) Why/whispering
   c) What/looking at   d) Why
2. Ask and answer these questions about Frank and his family:
   a) Susan and her mother/television
   b) Frank/an opera
3. Ask and answer what each person in the picture is doing!

4

It is 11 o'clock. Susan is talking to Tom. He is phoning from Paris. "Are you having a good time? What's the weather like? Is it raining?" she wants to know.

Frank and his wife are getting ready for bed. He can hear Susan downstairs. "Who's she talking to?" he is asking.

1. What is Susan doing and where is Tom phoning from?
2. What are the questions Susan is asking?
3. Ask what Frank is doing and what he is asking!

Unit 2b   FORMATION AND MANIPULATION

1 Pronunciation

a) Practise the weak form of *is*, *are* and *am* in these typical examples
   i) Frank*'s* at the factory. He*'s* working
   ii) They*'re* watching an opera.
   iii) What*'s* she doing?
   iv) Where*'re* you going?

b) Practise the strong form in these simple questions (when *is*, *are* or *am* begin the questions)
   i) Am I speaking too fast?
   ii) Is the bus coming?
   iii) Are you waiting for the bus?

2

a) Notice the word after *he, you, I,* etc.

I	*am* ('m)	learning English
He / She	*is* ('s)	watching television
You / We / They	*are* ('re)	listening to the teacher / disturbing those people

b) Notice the position of *is*, *are* and *am* in questions

Am	I		
Is		my radio	*disturbing* you?
Are	we		

Make at least six sentences from 2 a) into questions

c) Notice how the *negative* is formed

I am	
She is	*not* listening
They are	

Pronunciation Note: In speaking, we usually say 'is*n't*' and 'are*n't*'. It is only with *I* that we *must* use *not* in its full form. ('I'm not listening')

Use 2 a) again to make two negative sentences each with *He, You* and *I* (6 sentences in all)

3

Notice the position of words like *to, at* and *for* (prepositions) in these questions with *Who* and *What*.

What		waiting *for*	
	are you	talking *about*	?
Who		listening *to*	

Look at the picture situations again. Start at situation 2 and think of questions like these for the people in the situations.

FORMATION AND MANIPULATION

Unit 2 b

Pronunciation, Stress and Intonation

Before doing anything else here, make the class repeat the examples given at the top of the page (a and b). Notice that the most common tune with the four examples in a) is the falling one. This is the safest and the one with widest cover to use as a model here.
The examples in b), however, would probably all be normally spoken with a rising tune.

Perhaps even more important than the tune to adopt (which can vary) is the stress (which is much less likely to vary). As a general rule, one can say that the words that are picked out and stressed are the nouns and main (not auxiliary) verbs. These alone are enough to give some rough idea of a sentence, whereas the unstressed words would make no sense at all if given alone. Compare:
'Frank ... working ... factory' with
'is ... in the ...'

In other words, get the class into the habit of stressing those words which the sentence could not do without. Stress is very important in English. Bad pronunciation is not the only thing that makes students sound foreign; bad stress is probably even more noticeable.

Fluency Practice

I'M PHONING FROM PARIS
1. He
2. talking about
3. football
4. They
5. me
6. watching
7. us
8. waiting for

HE ISN'T WATCHING THE OPERA
1. looking at
2. her
3. They
4. listening to
5. me
6. talking about
7. us
8. She

ARE YOU HAVING A GOOD TIME?
1. Tom
2. lunch
3. you
4. waiting for
5. the bus
6. she
7. disturbing you
8. I

WHO ARE YOU TALKING TO?
1. I
2. she
3. waiting for
4. you
5. What
6. looking at
7. they
8. listening to

Other Activities

1. Write various times on the board, all involving half hours. Make sure the class associates times like 'Half past five' with 5.30 and not 4.30, as happens, for instance, in German. This can be made into a paired drill. The teacher points to one of the times on the board, and one student asks another what time it is.

2. Put all the numbers from 1–10 on the board. Make sure the class knows them. Then see if they can quickly copy them out when given *orally* in the form of phone numbers, etc. (T: My number is 01-345-477.) Practise such things as '*double* 5' and '0' (pronounced here not as *nil* but as *oh*).

Unit 2

C

EXPLOITATION OF THE EPISODE

In this episode, a certain number of items are introduced for preview. They are marked (pr). These are things that have not yet been taught intensively but are in later units. The teacher should not try to practise such items intensively here. That will be done later. All that is needed is a brief explanation, and perhaps an indication that the item will be taught later.

Key Patterns and Vocabulary	*Explanation or Remarks*
a) The police *do* not (9)	Notice that we do not say *does*!
b) looking for a man who *escaped* (pr) (6)	If a man is in prison, and he runs away, he *escapes*. Coke escaped this morning.
c) snowing (10)	In Moscow, and in Zurich, and in Helsinki, it snows a lot in winter. Snow is white, it covers the ground.
d) arrest (27)	If the police find Coke, they will arrest him. Then they will take him back to prison.
e) arrested him four years ago (pr) (27)	It is now 19 . . . Baxter arrested Coke in 19 . . . That was *four years ago*.

Section 1
1. Sample general questions.
   a) What are people all over England doing? What are the police doing? Why?
2. Sample detailed questions.
   a) When did Coke escape? Where are the police looking for him? What is Coke wearing?

Section 2
1. After a few general and detailed questions, ask what a pub is and what people do in them. Explain that Soho is a part of the centre of London where there are a lot of foreign restaurants, cinemas, bars and strip-tease clubs. It is also a place where criminals often meet.
2. Optional fluency practice
   THEY ARE NOT VERY INTERESTED IN THE NEWS
   a) She
   b) music
   c) football
   d) Are you
   e) opera
   f) He

Section 3
1. If you have any questions involving the past tense, ask them so that they can be answered in a few words. Example: 'When did Baxter arrest Coke?' 'Four years ago.'

Other Activities
1. Short dictation phase, using part of the text, perhaps the news item (ll. 5–10).
2. Pair students and get them to ask each other questions about the text; give prompts to force questions about particular parts of the text.
   Examples for 1:
   a) What . . . weather?
   b) Where . . . people . . .?
   c) What . . . people?
   d) Who . . . police . . .? etc.

THE MAN WHO ESCAPED
Episode 2

Unit 2

C

1. It is six o'clock on a very cold winter evening. All over England people are sitting down in their living-rooms and are watching the news on television or are listening to it on the radio. There is one very important piece of news this evening. It is this.
    "In the West of England this evening, hundreds of policemen are looking for a man who escaped from Princeville Prison early this morning. The man's name is Edward Coke. He is 30 years old, six feet tall, and has black hair and blue eyes. He is wearing a dark blue prison uniform. The police do not think he can stay free very long. It is only a few degrees above zero and it is snowing."

2. The radio is on in an expensive pub in Soho, in the centre of London. Most of the people there are not very interested in the news programme, but one man is. His name is Eric Masters. He is about 45 and is wearing very expensive clothes. He is looking very afraid of something. There is another man standing next to him at the bar. Masters is asking him a question.
    "Did they say the man's name was Coke?"
    "Yes, that's right. Coke . . . Edward Coke. Why? Do you know him?"
    "Pardon?"
    "Do you know him?"
    "No . . . no, I don't know him . . . I . . . I just wanted to know the man's name, that's all."

3. In another part of London, a young detective is standing in the office of his chief at Scotland Yard. The young detective's name is Richard Baxter.
    "You knew Coke, didn't you, Baxter?"
    "Yes, sir. I arrested him four years ago."
    Baxter's chief is nodding his head.
    "Yes, I know that, Baxter. That's why I'm giving you this order, now. Find Coke again! You must find him immediately!"

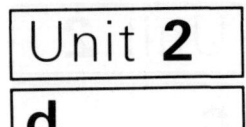

FURTHER PRACTICE

1. Invention Exercise

Make questions using the prompts
Example:
PROMPT: I/too fast?
RESPONSE: Am I driving too fast?
   or: Am I speaking too fast?
Prompts:

a) I/your seat?
b) you/a good time?
c) Julia/lunch now?
d) Frank/a football match?
e) we/too much noise?
f) you/the news?
g) those people/about me?
h) that woman/a cigar?
i) Deborah/up?

2. Conversation

A TALKATIVE OLD LADY

(The information office in a railway station. We can hear the sounds of trains coming and going and announcements over the loudspeakers)

OLD LADY: Good afternoon. I'd like some information about the trains, please.
CLERK: Yes, madam. Which train? Where are you going?
OLD LADY: To Bournemouth. You see, I have a sister there and . . .
CLERK: So your question is 'When's the next train to Bournemouth?' Is that right?
OLD LADY: Yes, that's right. When's the next train to Bournemouth, please?
CLERK: At half past four. That's in about a minute.
OLD LADY: Thank you very much. Oh! Can I get something to eat on the train? I always have something to eat when I travel. I find that a cup of tea and a sandwich always help my nerves.
CLERK: Yes, madam. There's a buffet car on the train.
OLD LADY: Oh, good! Er . . . how much does a cup of tea cost?
CLERK: I'm not sure, madam. Eightpence, I think.
OLD LADY: Eightpence! Oh dear! Things are getting so expensive!
CLERK: Yes, madam. Your train's going to leave in half a minute now.

OLD LADY: Thank you. Oh! Which platform does it leave from?
CLERK: Platform 13.
OLD LADY: Platform 13! Oh, dear! I never travel on trains that leave from platform 13! 13's an unlucky number. When's the next train after the 4.30?

Questions

a) Without looking at the text, ask the questions the old lady did, using these words:
   i) next train to Bournemouth   ii) platform   iii) something to eat
b) What does the old lady always do when she travels? Ask why and answer!
c) What is it that she never does? Ask why and answer!

Practice

a) Make questions of your own using these two patterns
   i) When's the next . . . to . . .?
      Prompts:
      bus/town-centre
      plane/London
      ship/Australia
   ii) How much does (or *do*) . . . cost?
      Prompts:
      those cigarettes. a bottle of whisky.
      that camera. those shoes.
      that sweater. a ticket to Manchester.

FURTHER PRACTICE

Unit 2
d

1. Invention Exercise

a) Follow the technique of giving this drill described in Unit One on teacher page 6.

b) Demonstrate the rising intonation of these questions first. Use the question 'AM I DRIVING TOO FAST?' and make sure the class can imitate the rise on 'too fast?' This drill is as much practice for intonation as it is for fluency.

c) Notice that the response for b) is '*having* a good time', for c) either *having* or *eating* lunch, for e) '*making* too much noise' and for f) either *listening to* or '*watching* the news'.

2. Conversation

Key Points
1. Meaning and Intonation of 'I'd like some . . ., please'
2. Practice with
   a) 'When's the next . . . to . . . ?'
   b) 'How much does/do . . . cost?'
3. Preview of 'going to do' in 'Your train's going to leave in half a minute now'
4. Falling Tune with questions beginning with *When/How much/Where*

Presentation Notes
1. Follow points 1, 2, and 3 to conversation in Unit One (see page 6).
2. Focus attention on the '*d* sound in 'I'd like some . . .' (line 1). Make the class repeat the sentence several times. Explain we use this form to ask for things politely. Practise the intonation as heard on the tape. Then, if time permits, practise it in sentences with different words in the position of *information*.
3. Preview 'going to do' (line 15) by asking questions like 'Is the train leaving when the clerk says this?' Explain the form will be practised intensively later. Most of the class will probably already have encountered the form. If necessary demonstrate its meaning by simple action sequences, such as:
T: Look at this book on the table. (reaches for it but does not pick it up yet) I'm going to pick it up in a second. What am I going to do? Ask me when! (Then picks it up).

Unit 2
e/f

e Summary

Notice that we have deliberately restricted the rule about the Present Continuous being used for things going on at the moment. We say 'in the situations in this unit' the tense is used this way. In fact, without this restriction, the rule is very inaccurate. It is a good beginning for the students to connect the tense with things going on now, but later they will have to grapple with such things as 'Greaves is running towards the goal. He shoots and scores!' and 'Deborah is usually lying in bed at 6'. The real distinction between Present Simple and Continuous is whether the action is seen as a whole or not. However, this would be far too complicated for the class at this particular stage. (For a full explanation of the distinction just referred to, see R. A. Close's *English as a Foreign Language* (Allen and Unwin). This is an excellent book for the guidance of teachers or *very* advanced students).

f Exercises for homework

1
It is a good idea to give as homework at least one set of exercises the class has already done orally in class. In fact, if the class appears still not to have grasped the main point of the unit, it is best to give only such exercises.

3
We suggest you also practise a few questions with these words. Point out how the preposition goes to the end with a *What* question. Example: WHAT ARE THE MEN IN THE CANTEEN WAITING FOR?
If the class can make sentences with the words easily, make them ask such questions with them as well.

4
Remind students why it is so important for them to have controlled practice in writing at this stage (see page 6).
It would be advisable, as with other exercises, to prepare this orally in class before allowing students to do it as a homework.

Unit 2
e/f

e Summary

Focal points in this Unit

1. Sentences like 'Where are you going?', 'Frank is watching television', etc. are in the *Present Continuous Tense*.
   Notice that in the situations in this Unit the tense is used to say what people are doing at the moment, at the time you see them. As soon as you want to talk about what they sometimes, always or usually do, you go back to the Present Simple tense. For instance, in situation 2 on page 9 we say 'Frank *is eating* in the factory canteen. He always *eats* there'.

2. Study the Formation and Manipulation page carefully. Notice how questions and negative sentences are formed. Notice that in the negative, we rarely say *not* in its full form.
   In speaking, we usually say:
   'He is*n't* coming' and 'They are*n't* watching an opera.'
   It is only with *I* that we must say *not* in its full form.
   'I'm *not* waiting for the bus'.

3. Notice that we usually use the Present Simple tense when we ask when a train leaves, or a bus arrives. (See Conversation, page 12). We do this because we are thinking of what the timetable says.

f Exercises for homework

1. Do all the questions and other exercises on pages 9 and 10.

2. Notice how these prompts are used to make *two* sentences.
   Deborah/always up/9.30=Deborah always gets up at 9.30. It is 9.30 now and she is getting up.
   Do the same with these prompts (two sentences each):
   a) Frank/breakfast/6.15
   b) Arthur/to work/8 o'clock
   c) Deborah/usually lunch/1.30
   d) Frank/usually/the television news/ 10 o'clock.
   e) I/the radio/6 o'clock

3. Make sentences of your own with these words:
   listen to. talk to. talk about. wait for. look at.
   Example: I'm waiting for a bus. Deborah never listens to the 8 o'clock news.

4. **Guided Composition**
   Read the news item from the Episode again carefully (page 11, lines 5–10) and then, using the same sentence patterns, write another piece of news with these prompts:
   North of Scotland/dozens of detectives/ young woman/a prison late last night// Jane Stone//26/five feet six inches/blonde/ blue//grey dress/black shoes//weather/ terrible//police/free very long//snow/very cold//

5. **Transfer Exercise**
   Write 5 true sentences about things that are happening or about what other people are doing *now* while you are doing this exercise.

Unit 3a

Simple past tense (Regular and irregular verbs)

1 
(a) late this morning?
(b) eat?
(c) drink?
(d) the dishes?
(e) much time?

2 
(a) friend's question?
(b) Where/manager?
(c) When/he Julia?

3 
(a) How often London?
(b) London yesterday?
(c) friend's question? (on time yesterday?)

4 
(a) Where/Arthur/this morning?
(b) Where/Deborah/station?
(c) Deborah's question?
(d) Who/Arthur/meet?
(e) train early?

5 
(a) Tom and Susan/this morning?
(b) What/now? (champagne/cake/good time)
(c) What/Susan's father?

6 
(a) Who/at the party?
(b) What/all do?
(c) Tom's mother?
(d) What/Frank?

Main Teaching-Points
1. Use of Simple Past tense with words and phrases like 'yesterday', 'last week', 'last night', 'this afternoon' etc.
2. Formation of some regular and irregular past forms (positive).
3. Formation of Negatives and Questions with *did*, and short answers 'Yes, I did', 'No, I didn't' etc.

Extra Points and Activities
1. Revision of the Past forms *was* and *were*.
2. The verb *arrive* + *on time/early/late* – importance of word order.
3. The meaning of *make* in 'He made a speech'.
4. The use of *so* in 'Susan's parents are there and *so are* Tom's' and 'Tom's parents were there and *so were* Susan's'.

HE WENT	HE ARRIVED	**Unit 3**
DID he GO?	DID he ARRIVE?	
HE DIDN'T GO	HE DIDN'T ARRIVE	**a**

1

Julia often gets up late and she got up late this morning. She ate some cornflakes and drank some tea. She did not wash all the dishes. She washed only some of them. She did not have very much time this morning.

1. Is Julia getting up now?
2. Is she eating cornflakes and drinking tea now?
3. Tell me three things she did this morning!
4. What did she do with the dishes and why?

2

Julia is having lunch with a friend. "Were you late again this morning?" her friend wants to know. "Yes, I was, and the manager was in the office, too!"
"Oh? Did he see you?"
"Yes, he did. He saw me when I came in."

1. What is Julia doing?
2. What are the exact words of her friend's question and Julia's answer?
3. Ask if the manager saw her!
4. Ask when!

3

Arthur often goes to London. He is going there today and he went there yesterday, too. He is talking to an old friend. "Does this train usually arrive on time?" his friend wants to know. "Yes, it does, but it didn't yesterday. It arrived late!"

1. Ask what Arthur often does!
2. Ask what he is doing now!
3. Ask if he did yesterday!
4. What is his friend's question?
5. What is Arthur's answer?

4

Arthur is back from London. He went there this morning. Deborah is at the station to meet him. "Did you have a good time in London?" she wants to know. "Yes, I did, and I met an old friend on the train this morning."
"Did the train get into London on time?"
"No, it didn't. It was late again!"

1. Ask and answer questions about Arthur:
   a) When/London   b) a good time
   c) When/old friend   d) Where
   e) train on time

5

Tom and Susan got married this morning. They are having a party now. Susan's parents are there and so are Tom's. They are drinking champagne, eating cake and having a good time. Only Tom's mother is unhappy. Susan's father is making a speech.

1. What did Tom and Susan do this morning?
2. Ask what they are doing now!
3. Ask questions with   a) eat   b) drink
4. Ask these questions:
   a) good time   b) Tom's mother
5. What is Frank (Susan's father) doing?

6

Tom and Susan had a party here this afternoon. Tom's parents were there and so were Susan's. Everybody ate cake, drank champagne and had a good time. Only Tom's mother did not eat or drink very much. She was unhappy. Frank made a speech.

1. Ask and answer questions with these words:
   a) When/a party   b) Tom's parents there
   c) Susan's too   d) What/drink and eat
   e) a good time   f) Tom's mother happy
   g) eat very much   h) Frank/speech

Unit 3 b

FORMATION AND MANIPULATION

1 a) Notice what happens to *regular* verbs in the past

> The train usually arri*ves* on time
> It arri*ved* late yesterday
> We usually arri*ve* on time
> We arri*ved* late yesterday

b) Notice how the question and the short answer are formed

> Did it arrive on time yesterday?
> No, it *didn't* (or 'Yes, it *did*')
> Did you arrive on time yesterday?
> Yes, I *did* (or 'No, I *didn't*')

Now do this yourself. Make 3 sentences for each of these, like this:
Julia usually washes the dishes = SHE WASHED THEM YESTERDAY
DID SHE WASH THEM YESTERDAY?
SHE DIDN'T WASH THEM YESTERDAY

i) The train usually arrives on time.
ii) We often arrive late.
iii) Work usually starts at 9.
iv) Frank usually watches television.
v) You usually listen to the news.
vi) Susan and Tom often talk about money.
vii) Arthur often works late.
viii) He usually phones her.

2 a) Notice what happens to *irregular* verbs in the past

> Arthur often *goes* to London
> He *went* there yesterday
> We often *go* to the opera
> We *went* there last week

b) Notice that we form the question and the negative *exactly as we do* with regular verbs

> He *went*
>
> *Did* he *go*?   He did*n't* go

Now do this yourself, like this: He went to London = WHEN DID HE GO TO LONDON?
i) Julia got to work.
ii) Tom and Susan got married.
iii) We had a party.
iv) They drank all the champagne.
v) I ate all the cake.
vi) Frank made a speech.

3 Notice which people we use *was* with and which people we use *were* with. Also notice the question form and the short answers

I He She It	was	late here in London early	yesterday last week last month
You We They	were		

Question: Was the train late yesterday?
Answer: Yes, it was (or 'No, it wasn't')

Make sentences from this table with all the various persons.
Then ask the person next to you questions with 'Were you . . .?'
Tell that person to give a short answer!

FORMATION AND MANIPULATION

Unit 3 b

Pronunciation, Stress and Intonation

Note: The emphasis in this Unit is to give students a clear grasp of the system behind the past tense in English. We have deliberately introduced only a few items. Far more regular and irregular past verbs are introduced in the coming units.

1. Point out the three different pronunciations of *ed* ending in regular verbs.
    Unvoiced
    Wash*ed* [t]
    Voiced
    Arrived [d], wanted [id]
    More examples of these, drawn from verbs previously introduced are:
    Unvoiced
    watched/talked/escaped/looked/asked/worked
    Voiced
    listened/phoned/whispered/disturbed/answered/earned.
    started/carried/wanted.

2. Give the class practice in saying *was* and *were* with weak stress, that is, with the vowel weakened to the neutral [ə]. The fluency practice provides many examples. Demonstrate the sound of the weak *was* and *were* first.

    Another useful feature of stress here is the weakening of *and* in 'Susan and Tom' to the unstressed *nd*. Give common examples of this, such as 'bacon 'n' eggs', 'Whisky 'n' soda' etc.

Fluency Practice

THE CHAMPAGNE WAS VERY GOOD
1. The lessons
2. The teacher
3. hungry
4. Susan and Tom
5. happy
6. I
7. late
8. The manager
9. angry

WAS JULIA LATE YESTERDAY?
1. you
2. on time
3. the train
4. all the trains
5. last week
6. she
7. this morning
8. everybody
9. we

Other Activities

1. Write these words on the board: 'got up', 'had breakfast', 'went to work/school', 'had lunch', 'got home', 'ate dinner', 'went to bed'. Use them for a 'chain exercise'. Student 1 asks Student 2 a question with 'When . . . yesterday?' Student 2 gives a short answer, the teacher then asks student 3 what happened at the time given, and student 3 answers.
    Example T: 'got up'
            St. 1: When did you get up yesterday?
            St. 2: At 7 o'clock
            T: (to St. 3) What happened yesterday at 7 o'clock?
            St. 3: He got up.

2. Practise quick comprehension of numbers 10–50. Give out sums and ask class to add them in English; explain this is *not* practice in adding, but practice in associating numerals with the English for them (23 = Twenty three, etc.).

Unit 3
c

EXPLOITATION OF THE EPISODE

Key Patterns and Vocabulary	*Suggested Explanations*
a) the wind is *still* blowing (1)	The wind started blowing earlier in the day, and it's blowing now. So we say 'the wind's (pause for response) still blowing'.
b) a man *is hiding* . . . (2)	If a man is escaping from the police and he thinks they might see him, he hides behind trees, or behind a building.
c) opposite him (10)	When you are sitting in a train and you are facing another person (so you can see his face), you are opposite him; and he is opposite you.
d) Would you like to . . .? (15)	This is a polite way of asking 'Do you want to . . .?'
e) a spy (22)	If a person works in a factory, or in the Navy or Air Force, and sees a lot of important secrets which he then sells to another country, he is a spy. Some people think Coke is a (pause for response) spy.

Section 1
1. Sample questions
a) What time of day is it?
b) What's the weather like?
c) How far from the prison is Coke now?
d) Who is 'the man in the field'?
e) What must Coke find soon?
2. Extra activity
After reading 1 (possibly in chorus), and asking a number of questions on it, read the text again, asking students to complete the sentences:
Example:
T. 'It is 6.30 in the . . .' (pause for response)
Ss. 'evening'
T. 'and the wind is' (pause)
Ss. 'still blowing.'
3. Optional fluency practice (pr)
IT'S GETTING COLDER
a) warmer
b) darker
c) The evenings
d) lighter
e) The mornings
f) It
g) easier

Section 2
1. After asking a variety of questions about the text (e.g. How far is London from the prison?/What is the man opposite Baxter doing?), get students to ask each other questions. Give prompts (orally or on the blackboard):
T. Baxter/uncomfortable compartment?
S.1 Is Baxter sitting in an uncomfortable compartment?
S.2 No, he isn't.
(Note: Encourage short answers. Do not ask students to give long answers which are unrealistic.)
2. Optional fluency practice
WOULD YOU LIKE TO READ ABOUT IT?
a) look at it
b) they
c) listen to the news
d) he
e) come to a party
f) you
g) go to the cinema
h) sit there

Section 3
1. Read the text or play the tape. Then ask students to read it silently for themselves.
2. Question phase as before.
3. Special optional activity. Ask students to agree with things you say, using the 'So do I/So does he' formula. Point out that you always have to use the matching auxiliary for the main verb in the statement:
I *hope* they catch him.
So *do* I.
I *went* to London yesterday.
So *did* I.
I *like* Paris.
So *do* I.
I *was* there last week.
So *was* I.
I *must* go now.
So *must* I.
I *have* a headache.
So *have* I.

THE MAN WHO ESCAPED
Episode 3

Unit 3

C

1. It is 6.30 in the evening now, and the wind is still blowing. It is getting colder. About ten miles away from Princeville Prison a man is hiding in a field. The wind is cutting through his thin prison uniform like a knife.

   A dog is barking somewhere in the distance. Is it a police dog perhaps? The man in the field does not know. There is only one idea in his mind at the moment: he must find food and some warm clothes, but where?

2. Two hundred miles away in London, Baxter's train is standing at platform 9 in Paddington Station. Baxter is sitting in a comfortable compartment. There is another man opposite him. Baxter does not know the man but he can see he wants to talk. The man is holding a newspaper in his hands.

   "I see someone escaped from Princeville Prison this morning."

   "Oh, really?"

   "Yes . . . Would you like to read about it? It's all here in the paper."

   "No, thank you."

3. The train is leaving the station now. Baxter is looking out of the window. He can see a thousand bright lights in the windows of pubs, cafés, houses and flats. Everywhere people are sitting down to warm meals and hot cups of tea. The world looks warm and comfortable.

   The man opposite Baxter is still talking.

   "The paper says the man was a spy . . . he gave important military secrets away. I hope the police catch him!"

   "Yes, so do I."

Unit 3 d

FURTHER PRACTICE

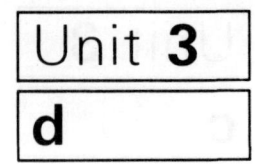

1. Invention Exercise

1) Use the prompts to make sentences:
   Example:
   PROMPT: to London last Thursday
   RESPONSE: I went to London last Thursday.
         or: We drove to London last Thursday.
   Prompts:
   a) late yesterday morning
   b) fish for breakfast yesterday
   c) television yesterday evening
   d) out for a walk last Saturday
   e) a good time at the party last night
   f) the news on the radio yesterday
   g) a good film last night
   h) football last Wednesday afternoon
   i) married in 1962
   j) 3 bottles of champagne last night

2) Now use the same prompts as in (1) to make negative sentences:
   Example:
   PROMPT: to London last Thursday
   RESPONSE: I didn't go to London last Thursday.
         or: They didn't drive to London last Thursday.

3) Now ask questions using the same prompts as in (1):
   Example:
   PROMPT: to London last Thursday
   RESPONSE: Did you go to London last Thursday?
         or: Did he drive to London last Thursday?

2. Conversation

Tom and Susan are in Tom's sports car. They are at a petrol station.

TOM: Three gallons of super, please.
ATTENDANT: Three gallons of super; yes, sir.
SUSAN: Tom . . . why don't we get a small family car?
TOM: What? You mean, sell my sports car? Never!
SUSAN: But it's expensive to run and it's old. You bought it long before I met you. When did you get it?
TOM: It's a very good car, and I never have any trouble with it!
SUSAN: But you had some trouble with it only last week. Don't you . . . ?
ATTENDANT: Er . . . excuse me. That's £1, sir.
TOM: Here you are. Oh, and would you check the battery, please?
ATTENDANT: Check the battery, sir? Certainly.
SUSAN: Don't you remember? It broke down just before we got married and it was in the garage for a whole week!
TOM: This is a wonderful car! It always starts first time!
ATTENDANT: The battery's all right, sir.
TOM: Thank you.
SUSAN: It didn't start first time yesterday morning!
TOM: That was only because it was so cold! It's a wonderful engine. Just listen to it when I start it now! (Presses starter. Sound of engine turning over but not starting.)
SUSAN: I'm listening, Tom.

Questions

1. How does Tom ask the attendant for petrol and to check the battery?
2. When did Tom buy the car and what does Susan say about it?
3. What happened the week before they got married?
4. What happened yesterday morning? What explanation does Tom give?

FURTHER PRACTICE

Unit 3
d

1. Invention Exercise

a) Follow the technique of giving this exercise used in Units 1 and 2 (pp. 6 and 11).

b) Notice that responses expected call for a repetition of some of the verbs used in the Past in the Presentation and Formation and Manipulation pages, and for the production of the Past forms of other verbs used in the first two units of the book. Thus the response for a) is either '*got up* late' or '*went* to work late', for b) '*had* fish' or '*ate* fish', for f) '*listened to* the news' or '*heard* the news', for g) *saw* or *watched* or '*went to* a good film', for h) *played* or '*watched* football', and for j) *had* or '*drank* 3 bottles'.

c) After students have given responses to all three exercises (and the teacher might ask for some of the responses to be written), pair students and get them to ask each other questions from the prompts given in 1) and give short answers.

Example: S.1: Did you get up late yesterday morning?
S.2: No, I didn't. I got up very early.

2. Conversation

Key Points
1. Meaning and intonation of 'You mean, sell my sports car?' and 'Never!'
2. Practice with 'Excuse me, . . .'
3. Practice with
   a) 'Why don't we . . .?'
   b) 'Would you . . ., please?'
4. Revision of imperative form as in 'Just listen to it!'
5. *buy* and *sell*

Presentation Notes
1. Follow points 1, 2, and 3 to the conversation in Unit One (see page 6).
2. Focus students' attention on the polite way of suggesting something with '*Why don't we* get a small family car?'

Make students suggest other things to each other. Give prompts such as 'go out this evening'/'watch the film on television'/'go for a walk'/'have fish for dinner'/'have a party tonight' etc.
Make sure that students use the intonation as heard on the tape.

3. Focus attention on this part of the conversation:
'I never have any trouble with it!'
'But you had some trouble with it only last week!'
Get students to practise this short dialogue, replacing 'have any trouble with it' by other ideas, such as 'play football':
Example: Prompt: play football
S.1: I never play football!
S.2: But you played football only last week!

Other prompts:
go to the beach/travel by train/write letters/talk about the boss/smoke French cigarettes
(Note: Once again, it is important that students should try to mimic the intonation used for these sentences on the tape.)

Unit 3
e/f

e Summary

1
Notice that we have only used a small number of 'time-pointer' words and phrases (e.g. 'yesterday') with the Simple Past tense in this Unit. You could certainly add more, particularly 'last month', 'last year' and 'last Sunday' (or any other days) so that the connection of the Simple Past tense with such times is made stronger in students' minds.
Where we have used 'this morning' and 'this afternoon' as time phrases we have been careful to show that the speaker is referring to the past (see situations 1, 2, 5 and 6), not the present or the future.

2
We have only introduced a certain number of irregular verbs in this Unit. More will be introduced in later Units.
Some are used only in the Conversation (page 18) – *bought, met, broke down* – and students' attention might well be drawn to them at this point.

f Exercises for homework

1
It is very useful for students to do, for homework, exercises which they have done orally in the classroom, as we said in the last Unit. In the same way, although it is not set on the student page as a homework, they might well be asked to do at least some of the Invention Exercise on page 18.

2·
As this is the first time we have used this particular type of exercise in this book, it should definitely be prepared in the classroom – unless, of course, you feel you want to use this exercise as a kind of small test.

3
This particular Guided Composition is to try and show students once again the opposition between 'I often do . . .' and 'I did . . . yesterday'.
Since the exercise is quite short, they could also perhaps write another paragraph of the same type about themselves or someone they know. Example: 'My brother usually plays football on Saturday, but he didn't play last Saturday because he was ill.' etc.

Unit 3
e/f

e Summary

Focal points in this Unit

1. *Ate, drank, washed, arrived,* etc. are all verbs in the *Simple Past Tense*.

2. We use the Simple Past tense with Adverbs of Past Time, like 'yesterday', 'last week', 'last Friday' etc.

3. Sometimes we do not actually put these Adverbs of Past Time in the sentence. They are only in our minds. We still use the Simple Past tense.

4. There are two main types of verb.
   a) *Regular verbs:* 'wash*ed*', 'watch*ed*' 'play*ed*'
   b) *Irregular verbs:* 'see/*saw*', 'get/*got*', 'go/*went*' etc.

5. We use the same system to form questions and negatives in the past as we do in the simple present. In other words, the past form of 'Do/Does', which is 'Did', is used with the base form of the verb:
   Examples: 'He went there' – 'He did not *go* there.' 'Did he *go* there?'

6. *Was* and *Were*, of course, do *not* use this system. Just like *Am/Is/Are*, questions are formed through *inversion,* and the negative with *not*.
   Examples: 'Was he here yesterday?' 'He was not here yesterday.' 'Were you here last week?' 'We were not here last week.'

7. In speaking, we usually use the weak form of *not*.
   Examples: 'He did*n't* come.' 'He was*n't* here.'

f Exercises for homework

1. Do all the questions and exercises on pages 15 and 16.

2. Make questions with 'What/Where/When did you/they etc. do . . .?' to which the following prompts are possible short answers.
   Example:
   PROMPT: On the train
   You write: Where did you meet him?
   or: Where did you see her?
   or: Where did he read that newspaper article?

   Prompts:
   a) Last Saturday   f) Cornflakes
   b) About 11.30   g) In September 1965
   c) To the opera   h) A new hat
   d) At the station   i) Last summer
   e) In London   j) Champagne, of course

3. **Guided Composition**

   Read situations 1 and 3 (page 15) carefully again, and then write about this person, using the prompts:
   Charles Brown/often/Paris//there today/last Monday too//late this morning//only time/coffee//train to London/late too//now/10 o'clock plane//usually/9 o'clock//

4. **Transfer Exercise**

   Write 5 true sentences about things you did, people you met or places you went to yesterday.

Unit 4
a
Mass and unit

1 
(a) Arthur/shop?
(b) newspaper man's questions? (men?/money?/hours?)

2 1948
(a) When/in a factory?
(b) 36 hours?
(c) How much/earn?
(d) Where/Joan?
(e) she/48 hours?
(f) she/£10?

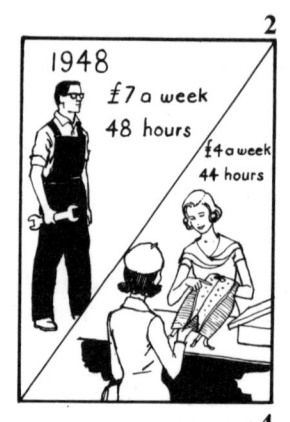

3 1950
(a) What/1950?
(b) Why/job?
(c) Why/Arthur/better job?

4 1951
(a) When/Arthur/better job?
(b) hours?
(c) earn?
(d) What/buy?

5 1960
(a) own factory?
(b) How many hours?
(c) money?
(d) life easier?
(e) cigars?
(f) small car?
(g) wife/car?

6 1963
(a) What/1963?
(b) Who/come?
(c) Who/children?
(d) When/Arthur/Deborah?
(e) When/they/married?

Main Teaching-Points
1. Use of 'How much?' with words like *money, time, petrol* and the use of 'How many?' with words and phrases like *men, hours, glasses of wine*.
2. Formation and use of the verb 'have to do' in Present and Past, statements and questions.

Extra Points and Activities
1. Practice with more verbs in the Past: 'started/earned/sold/found/bought/smoked/drove/died'.
2. Phrases like '£30 *a week*' and '48 hours *a week*'.
3. Revision of simple Comparatives: *better* and *easier*.
4. Position of *enough* in 'They didn't have *enough* money'.
5. Ordinal numbers *first* and *second*.
6. Phrasal verbs 'give up' and 'look after'.

Unit 4 a

HOW MUCH / MANY ?   HAVE / HAD TO DO

1

Arthur owns a factory. A newspaper man wants to write an article about it.
"How many men work for you?"
"About 200"
"How much do they earn?"
"£30 to £40 a week"
"How many hours do they work?"
"40 hours a week"

1. Why is the newspaper man asking these questions?
2. Ask the same questions:
   a) men   b) earn   c) hours

2

Before Arthur started his own factory he worked in one. He started in 1948. He worked 48 hours a week or more. He never earned more than £7 a week. He had another wife then. Her name was Joan and she sold underwear in a department store. She worked 44 hours a week and earned £4. Life was not easy.

1. What did Arthur do before he started his own factory?
2. What did his wife do?
3. Ask these questions about them both:
   a) hours a week   b) earn

3

Joan had to give up her job in 1950, when she had a baby. She did not want to, but she had to. She often said "You have to find a better job, Arthur. You simply have to!"

Arthur had to find a better job because they did not have enough money.

1. What did Joan have to do in 1950?
2. Ask why!
3. What did she often say?
4. Why did Arthur have to do this?

4

Arthur came home one day in 1951 and said "I found a better job today" "Oh? How many hours do you have to work? How much do you earn?" Joan asked. "£70 a month for 44 hours a week" he said. Joan had another baby that year and he bought a house.

1. Ask and answer questions with "When...?"
   a) home and say "a better job"
   b) another baby
   c) a house
2. Ask questions with "How much" or "How many"
   a) hours a week
   b) money a month
   c) children at the end of the year

5

Arthur started his own factory in 1960. He had to work 60 hours a week at first but he earned £4,000 that year. Life was not easier but it was better. He smoked 5 or 10 cigars a day and drove a large car. His wife had a car, too.

1. What happened in 1960?
2. How many hours a week did he have to work at first?
3. Ask questions with a) cars   b) cigars

6

His first wife died in 1963. His children were young and his sister had to come and live with them. She had to look after the children. He met Deborah in 1968 and married her the same year. Deborah is his second wife.

1. What happened in 1963?
2. What did his sister have to do?
3. Ask why!
4. What happened in 1968?
5. Is Deborah his first wife?

Unit 4 b

FORMATION AND MANIPULATION

1 Notice the words that go with 'How *much*' and those that go with 'How *many*'

a)

| How *much* | time
money
petrol
beer
wine | have you got? |

b)

| How *many* | cigarettes
hours
bottles of beer
glasses of wine | did he have? |

Which of these words do you think go with 'How much' and which with 'How many'? Make questions with '... have you got?/do you want?'

i) chocolate
ii) pieces of chocolate
iii) bread
iv) sandwiches
v) eggs
vi) bacon
vii) steak
viii) pieces of steak
ix) champagne
x) wine
xi) glasses of beer
xii) children
xiii) petrol
xiv) tobacco
xv) cigars

2 Look at this:

| Frank *has* | |
| I *have* | to get up early every day and he/I *had* to get up early yesterday |

i) Make sentences like this about someone you know and about yourself.
   Example: 'My teacher has to give a lesson every Monday at this time and I have to listen to it. He had to give one yesterday and I had to listen to it.'
ii) How do you ask questions with this form? If you don't remember, look at situation 4. Ask some questions yourself. Use words like 'you', 'your brother', 'our teacher'.
iii) What is the *past form* of questions with 'have to'? Look at situation 5, question 2. Then ask someone else questions like that with:
   get up very early yesterday, do a lot of homework last week, work very hard when you were a boy/girl?, etc.
   Notice that the answers are 'Yes, I *did*' or 'No, I *didn't*'

3 Look at this:

| He *found* a better job. | When did he *find* a better job? |

Ask the same sort of question with these new irregular verbs, all of which are from the situations.
   sold underwear, *came* home, *bought* a new house, *said* 'I found a better job today'

FORMATION AND MANIPULATION

Unit 4 b

Pronunciation, Stress and Intonation

Note: The focal point of this Unit is the use of 'How much' and 'How many' and the discrimination between Mass and Unit words. Closely connected with this (and the practice in this Unit) is the use of 'has/have got' instead of simply 'has/have'.

1. a) Use the prompts (words and phrases) in **1** for a simple discrimination exercise.
   Write on the board   1   2
                         bread   sandwiches
   Give a number of words and phrases orally and ask students simply to say whether they are like 1 or 2. Then ask the class for more examples of 1, and then more examples of 2. Finally point out that words like 1 are Mass words; we use 'How much' with them: and words like 2 are Unit words; we use 'How many' with them.
   Finally get students to ask each other questions with the prompts in **1** to practise both 'How much'/'How many' and the 'have you got' forms.

   b) **Additional fluency practice**
   HOW MUCH TIME HAVE YOU GOT?
   1. cigarettes   6. he
   2. he   7. they
   3. brothers   8. petrol
   4. you   9. we
   5. money   10. time

   c) Point out the weak forms of *has* and *have* in the sentences practised above. Point out also that the past form of 'I've got' is 'I had'.

   d) Make a special point of showing that although we use the 'has/have got' form in the Present, it cannot be used in the Past. Examples:

Present	*Past*
I've got a car.	I had a car.
Has she got a car?	Did she have a car?
You haven't got a car.	You didn't have a car.

2. a) Point out the meaning of the verb 'has/have to do' as necessity or obligation. As well as referring back to the relevant situations on page 20, give other examples:
   i) 'I have an appointment at the dentist's at 3 this afternoon. I don't really want to go, *but I have to*. And *I have to be there* at 3 o'clock.'
   ii) 'I had a terrible toothache last Monday. I didn't really want to go to see the dentist, but the pain was so bad *I had to go*.'

   b) Point out the strong pronunciation of *has* and *have* in 'He *has* to do that work today.'/'Does he *have* to do it?' and 'I *have* to be there.'/'Do you *have* to be there?'

Fluency Practice

I HAVE TO GO OUT
1. He   6. get up early
2. be there   7. you
3. Do you   8. talk so much
4. stay home   9. she
5. she

I HAD TO SEE HIM
1. go out   6. He
2. She   7. be there
3. buy more wine   8. ask everybody
4. write a letter   9. I
5. invite them   10. finish the job

Unit 4
C

EXPLOITATION OF THE EPISODE

Note: From this point on, each episode will be prefaced by a synopsis, a short summary of the story so far. The main aim of the synopsis is simply to remind students of what has happened in the story so far. It can, of course, already provide the class with practice and revision not only of the facts, but also of vocabulary and structures they learnt in the last episode.

Key Patterns and Vocabulary	Suggested Explanation
a) 'he could *hardly* feel' (5)	There was very little feeling in his arms and legs.
b) 'It must be a house' (13)	Coke cannot be sure but that is the only possible thing it could be. Another example of *must* in this sense is Q: Who is that man in the blue uniform? A: I don't know. He must be a policeman.
c) 'I have to take the chance' (24)	Coke knows it is dangerous, but he still has to do it.

Also observe Comparatives
'later/darker/colder/larger/better' introduced for *preview*.

Section 1
1. Sample questions
a) Where were Baxter and Coke at 6?
b) Was it a warm, summer evening?
c) What did Coke have to find soon?
d) What was the weather like?
2. Ask students to read the text again silently.
3. Optional fluency practice
   THE EVENING GOT DARKER AND COLDER
a) morning
b) colder and colder
c) weather
d) better and better
e) summer
f) hotter and hotter
g) day

Section 2
1. Listening phase (teacher or tape) followed by choral reading and questions.
2. Completion exercise (as used for Section 1 of Episode 3).
3. Optional invention exercise
   Model: IT CAN'T BE A CAR. IT MUST BE A HOUSE.
   Example:
   Prompts:
      an Englishman/an American
   Response:
      He can't be an Englishman.
      He must be an American.
   Prompts:
a) a policeman/a private detective
b) a house/a hotel
c) the London train/the Brighton train
d) a secretary/a teacher
e) a workman/the boss
f) tea/coffee

Section 3
1. After normal listening phase, ask a number of questions on the text.
2. Ask students to read the text carefully and try to write some sentences of their own based on sentences in the texts as pattern models.
Examples: Text: 'Ten minutes later he was outside the house.'
Possible Student sentence:
'Half an hour later we were inside the cinema.'
Text: 'This is the only place I can find warm clothes and food.'
Possible Student sentence:
'That is the only time I can come.'

THE MAN WHO ESCAPED
Episode 4

Unit **4**

c

NOTE: From this point onwards, there is a synopsis at the beginning of every episode. The synopsis tells in a few words what happened in the last episodes.
The story is also told in the *past tense* from now on.

SYNOPSIS: *A young detective, Richard Baxter, arrested Coke four years ago. Coke escaped from prison because he wanted to find two men, Eric Masters and someone called 'Hugo'. That was all Coke knew about the second man. He knew Masters when they were officers in the army. Baxter, the detective, left London on the same day Coke escaped. His job was to catch Coke again.*

1 Baxter got on the train at 5 o'clock. An hour later, at 6, he was asleep in the warm train compartment. Coke was still in his hiding-place in a field, 100 miles away. The winter evening got darker and colder. The wind cut through Coke's thin uniform like a knife. Coke was hungry and tired, and his arms and legs were so cold that he could hardly feel them. He knew he had to find food, warm clothing, and a warm place somewhere. "I have to make a move! I can't just stay in this field and die of the cold!" he thought.

2 Coke got up and began to walk. "Where am I? Which direction am I walking in? Am I going back towards the prison?" he asked himself. A few minutes later, the moon came out and Coke could see better. He stopped and looked around. Suddenly he saw a small light not far away. "What can it be? It can't be a car. It isn't moving! It must be a house!" he said to himself and began to walk towards it. The light got larger. It was a house! He could see the form of the roof in the darkness.

3 Ten minutes later he was outside the house. He stopped and listened. "Strange!" he thought. "I can't hear anything, not even a radio or a television, but there must be someone in there! There's a light on!" Just at that moment, a thought struck him.
"This is probably the only house around for miles! The police know I'm probably around here somewhere; and if they're anywhere, they're in that house, waiting for me!"
Coke did not move. The wind became colder. His feet and hands felt like ice in the snow. "I have to take the chance! I have to! This is the only place I can find warm clothes and food!" he thought.

Unit 4 d

FURTHER PRACTICE

1. Invention Exercise

You are talking to Tom Atkins about his job. He teaches languages at a Technical College, remember. Ask him questions with 'How much/How many . . .?' using the prompts.

Example:

a) PROMPT: students/at the College this year
   RESPONSE: How many students are there at the College this year?
b) PROMPT: homework/every evening
   RESPONSE: How much homework do the students do every evening?

Prompts:

a) free time/every week
b) teachers/at the College this year
c) lessons/every day
d) students/your class this year
e) work/in the evenings
f) books/in a month

Now use the same prompts again to ask questions about *last year, yesterday, last week* etc.

2. Conversation

Tom and Susan bought a house last month. They have not got very much money and Susan is adding up all the money they spent on food and other things last week.

SUSAN: We spent £12 last week. £12! That's too much!
TOM: Er . . . that reminds me . . . did I tell you about the party?
SUSAN: Party? What party?
TOM: Well . . . er . . . you see, there's a tradition at the College. When a teacher there buys a house he has to . . . he has to . . .
SUSAN: 'has to give a party'? Is that what you're going to say?
TOM: Yes, I'm afraid so. So we need some beer and wine and cheese for tomorrow evening.
SUSAN: What? Tomorrow evening! Why didn't you tell me this before?
TOM: Well . . . I suppose I forgot. I'm terribly sorry. I really am!
SUSAN: Oh, well, I suppose if we have to give a party, we have to. Anyway, we have some beer already.
TOM: Oh, how much?
SUSAN: At least a dozen bottles. Perhaps more than that.
TOM: How many? Only a dozen bottles? That isn't enough.
SUSAN: What do you mean? How many people did you invite? Only three or four, I hope.
TOM: Er . . . more than that, actually. Now, don't worry about the money.
SUSAN: What do you mean 'Don't worry about the money?' Someone has to! You never worry about it! Now, how many teachers did you invite?
TOM: Well . . . naturally I had to invite all the teachers and not just some of them. I *had* to!
SUSAN: All the teachers? But how many teachers are there at the college?
TOM: Not many, really . . . only 35.
SUSAN: What? 35 teachers! Are you mad, Tom? It isn't just beer and cheese and wine we need! We need much more than that! Much more!
TOM: I don't understand. What do you mean?
SUSAN: We need a bigger house!

Correct these statements

STATEMENT: They spent £10 last week.
RESPONSE: No, they spent £12!

1. They have to give a party because they bought a new car.
2. They have to give the party next week.
3. Tom often worries about money.
4. Tom invited only some of the teachers.
5. Susan thinks they need a bigger kitchen.

Now ask and answer the questions:
1. Ask when they have to give the party!
2. Ask why!
3. Ask what they need for the party!
4. Ask questions with 'How much' or 'How many':
   a) teachers at the college
   b) bottles of beer and wine tomorrow
   c) cheese

FURTHER PRACTICE

Unit 4
d

1. Invention Exercise

a) Follow the technique of doing this exercise in the classroom described in Unit One (teacher page 6).

b) Notice that the prompts call for a variety of verb-forms apart from a discrimination in the use of 'How much' and 'How many'. Thus the response for:
  i) is either 'How much free time *do you get*' or '... *do you have* ...'
  ii) 'How many teachers *are there* ...' or '... *have you got* ...?'
  iii) 'How many lessons *do you give* ...' or '... *do you (have to) take*'
  iv) 'How many students *are there* ...' or '... *have you got* ...?'
  v) 'How much work *do you do* ...' or '... *have you got* ...' or '... *do you have to do* ...'
  vi) 'How many books *do you read* ...' or '... *do you have to read* ...' or perhaps even 'How many books *do you buy* in a month?'

c) Get students to use the prompts to ask each other questions. The answers they give should be true.

2. Conversation

Key Points
1. Use of 'spend (money) on ...'
2. Meaning and intonation of 'that reminds me'
3. Intonation patterns in 'Party? What party?'
4. Intonation of the introductory 'Well ... you see ...'
5. Preview again of 'going to' in 'Is that what you're going to say?'
6. Intonation and use of 'I'm terribly sorry. I really am!'
7. Meaning and use of 'at least' and 'worry'.
8. Preview of *some*

Presentation Notes
1. Follow points 1, 2 and 3 to the conversation in Unit One (see page 6).
2. Focus students' attention again upon the past form of 'have to' used in the conversation with 'I had to invite all the teachers ...'
Simple Substitution Drill:
Model: I HAD TO INVITE ALL THE TEACHERS.
Prompts: stay home last night/save more last year/take a chance/call the police/walk there/sell the car/get a taxi.
3. Paired conversation phase with this part of the conversation –
'That reminds me. Did I tell you about the party?'
'Party? What party?'
–using the following prompts in place of 'the party' and trying to copy the intonation on the tape as closely as possible:
Prompts: the film/the football match/the new car/the gas bill/the examination results/the accident/my sister.
4. If you are using the tape, test whether the class has grasped the correct intonation of various items and sentences in the conversation by asking them to say the sentences they remember from the prompts below. Books should be closed.
Example: £12 last week = WE SPENT £12 LAST WEEK.
  a) tradition   e) beer already
  b) afraid   f) the money
  c) before?   g) invite?
  d) terribly   h) house

Unit 4
e/f

e Summary

1 and 2
It is extremely important that students can immediately discriminate between Mass and Unit words because this basic distinction governs not only the use of 'How much' or 'How many', but also the use of 'a few' and 'a little', for example. (See Unit 5)
Point out also that both phrases 'How much' and 'How many' are often used alone when the speakers in a conversation know what they refer to:
Example: 'I'd like some cheese, please'.
'How much would you like?' (*cheese* is understood)
And in the question 'How much do they earn?', *money* is understood.

3
Notice that we have not introduced the negatives 'doesn't/don't have to' or 'didn't have to' or 'won't have to' in this Unit as it brings with it the problems involved in the discrimination of 'don't have to', 'needn't' and 'mustn't'.

f Exercises for homework

2
Once again it is advisable to do this exercise in class (time permitting) before asking students to do it as a written homework exercise. They could also be asked to use it for asking questions about each other or each other's relations or friends. Again it is important that such question and answer work is as realistic as possible.

3
As in the last Unit, this type of Guided Composition exercise may also be applied to the student's individual experience, so that he can use the structures and sentence patterns in describing his own or the life story to date of a friend or relative.

Unit 4

e/f

e Summary

Focal points in this Unit

1. 'How *much*' is used with *Mass* words. Typical mass words are *beer, milk, cheese, coffee, money, time*.

2. 'How *many*' is used with *Unit* words. Typical unit words are 'bottles of beer', 'glasses of milk', 'pieces of cheese', 'cups of coffee', 'coins', 'seconds' and 'minutes'.

3. a) 'Have to do' means 'It is necessary to do'.
   b) The past of 'have to' is 'had to'.
   c) Questions are formed with 'Do/does . . . have to . . .?' in the present and 'Did . . . have to . . .?' in the past.
   d) The future is 'Will have to', which is usually pronounced 'I'll have to'.

4. It is not a good thing to try and explain the difference between *have to* and *must* at this point. You need a lot more practice in English first to understand the practical difference. However, notice these points:
   a) *must* has no past and no future form. That is, 'had to' and 'will have to' express the past idea and the future idea.
   b) We usually use *have to* rather than *must* to talk about necessity. A common situation in which we frequently use *must* is when we give someone very strong advice, such as 'You know, you really must save more money!'

f Exercises for homework

1. Answer the questions to the situations on page 21 and do the exercises on page 22.

2. In English, we can say 'How many children have you?', but it is more usual to say 'How many children have you got?', using 'have got' instead of simply *have*. Ask questions with 'How much/How many . . . has he/have you got?' with the prompts.
   Examples:
   a) PROMPT: children/they
      RESPONSE: How many children have they got?
   b) PROMPT: money/he/in the bank
      RESPONSE: How much money has he got in the bank?

   Prompts:
   a) friends/they
   b) cars/they/in that garage
   c) boyfriends/she
   d) cigarettes/you
   e) rooms/you/in your house
   f) brothers/your friend
   g) meat/we/in the fridge
   h) modern furniture/they/in their house
   i) children/your sister
   j) clothes/she

3. **Guided Composition**

   Read again what happened to Arthur from 1948 to 1960 (situations 2, 3, 4 and 5; page 21) then write about this person:

   Jim Brent/teacher/language school/1955// 25 lessons a week/£65 a month//wife/book shop//40 hours/£9 a week//she/give up/1959/baby//Jim/better job/money//new house/1961/wife/another baby//own school/1963//Jim/55 hours/but/£3,500//another new house/new car//wife/new car, too//

4. **Transfer Exercise**

   Write at least 5 true sentences about things you *have to do* today or tomorrow, or about things you *had to do* yesterday or last week.

Unit 5
a Some, any, a few, a little

1
(a) demonstrators?
(b) policemen?
(c) soldiers?
(d) tourists?
(e) reporters?
(f) birds interested?

2
(a) What/Susan?
(b) What/want to use?
(c) How much sugar/usually always
(d) chocolate?

3
(a) When/strike?
(b) Where/policemen and strikers?
(c) What day?
(d) What/most of the men?
(e) reporters there?

4
(a) What/Arthur/order?
(b) waiter bring?
(c) many people?

5
(a) How many men?
(b) any women?
(c) What time?
(d) What/Fred?
(e) What/want?
(f) Fred/any money?

Main Teaching-Points
1. Use of *some* and *any* with Mass and Unit words: *some* in positive sentences and *any* in negative sentences.
2. Revision of *There's* and *There are* (unstressed *is* and *are*) with *some* (also in unstressed pronunciation [səm]).
3. Use of 'a few' with Unit words and 'a little' with Mass words as indicators of quantity.

Extra Point and Activities
1. Practice with 'interested in'.
2. Preview of 'going to' in 'Susan is going to bake a cake'.
3. Prepositional uses; e.g. *in front of* the factory/*at* the match/*in* the trees.
4. Sentences like '*There aren't any* soldiers *there*'. Discrimination of the two *there*'s.
5. Preview of *ago* in the sentence 'The waiter brought him . . . a few seconds ago'.

Unit 5 a

SOME, ANY, A FEW, A LITTLE

1

This is a small demonstration in a London park. There are some demonstrators and some policemen in the park, but only a few. There are not any soldiers there but there are a few tourists. There are also some reporters there; in fact, there are quite a few. There are also some birds in the trees but they are not very interested in the demonstration.

1. Ask questions with "Are there any . . .?"
   Answer with 'some' or 'not any'
   a) policemen   b) demonstrators
   c) soldiers   d) tourists
   e) reporters   f) birds
2. Now ask questions with "How many . . . are there?"
   Answer with 'a few' or 'quite a few'

2

Susan is going to bake a cake. She has some eggs, butter, sugar and milk. She wants to use only a few eggs and a little butter. She always uses a lot of sugar. She has not got any chocolate. She needs some. It is going to be a chocolate cake.

1. What is Susan going to do?
2. Ask questions with 'any'
   a) eggs   b) butter
   c) sugar   d) milk
3. What does she need? What hasn't she got? Why does she need it?
4. Ask "How much/many . . . is she going to use?"

3

This strike began last week and it is still going on. There are some policemen and strikers in front of the factory but only a few. It is Saturday and most of the men are watching a big football match. The strange thing is that there are not any reporters or television cameramen there; perhaps they are at the match too.

1. Ask questions with 'any'
   a) strikers   b) policemen
   c) T.V. cameramen d) soldiers
2. Are there a few or quite a few people here?
3. Where are all the others?

4

Arthur ordered a steak with some salad and potatoes. The waiter brought him some salad with his steak a few seconds ago but he did not bring him any potatoes. Arthur is telling him to bring him some now. There are only a few people in the restaurant. Perhaps it is not very good.

1. Ask what Arthur ordered and what the waiter brought him!
2. What is Arthur telling him and why?
3. Ask how many people there are!

5

There are quite a few men in this pub. There are also a few women. It is almost closing-time (11 o'clock). The man looking at his wallet is called Fred Collins. He wants some more beer. The trouble is he has not got any money.

1. Ask questions with "Are there any . . . ?" or "Is there any . . . ?"
   a) men   b) women
   c) money in Fred's wallet
2. What is Fred doing and why?

Unit 5 b

FORMATION AND MANIPULATION

1 Study this. Notice when we use *is a*, *is some*, and *are some*:

There *is a*	piece of bread packet of butter bottle of milk cigarette detective	over there

There *is some*	bread butter milk tobacco	over there

There *are some*	pieces of bread packets of butter bottles of milk cigarettes detectives	over there

Now use one of these three models for these words
- i) oil
- ii) tins of oil
- iii) glass of wine
- iv) hot coffee
- v) warm clothes
- vi) warm jacket
- vii) police dog
- viii) policemen
- ix) hot water
- x) food
- xi) sandwich
- xii) sandwiches

2 Study the use of *any* in:

a) Negative sentences

There	is not any	food wine money	left
	are not any	sandwiches potatoes cigars	

b) Questions

Is there any	food wine money	left?
Are there any	sandwiches potatoes cigars	

a) Use these tables to make more sentences of your own.   b) Make sentences with these words:
- i) I didn't use
- ii) Have you got
- iii) They didn't want
- iv) Did you get
- v) Did she buy
- vi) She didn't buy

3 Study the use of 'a little' and 'a few'

There is We have got	only a little	work time money petrol butter

There are We have got	only a few	cinemas good hotels cheap restaurants here intelligent people big factories

Can you make some sentences of your own, with words like: beef in this beef soup, good bookshops here, parks in Birmingham, wine in the bottle?

FORMATION AND MANIPULATION

Unit 5 b

Pronunciation, Stress and Intonation

Note: The emphasis in this Unit is to give students a clear grasp of the use of *some* in positive statements and *any* in negative statements and questions. (See also *Special Note* below.) The other pairs (something/anything; somewhere/anywhere; someone/anyone; etc.) are also introduced at various points in the unit, but are not practised explicitly. There is no reason why the teacher should not practise these forms, however, since their usage corresponds to that of *some* and *any* practised here.

Special Note: In **2** (student page) we show how *any* is used in questions. Since students will hear both *some* and *any* used in questions by English speakers, it might be worth giving examples of both:
  i) *Have you got any matches?/Is there any food left?*
  ii) *Would you like some tea?/Do you want some apples?*
In (i) the speaker has no particular quantity in mind; thus he uses *any*. In (ii) the speaker has a positive idea of the quantity, (perhaps a cup of tea, or 3 or 4 apples for the other person to eat while he's out for a day in the country); so he uses *some*.

1.
1. Practise the tables orally as Simple Substitution Drills. Focus students' attention on the unstressed forms [ðəzə], [ðəzsəm] and [ðərəsəm]. Also insist on the unstressed [əv] in 'a piece of bread'.
2. Give the prompts i to xii orally for choral or individual responses. If individual responses are required, give the prompt before indicating the individual from whom you want the response.
   Give a short writing phase, asking students to write down one or two sentences that have been given orally.

2. a)
1. Explain the use of *left* in this context. (Suggested explanation: 'If I have 5 books, and I take away 3, there are 2 left.')
2. Once again, focus attention on the short forms in spoken English – 'There *isn't*' and 'There *aren't*'.
3. **Suggested paired practice phase** using statements from the Table (2 a):
   Model: S.1: There isn't any food left.
          S.2: Oh, isn't there? I'll get some more, then.

2. b)
1. Choral repetition of questions from the Table to establish the intonation of this type of question and the word stress attached to different words (e.g. potatoes/cigars).
2. Short writing phase using prompts i to vi.
3. If felt necessary, give examples also with *some* in questions. (See *Special Note*.)

3.
1. Firstly give the class a short discrimination exercise (as described in 1 a) Unit 4), this time putting the following on the blackboard:

1	2
only a few	only a little

   Give the class a number of words and phrases (e.g. bread/pieces of bread) and ask whether they are 1 or 2 words. Repeat the same words, this time asking students to say 'only a few . . .' or 'only a little . . .'
   Example: T: cheese   Ss: only a little cheese.

Fluency Practice

I'VE GOT A FEW BOOKS
1. friends
2. He
3. shops
4. They
5. We
6. bottles of wine

THERE'S ONLY A LITTLE TIME LEFT
1. money
2. petrol
3. food
4. milk

Unit 5 C

EXPLOITATION OF THE EPISODE

Key Patterns and Vocabulary	Suggested Explanations
a) Coke could hardly believe his ears. (20)	He could not really believe what he heard.
b) Coke *stared at* her . . . (26)	He looked at her for a time. It is impolite to stare at someone.
c) . . . Coke *froze* (13)	He stood perfectly still. (Point out that *froze* is the past form of *freeze*.)

Special Preview
The pattern 'There was . . . -ing' is used twice in this episode (lines 2 and 6) and it is worth practising before studying the text with the class. Quote the two examples from the text –
  There was smoke coming from the chimney and
  There was a fire burning in the fireplace
– then give this Substitution Drill for fluency practice:

THERE WAS A MAN WAITING IN THE OFFICE
1. girl
2. sitting
3. three girls
4. working
5. a policeman
6. standing
7. salesman

Section 1
1. Listening phase followed by comprehension questions as suggested in earlier episodes.
2. Completion of text technique as used with Episode 3.
3. Point out the word *furniture* in line 7. It often provides a problem because in English it is a Mass word and is therefore used with 'How much', 'not much', 'a little' etc., and has no *s* plural. Get students to ask each other questions:
For example:
How much furniture have you got in your bedroom?
How much modern furniture have you got at home?
Have you got any old-fashioned furniture at home?

Section 2
1. Listening phase followed by questions, then silent reading.
2. Fluency practice:
SHE DIDN'T LOOK AFRAID
a) surprised
b) He
c) ill
d) He looked very
e) She
f) old
g) Did she . . . ?
h) he
i) young

Section 3
1. After asking a variety of questions about the text, (e.g. Why didn't the old woman hear Coke?/Was his uniform clean?/What did the old woman give him?) get students to ask each other questions. Give prompts (orally or on the blackboard):
Example:
T: Why/not hear?
S.1: Why didn't the old woman hear Coke?
S.2: Because she was deaf.
T: Old woman/know/ prisoner?
S.1: Did the old woman know he was a prisoner?
S.2: No, she didn't.
2. The pattern *She gave him some hot water* could be practised briefly here with a Substitution Drill:
SHE GAVE HIM SOME HOT WATER
a) some food
b) me
c) a book
d) He
e) some sugar
f) potatoes
g) They
h) a piece of steak

THE MAN WHO ESCAPED
Episode 5

Unit 5

C

SYNOPSIS: *Coke escaped from prison and hid in a field. It was very cold and he knew he had to find warm clothes and food somewhere. He saw a house in the country, isolated and far away from the nearest town. He stood outside the house before going in. He could not understand why there was no noise coming from it, not even the sound of a radio or television.*

1 Coke listened for several seconds but he could not hear anything at all. And yet there was smoke coming from the chimney and there was a light on in the front room! "Why is it so quiet? Is it a trap? Are the police waiting for me in there?" he asked himself. He went to the front door and pushed it. To his surprise it was open! He went in very quietly. In the front room there was a fire burning in the fireplace. The room was clean, small and very warm. There was very little furniture in it— only a couch and a table in front of the fire and two old-fashioned chairs. There were also some photographs on the shelf above the fire. They were yellow and old. One of them was of a young man in a World War I uniform. There were also a few of the same young man and also a woman in old-fashioned wedding-clothes.

2 Suddenly Coke froze. There was someone else in the room. He knew it. He could feel it! He turned around quickly and, at the same time, put his hand in his pocket. There was a small knife there. He saw an old woman. She had a covered dish in her hands and there was a delicious smell of meat and vegetables coming from it. She did not look afraid. She did not even look surprised.
"I'm sorry," she said, and put the dish down on the table.
Coke could hardly believe his ears. Here he was, a stranger in her house and yet she said *she* was sorry!

3 "I'm sorry," she said again. "I didn't hear you. Did you knock? I'm deaf, you see." She pointed to her ear, shook her head and said "deaf" a second time. "People often come to the door and knock, but I don't hear them. I'm glad you came in."

Coke stared at her for a second and then finally found his voice. "I . . . I'm sorry. I just stepped in."
He looked down at his clothes. His prison uniform was so dirty that it was impossible to tell what kind of uniform it was. Then he suddenly had an idea.

"I'm a mechanic from a garage in town. I came to repair a lorry somewhere out here but the road was icy. I had an accident. I . . . I fell off my motorbike."

He had to say this several times before she finally understood him. When she did, she gave him some hot water and soap and afterwards some food. The only thing he needed now was a change of clothes!

Unit 5 d

FURTHER PRACTICE

1. Special Transformation Exercise

MODEL: I need some eggs
We haven't got = We haven't got any eggs
cold beer = We haven't got any cold beer

Prompts:

a) sugar
b) There isn't
c) potatoes
d) coffee
e) I'd like
f) breakfast
g) We didn't have
h) rain
i) There wasn't
j) good films
k) I saw
l) They went to

2. Conversation

Arthur and his chief engineer, Don Anderson, went to a small town near Manchester last week. They went on business and they had to stay the night in a small hotel. They had to eat in the hotel, too.

DON: Can't we eat somewhere else, Arthur? Very few small hotels like this serve good food.
ARTHUR: I know, but there isn't anywhere else in this town. Besides, the waiter's coming over for our order, now.
WAITER: Good evening. Would you like to order now? I can recommend the roast beef. It's very good.
ARTHUR: No, I'm afraid I don't like roast beef. Let me see . . . what else have you got on your menu. You order first, Don.
DON: All right. Roast beef for me, please. But I don't want any potatoes. I'm trying to lose some weight.
ARTHUR: I think I'd like some fish. Yes, some Scotch salmon, please.
WAITER: Er . . . I'm afraid we haven't got any salmon this evening, sir. The roast beef's really very good indeed, sir.
ARTHUR: No. If I can't have any salmon, I'd like some trout.
WAITER: I'm terribly sorry, sir, but I'm afraid we . . . er . . .
ARTHUR: You mean you haven't got any trout, either!
WAITER: No, sir. I'm afraid not, sir.
ARTHUR: Well . . . hmm . . . I suppose you have some Dover sole, then?
WAITER: Dover sole, sir? Did you say Dover sole, sir?
ARTHUR: Yes, that's right, I'd like some Dover sole with some . . .
WAITER: There's very little good Dover sole on the market at this time of the year, sir. Our roast beef's much better!
ARTHUR: I'm sure it is, but I don't like roast beef. I'd still like . . .
WAITER: Try the roast beef, sir.
ARTHUR: Why? I don't like roast beef! I never eat roast beef! In fact, I hate roast beef!
WAITER: Well . . . I'm afraid we haven't got anything else, sir.

Questions

1. Where does Don want to eat at the beginning and why can't they do this?
2. Ask and answer these questions:
   a) How many small hotels/good food?
   b) Why/Don/potatoes?
3. Ask and answer why Arthur can't get any
   a) salmon   b) trout   c) Dover sole
4. What does the waiter say about the roast beef?
5. Why doesn't Arthur want it?

FURTHER PRACTICE Unit 5 d

1. Special Transformation Exercise

a) This exercise is designed to help the students produce *some* with a positive idea and *any* with a negative idea. It is designed to increase the fluency of students' speech and should therefore definitely be practised in the classroom before any written work is done.

b) We have not included any question items here, although the exercise (2b) on the Formation and Manipulation page (28) could well be given also as written work.

c) Paired practice with this Model:
   S.1: I need some eggs.
   S.2: I'm sorry. There aren't any left.
or S.1: I need some bread.
   S.2: I'm sorry. There isn't any left.
Prompts: eggs/coffee/books/cheese/cigarettes/ butter/food/warm boots/tobacco.

2. Conversation

Key Points
1. Practice with 'somewhere else' and 'anywhere else'
2. Meaning and use of *recommend*
3. Meaning and intonation of 'I'm afraid' + negative idea
4. Meaning and use of 'I'm afraid not'
5. Practice with 'If I can't have any . . . I'd like some . . .'
6. Use of *much* + Comparative as in 'Our roast beef's *much better*'
7. Practice with 'in fact' as in 'I never . . . In fact, I hate . . .'

Presentation Notes
1. Follow the initial presentation procedure as for the previous Conversations (outlined on Teacher page 6).
2. *Simple Substitution Drill:*
   Model: CAN'T WE EAT SOMEWHERE ELSE?
   (Prompts to replace WE and EAT.)

a) go   e) he
b) you   f) stay
c) play   g) your parents
d) the children h) we

3. Explain the meaning of the word *recommend*. (Suggested explanation: If a friend likes Western films and you see one you think he will like, you might say: 'You'll like that film.' You recommend it.)
   Practice: I CAN RECOMMEND THE ROAST BEEF. IT'S GOOD.
   a) that book/interesting
   b) this wine/good
   c) that film/exciting
   d) that TV programme/amusing.

4. Focus students' attention on the type of phrase used after *I'm afraid*:
   'I'm afraid   I don't like roast beef.'
                  we haven't got any salmon.'
                  we haven't got anything else.'
   Practise in pairs this short dialogue using the prompts given above (Transformation Exercise, c).
   S.1: I'd like some matches, please.
   S.2: I'm afraid we haven't got any matches.

5. With student books closed, use the following prompt-words and phrases as a Recall exercise for some of the key sentences:
   a) try/weight
   b) can't have salmon/trout
   c) mean/trout, either

Unit 5
e/f

e Summary

1, 2 and 3
The use of *some* and *any* in positive and negative sentences respectively should not cause students a great deal of difficulty, and it is well worth while extending their grasp of the overall concept to the other pairs of words which function the same way: *somebody/anybody*, *someone/anyone*, *something/anything* and *somewhere/anywhere*.
Give examples:
'I can hear *somebody*.'/'I ca*n't* hear *anybody*.'
'It's here *somewhere*.'/'It is*n't* anywhere in the room.'
'I've got *something* for you/'I have*n't* got *anything* for her birthday.'
If the students have been given examples of questions using both *some* and *any*, remind them of the reason why we use one rather than the other in English (see Formation and Manipulation teacher page 28).

4
Notice that we have only asked the student to use actively the forms 'a few' and 'a little' (with modifiers *only* and *quite*). We have not asked students to use the forms 'few', 'very few', 'little' or 'very little', which imply a definite negative attitude to the number or quantity being talked about. They do, however, occur in the Conversation for recognition ('very few small hotels' and 'very little good Dover sole').

f Exercises for homework

2
We have asked students here to ask questions using *any*. As noted above and on page 27 they might also be shown that such questions can also be asked with *some*. The prompts given might also be used for a short Paired Practice phase whilst preparing for the homework. Some of the prompts could be changed slightly to fit the situation:
Example:
Prompt: good detective novels at home
S.1:   Have you got any good detective novels at home?
S.2:   No, I haven't; but I've got some good Westerns.
OR: Yes, I have. I've got quite a few.

3
Point out to the students that although the original situations 1 and 3 (page 26) are in the Present tense, they are asked to write their short composition in the Past.

Optional Homework:
As a further written exercise, students could be asked to study the Conversation on page 29 again very carefully, and then to write another shorter conversation like it, using some of the sentences (e.g. 'I can recommend . . .'/'What else have you got . . .?'/etc), beginning like this:
Julia is in a café waiting for lunch.
Waitress: Good morning, madam. Would you like to order now?
Julia: Yes . . . What can you recommend?
                                    and so on.

Unit 5
e/f

e Summary

Focal points in this Unit.

1. When we have an idea of the quantity of something but we do not think it is necessary to give the exact amount, we use *some*. We use *some* in positive sentences, with Mass and Unit words:

   Examples:

   There are some policemen in the park.
   There is some chocolate on the table.

2. When we ask questions about something or a number of things, and we have no idea of the quantity, we use *any*:

   Examples:

   Is there any food left?
   Are there any sandwiches for me?

3. We use *any* (instead of *some*) in negative sentences:

   Examples:

   There isn't any food left.
   There aren't any policemen in the park.

4. 'a few' and 'a little':
   a) *a few* means a small number, and we use it with Unit words – a few policemen/ a few people/a few strikers. We sometimes add the word *only* ('only a few') or *quite*. 'Quite a few people' means 'A lot of people'.
   b) *a little* means 'a small quantity', and we use it with Mass words – a little sugar/a little petrol/a little food. We also add the word *only* ('only a little'), but we rarely add the word *quite*.

f Exercises for homework

1. Ask the questions to the situations on page 27, and do the Special Transformation exercise on page 30.

2. Make statements and ask questions about the following things:

   Example:
   PROMPT: good detective novels in that shop.
   RESPONSE: a) There are some good detective novels in that shop.
             b) Are there any good detective novels in that shop?

   Prompts:
   a) money in his bank account
   b) bread in the cupboard
   c) tomatoes in that box
   d) milk in the fridge
   e) chairs in the room
   f) Russian students at the University
   g) petrol in the tank
   h) very good Continental restaurants in London
   i) cigarettes left in that packet
   j) time left

3. **Guided Composition**

   Read situations 1 and 3 on page 27 again carefully, and then write about a demonstration last week. Use the prompts and begin with this sentence:

   'There was a small demonstration in Hyde Park last week.'
   demonstrators/students/policemen//not any soldiers/but/tourists//reporters/but not many//Saturday/most/football match// also/other young people/Park/not interested /demonstration//

4. **Transfer Exercise**

   Write 5 true sentences about yourself using *some* and 5 using *any*. Here are two examples:
   'I met some friends in the town yesterday.'
   'I didn't have any breakfast this morning.'

Unit 6
a

Past tense with 'Ago' and questions with 'How long ago?'

1 
(a) When/open?
(b) What/shoppers?
(c) What/sales people?
(d) Where/detective?
(e) What/wear?
(f) Who/watch?

2 
(a) What time?
(b) When/close?
(c) shoppers?
(d) detective?
(e) sales people?
(f) When/last one?

3 
(a) When/London express?
(b) What/want to know?
(c) What/answer?

4 
(a) Why/a hurry?
(b) When/film?
(c) new film?
(d) When/made?
(e) When/Julia/film before?

5 
(a) Where/Fred?
(b) Fred's wife's question?
(c) What time?
(d) When/he/work?
(e) How long ago?

6 
(a) What time?
(b) When/lecture?
(c) Why/hesitate?
(d) What/lecture on?

Main Teaching-Points
1. Use of the word *ago* with phrases like 'half an hour', 'fifteen minutes', '10 years', etc. in the past.
2. The use of 'How long ago?' with questions in the past; therefore revision of and practice of past question 'Did you/he/they?' etc.

Extra Points and Activities
1. More practice with times using *ago* – 'half an hour ago', 'a quarter of an hour ago', etc.
2. Practice with more verbs in the past: 'closed/left/watched/counted/thought/saw'.
3. Practice with the patterns:
   a) 'He thought it left at 11.10.'
   b) 'I wonder where he is.'
4. Practice with the words *home* and *work* in 'They went home' and 'He always *leaves work* at 5.30'.

| He did something ...... years/hours ago | **Unit 6** |
| How long ago did he ....? | **a** |

1

This is a department store. It is open six days a week, from 9 to 5.30. It is closing now. The shoppers are all leaving and the sales people are counting money. The man in the jacket by the door is a detective. He is watching everybody.

1. What kind of store is this?
2. When is it open?
3. What are the shoppers doing?
4. Ask why!
5. What else is happening?

2

It is 6 o'clock now. The store closed half an hour ago. All the shoppers left the store half an hour ago. The detective watched them. Then the sales people counted their money and went home, too. The last one left fifteen minutes ago. That was at 5.45.

1. What did all the shoppers do half an hour ago and why?
2. What did the detective do?
3. What did the sales people do?
4. When did the last one leave?

3

Arthur thought the London express left at 11.10. In fact it left at 11.05. It left before he got to the station. "How long ago did it leave?" he wants to know. "Five minutes ago, at 11.05" is the answer.

1. What time is it now?
2. What happened before Arthur got to the station?
3. When did he think it left?
4. Ask two questions about the train with
   a) When   b) How long ago

4

Julia and her boyfriend are in a hurry. The film started fifteen minutes ago. They do not want to miss too much of it. It is one of Charles Kay's old horror films. It was made 10 years ago. Julia does not remember but she saw the film on television a few months ago.

1. Ask and answer why Julia and her boyfriend are in a hurry!
2. Ask how long ago the film began!
3. How long ago was it made? What year was that?
4. What is it that Julia does not remember?

5

Fred Collins spends most of his time in pubs. We met him in Unit 5. This is his wife. "I wonder where Fred is?" she is saying. Actually she has a pretty good idea. It is 8 o'clock now and she knows he always leaves work at 5.30. How long ago was that?

1. Is Fred at home?
2. What is his wife saying?
3. Ask these questions about Fred
   a) most of his time   b) When/work
   c) How long ago/work
4. Where do you think Fred is?

6

Tom does not know whether to go to the lecture or not. It is already 3.15 and it started at 3. How long ago was that? Tom is hesitating because he does not want to disturb anyone in the hall. The lecture is on language-teaching.

1. Ask two questions about the lecture:
   a) When   b) How long ago
2. Ask what Tom is doing and why!
3. What is the lecture on?
4. Make a sentence of your own with 'didn't know whether to ... or not'.

Unit 6 b

FORMATION AND MANIPULATION

1 Notice that the word *ago* comes after phrases like 'fifteen minutes', 'half an hour', '10 years'.

A	B	C	D
They	left	the cinema	half an hour	ago

i) How many words can you think of to replace 'They' in box A? (for example: 'he').
ii) Now think of words to replace 'the cinema' in box B.
iii) Now look at the situations on page 33 and find other time phrases to replace 'half an hour'.
iv) Make as many sentences as you can using the words you have for exercises i), ii) and iii).

2 Notice the question form with *How long ago*.

A	B	C
How long ago did	the film	start?

i) Find as many words as you can to replace 'the film' in box B and 'start' in box C.
ii) Now ask questions with the words you have from exercise i, and with the words you have from exercise **1** iii, answer them like this:

    Question: How long ago did they go home?
    Answer: Ten minutes ago.

3 Verbs like *start, arrive* and *wash* are regular verbs. They end in *-ed* in the past: *started, arrived* and *washed*.
Verbs like *leave, see* and *read* are irregular and have different types of past forms: *left, saw* and *read*.

4 You must learn the past forms of regular and irregular verbs by heart. There is a list of verbs at the back of this book. Learn five verbs each day. Start today and learn these verb-forms

    do – did   get – got   find – found
        start – started   look – looked

FORMATION AND MANIPULATION

Unit 6 b

Note: The emphasis in this Unit is on the correct manipulation of the question forms of regular and irregular verbs in the simple past tense. Oral practice of the question form using 'How long ago . . .?' must be continued until there is no hesitation at all by students. A short writing phase (two or three minutes) can be used to give the students a rest from high-speed oral production. Both oral and written work should be based on the substitution tables on student page 34.

1. and 2.

Students have a tendency to say 'did he opened?' This is because it is more difficult to hear a difference between *open* and *opened* than between *go* and *went*. Use this simple discrimination drill to remedy this.
Write *open* and *buy* on the blackboard and label them *a*.
Write *opened* and *bought* on the blackboard and label them *b*.
Ask students to tell you whether the forms of the verbs you give them are like *a* or *b*:
Verb-forms: watched, think, talk, took, talked, sent, sold, send, say, happen, played, met, looked, learned, happened, went, give, got, fly, finished, turn, drive, did, brought, turned, ask, answered, listened, stared.

3. and 4.

The importance of learning the correct forms of verbs must be constantly emphasised. Unless students make a conscious effort to learn the forms by heart, much of what they produce will be needlessly inaccurate.
Help the students to get into the habit of learning by heart. Spend ten minutes today in class allowing the students to learn some of the verbs at the end of the book. Spend as long as is necessary and test the students thoroughly to show them that this is a serious business.

Learning a few verb-forms each day can then become a regular part of the homework schedule.

Testing Techniques

1. Full answers. Ask students simple questions and get full answers e.g.:
   Teacher: Did you see the film?
   Student: Yes, I saw it.
2. Question-forming. Use this form of eliciting questions:
   Teacher: Richard cooked a meal yesterday.
   Student: Yes, but did John cook anything?
3. Simple transformation of forms:
   Teacher: I say *look* and you say *looked*
   and   I say *bought* and you say *buy*.
4. Ask students to write out both forms of the verbs learnt.
5. Write one form and ask the student to write the other.

N.B. YOU WILL BE REMINDED ABOUT REVISING THESE FORMS THROUGHOUT THE BOOK.

Unit 6 c

EXPLOITATION OF THE EPISODE

Key Patterns and Vocabulary	*Suggested Explanations*
a) wonder (5)	'I don't know, but I would like to.'
b) even (9)	She doesn't listen to the radio or watch television, so you think she reads papers, but she doesn't read them either.
c) bike (14)	bicycle.
d) Besides, . . . (14)	and also.
e) social formalities (19)	'Hello', 'How do you do', and shaking hands are examples of social formalities.
f) before another 24 hours are up (20)	in the next 24 hours.
g) Let's get going! (27)	We should start now!

Also observe the past tenses used in the episode:
'could/died/answered/wondered/found/shook/blew.'

Section 1
1. Sample questions
a) What sort of a night was it?
b) How far was the police station away from the old lady's house?
c) When did the old lady's husband die?
d) Why doesn't she listen to the radio?
2. Fluency Practice:
I WONDER HOW MRS. BENTLEY IS
(discrimination of *how* and *where*)
Example:
T: Arthur
S: I wonder how Arthur is.
a) Arthur
b) where
c) Julia
d) how
e) the children
f) where
g) my wallet
h) Susan
i) how

Section 2
1. Sample questions
a) Who met Baxter at the station?
b) Who told Halls to meet Baxter?
c) When did Coke escape?
d) How soon does Baxter want to catch Coke?
2. Ask students to make sentences of their own with these words: they should use the words *in the same way as they are used in the text*:
a) get off
b) shake (someone's hand)
c) interested
d) half-way

Section 3
1. Ask students to read the text silently. Then ask short-answer questions about the passage.
2. Get students to ask each other questions about the passage using these prompts:
a) policeman/happy?
b) Why/angry?
c) Why/get off/bike?
d) What/from the top of the hill?
e) Where/light?
3. Focus students' attention on the phrase '. . . he saw a light go on . . .' (line 36) and in particular on the form of the verb *go*. (He *saw something happen*.) Use this table (on the blackboard) for more examples of the same type of sentence. Point out what types of verb we use and therefore what types of situation we use the structure in.

I He She They	saw	a light go on the man fall down the car stop the prisoner run away

Note: Point out that the actions 'go on', 'fall down', 'stop' and 'run away' are quick, complete actions.

Ask students to write 2 or 3 sentences of their own with the pattern.

THE MAN WHO ESCAPED
Episode 6

Unit 6

C

SYNOPSIS: *After Coke escaped, he hid in a field all day. Then, when it got dark, he went into a small house in the country. There was an old deaf lady in the house. She gave him food. The young detective who arrested Coke four years ago, Baxter, left London by train. Scotland Yard's orders were "Find Coke immediately!"*

1 It was a cold and miserable night. Only a few miles away from the house Coke was in, two policemen in a small village police station could hear the wind outside. One of them was a sergeant. The other was much younger.
"I wonder how Mrs Bentley is?" the sergeant asked.
"Mrs Bentley? Oh, you mean that old lady whose husband died a few years ago?"
"That's right. She's deaf, you know, so she never listens to the radio or watches television. In fact, she doesn't even read the papers."
"Oh?" the young policeman said. He wondered why the sergeant wanted to tell him all this. Then he found out.
"Why don't you go out to her place and see if she's all right?"
"Who? Me? On a night like this?"
"It's not far. Besides, you've got your bike, haven't you?"

2 Baxter got off the train at a small station. There was a detective waiting for him on the platform. He shook Baxter's hand.
"My name's Halls, Tom Halls. Scotland Yard phoned us and told us to meet you here. There's a car waiting."
Baxter wasted very little time on social formalities.
"Coke escaped more than 24 hours ago. I want to catch him before another 24 hours are up."
Halls looked at Baxter for a few seconds before he answered.
"A lot of us wonder why Scotland Yard is so interested in this fellow Coke. He isn't the first one to escape. Another man did only about six months ago, but Scotland Yard didn't send anyone to help us then."
Baxter was already half-way to the car before he said anything.
"Coke isn't just an ordinary prisoner. He's very special. Let's get going!"

3 The young policeman was angry. He was on the road now. The wind was cold and blew snow into his face. "That stupid sergeant!" he thought. "We must be one of the last stations in England that still uses bikes, and he sends me out on one on a night like this!"
He had to get off the bike and push it up a hill. It was the last hill between the station and the old lady's house. When he got to the top of it he could see the house down below, at the bottom of the hill. Just as he looked down at it, he saw a light go on in one of the rooms upstairs. "Stupid! That's what it is, sending me out on a night like this!" the policeman said again. Then he got on his bike and began to go down the hill very fast, towards the house.

Unit 6 d

FURTHER PRACTICE

1. Invention Exercise

This exercise practises the Past tense with *ago*, but we have also added the words *first* and *last*. Notice where we put these words in the Model. *First* here means 'the first time', *last* means 'the last time'.

Make sentences using the prompts:
Example:

MODEL: I {first/last} went to London 10 years ago.
PROMPT: She first/Buckingham Palace/3 years
RESPONSE: She first saw Buckingham Palace 3 years ago.
or: She first visited Buckingham Palace 3 years ago.

Prompts:

a) She last/London/3 weeks
b) They first/the cinema/25 years
c) I last/him/five minutes
d) We last/champagne/at a party/a fortnight
e) Tom and Susan last/a wine and cheese party/about 6 weeks
f) He first/a pipe/10 years
g) I first/a novel by Nevil Shute/6 years
h) She first/a television programme/3 years
i) Arthur last/a new car/2 months
j) That man first/to prison/25 years

2. Conversation

Arthur Tigers went out to lunch at 12 o'clock. It's now 2.30 and he's just walking into his office. His secretary is typing. Before Arthur went to lunch, he told his secretary, Miss Bradley, to ring him at the restaurant if a man called Mr Powell came to see him. Arthur came back from lunch only a second ago.

MISS BRADLEY: (nervously) Good afternoon, Mr Tigers. Did you have a good lunch?
ARTHUR: Yes, thank you, Miss Bradley. It was very good. Did anyone phone while I was out?
MISS BRADLEY: No. Nobody phoned, but . . . er . . . Mr Powell came.
ARTHUR: What? But he's the man I told you about!
MISS BRADLEY: Yes, I know, but . . .
ARTHUR: Well, if you knew, why didn't you phone me? Mr Powell has some very important information. I wanted to talk to him as soon as possible. I told you all that before I left. Didn't you understand me?
MISS BRADLEY: Yes, of course, I understood you, Mr Tigers, but . . .
ARTHUR: I even gave you a card with the name and phone number of the restaurant! I put it on your desk.
MISS BRADLEY: But that's just it! You didn't give me the card. You didn't put it on my desk!
ARTHUR: What do you mean? Of course I did. I took the card out of my wallet just before I went to lunch! Look! It isn't in my wallet now! (suddenly) Oh!
MISS BRADLEY: Mr Tigers, what's that card on the floor? It fell out of your wallet a second ago.
ARTHUR: That card? It's . . . er . . . it's the card I thought I gave you.
MISS BRADLEY: You see! You forgot! That's why I didn't phone. I didn't know where you were.
ARTHUR: No. I'm very sorry, Miss Bradley. It wasn't your fault. I apologise.
MISS BRADLEY: That's all right. Please forget it.

Questions

1. Ask (and answer) when Mr Powell came!
2. Why is Arthur so angry when Miss Bradley tells him this?
3. What does Arthur think he did before he left? Ask and answer if he did! (her the card. on her desk)
4. Why didn't Miss Bradley phone Arthur?
5. What are Arthur's exact words when he apologises?
6. What is one thing we can say in English when someone apologises to us?

Practice

Which form of these words do we use in questions in the past? Which form do we use in statements about the past? Make sentences with each!

a) have/had
b) tell/told
c) phone/phoned
d) understand/understood
e) give/gave
f) know/knew
g) forget/forgot
h) go/went
i) come/came
j) fall/fell

FURTHER PRACTICE

Unit 6
d

1. Invention Exercise

a) Follow the technique of doing this exercise as suggested in earlier Units.

b) Notice that the exercise is designed to give more practice with *ago*, but that it also adds the new elements *first* and *last* which are frequently used with the Simple Past tense and *ago*, as in sentences like
'I *first* visited this part of the country 20 years ago.'
or 'My parents *last* went abroad 18 months ago.'
The position of *first* or *last* in this type of sentence is very important.

c) Notice too that the prompts call for a variety of verbs in the Simple Past. Thus, the verbs which could be used in the items are:
for a) *went to, lived in, visited,* or *saw*; for b) *went to*; for c) *saw, met* or *spoke to*; for d) *drank* or *had*; for e) *went to, had* or *held*; for f) *smoked* or *bought*; for g) *read* or *bought*; for h) *watched* or *saw*; for i) *bought* (or *sold*); for j) *went to*.

2. Conversation

Key Points
1. Question intonation in
   a) 'Did you have a good lunch?' and 'Did anyone phone while I was out?' and
   b) '... why didn't you phone me?'
2. Meaning and use of *information*: Mass word in English
3. Meaning and use of 'But that's just it!' in an argument
4. Meaning and use of 'You see!' when proving a point in an argument
5. Apologies and acceptance:
   'I'm very sorry ... I apologise'
   'That's all right. Please forget it'

The conversation also practises the past forms of a number of common verbs (see Practice on the student page).

Presentation Notes
1. Follow points 1, 2 and 3 to the conversation in Unit 1 (see page 6).
2. Go back to the questions used in the conversation and drill them for intonation.
3. Focus students' attention on the word *information*. Point out that this word is always in the singular form in English and that it is a Mass word.
Other words like this are: *furniture, advice* and *fruit*.
Use this Substitution Drill for fluency:
HE HAS SOME VERY IMPORTANT INFORMATION.
   a) She   e) interesting
   b) very useful   f) they
   c) advice   g) furniture
   d) Have you any ...?
4. Focus students' attention on this part of the conversation:
   Arthur: I *gave* you a card ... I *put* it on your desk.
   Secretary: But that's just it. You *didn't give* me a card. You *didn't put* it on my desk.
Pair students to practise short dialogues like this using the verbs given under Practice on the student page.
For example:
S.1: I told you about it yesterday. I phoned you.
S.2: But that's just it. You didn't tell me about it. You didn't phone me.
Ask students to try and make up as many such dialogues as they can.

Unit 6
e/f

e Summary

1 and 2
Before extending the range of expressions which can be used with *ago*, a check should be made that the students have gained fluency in handling the forms already presented. If any hesitancy is evident, the substitution tables (student page 34 1 and 2) should be revised.
Other expressions used with 'ago'. Practise these forms orally using a substitution table (the table on student page 34 (B 1) will do):
Not so long, ages and ages, weeks and weeks, years and years, days and days, months and months, a very long time, a quarter of an hour.

3
As a final check on the students' ability to handle the question form of HOW LONG AGO make the students ask each other questions (and answer them) using prompts written on the blackboard.
Example: S.1: How long ago did you *get up*?
S.2: About 2 hours ago.
Prompts: get up, have your breakfast, get here, sit down, start learning English, have a drink, see your friend, have a holiday.

4
Remember to tell students that *first* and *last* are used when the verbs qualified refer to actions which are normally frequently repeated, so that it is necessary to distinguish the first or last time such an action happened.

f Exercises for homework

2
This exercise can be extended by getting students to ask and answer questions about recent news items.
For example:
How long ago did the President arrive?
About 3 days ago.
How long ago did the accident happen?
2 days ago.

4
The teacher can provide an interesting introduction to this exercise by giving various examples of what he or she did . . . ago.

Unit 6
e/f

e Summary

Focal points in this Unit.

1. The word *ago* goes after phrases like 'two minutes', 'three years', 'a long time', 'half an hour', and means a certain time ('two minutes', 'three years' etc) *back from now*. Remember and look at the examples you have learned in this Unit:

    'It is 6 o'clock now. The store closed at 5.30. That was *half an hour ago*.'

2. Use the Simple Past tense with the word *ago*:

    'It *left* 5 minutes *ago*'/'The film *was made* 10 years *ago*.'/'Arthur *came* back from lunch only a second *ago*.'

3. To ask a question with *ago*, we often use 'How long ago . . .?':

    '*How long ago* did it leave?'/'*How long ago* was that?'

4. Remember how we use the two words *first* and *last* with the Simple Past and *ago*. Look at the Invention Exercise on page 36 again. Here is one example to remind you:

    'I *last* saw him 5 minutes ago.'

f Exercises for homework

1. Do all the exercises and questions on pages 33 and 34.

2. Ask and answer questions using *ago*.

    Example:

    It is 8 o'clock and I am watching television. I turned it on at 7.

    You write:

    Q: How long ago did you turn the television on?
    A: I turned it on an hour ago.

    a) It's March now, and Mary is living in France. She went to France in January.
    b) It's 4.30 now, and Arthur is sitting in his office. He came back from lunch at 2.30.
    c) Tony is standing outside a shop (It's 6.30). But the shop closed at 5.30.
    d) It's 3 o'clock, and Deborah is sitting in the airport lounge looking sad. Her plane left for Paris at 1 o'clock.
    e) Tony is staying at the Hilton Hotel. (It's January, 1970) He last stayed there in July, 1969.

3. **Guided Composition**

    Read the conversation again on page 36. Mr Powell came while Arthur was at lunch. Write the short conversation between Mr Powell and Arthur's secretary, using the following prompts:

    MR POWELL: afternoon//Mr Tigers?//
    MISS BRADLEY: afternoon//No/lunch/half an hour//
    MR POWELL: Where?//important information //must/soon as possible//
    MISS BRADLEY: don't know where//told me/no address or phone number//Mr Tigers/not/card//sorry//
    MR POWELL: all right//not/fault//tell/ring later//Good bye.
    MISS BRADLEY: really/sorry//tell Mr Tigers// Good bye.

4. **Transfer Exercise**

    Write 5 or more true sentences about yourself, friends or relations, using the word *ago*.

    Example:

    I left school 5 years ago.
    My parents and I spent 2 months in Italy 3 years ago.

Unit 7
a
Adjectives and adverbs

1 
(a) How/tall player?
(b) How/short player?
(c) What/yesterday?
(d) won?
(e) lost?

2 
(a) Where/yesterday?
(b) beginning?
(c) end of the film?
(d) Why/in the middle?
(e) Where/Arthur and Deborah?
(f) Why/walk out?

3 
(a) How/piano?
(b) How/tennis?
(c) good cook?
(d) How/French and German?

4 
(a) Fred/bus-driver?
(b) Why/3 accidents?
(c) worst accident?
(d) What/after that?

5 
(a) How/Arthur/when/younger?
(b) How many hours?
(c) How/now?
(d) How many hours/now?

6 
(a) What/Carter and Flash do?
(b) How/houses?
(c) Why/man/shout?

Main Teaching-Points
1. Formation and use of adverbs of manner: three main types:
   a) good → well
   b) hard → hard
   c) dangerous → dangerously
2. Position of adverb as in 'She sings *well*'.
3. Comparison with 'as . . . as' in 'He works *as hard as* his father did'.
4. Formation and use of 'so + adverb + that' as in 'He drove *so dangerously that* he lost his job'.

Extra Points and Activities
1. Unstressed form [əz] in 'as hard as'.
2. More verbs in the past: 'won/lost/missed/sang/ran/built/fell/bought'.
3. Use of *the* with instruments, as in 'She *plays the piano* very well'.
4. Revision of 'used to be'.
5. *Better* as Comparative Adjective (revision) and as Comparative Adverb (preview).

> She's a GOOD singer. She sings WELL.
> He works AS HARD AS his father did.
> He drove SO DANGEROUSLY THAT he lost his job.

Unit 7
a

1

These two often play tennis. The tall player is good. He is playing well. The short one is bad. He is playing badly. One always wins and the other always loses. They also played yesterday. Who do you think won? Who lost?

1. What do these two often do?
2. Ask a question about 'now'!
3. What kind of a player is the tall one?
4. How is he playing?
5. Ask the same questions about the other!
6. What happened yesterday?

2

Julia and her boyfriend went to a film yesterday. They missed the beginning and they did not see the end. It was so bad that they walked out in the middle.

Deborah and Arthur went to the opera. The singers sang so badly that they walked out too.

1. Ask these questions about Julia and her boyfriend:
   a) What/yesterday   b) the beginning
   c) the end   d) Why/in the middle
2. Ask what Deborah and Arthur did!
3. How did the singers sing?

3

Carol Stuart plays the piano and tennis very well. She is a very good cook and swimmer. She speaks French and German perfectly. She is beautiful, too. That is why she was Miss Europe last year.

1. Ask how well she does these things:
   a) tennis   b) the piano
   c) French   d) German
2. Make sentences with 'good' or 'well' about her with these words:
   a) swimmer   b) swims
   c) cooks   d) a cook

4

Fred Collins used to be a bus driver but he is not any more. He drove so badly and dangerously that he had three accidents in one month. The worst was when he ran into a police car. He lost his job after that.

1. Is Fred still a bus driver?
2. What can you say about Fred
   a) as a driver   b) the way he drove?
3. Ask how many accidents he had! (answer)
4. What was the worst and what happened after that?

5

When Sir Arthur was younger he worked very hard. He worked at least 60 hours a week and always did a lot of work. He still works hard but not quite as hard as he used to. He works about 45 hours a week now.

Ask these questions and answer them:
   a) How many hours/   b) How many now?
      younger?
   c) hard then? hard   d) hard as he used to?
      now?

6

R. Carter and J. Flash both build houses but Carter builds them much better. He is a much better builder. Flash builds houses quickly but badly. Once he built a house in a week. It fell down a week later. The man shouting at Flash is the man who bought the house.

1. What can you say about Carter's houses and also the way he builds them?
2. How does Flash build his houses?
3. What happened once?
4. Who is the other man in the picture shouting at Flash?

Unit 7 b

FORMATION AND MANIPULATION

1 Study this. Notice how we use the words *good* and *bad*, and *well* and *badly*. Notice too their position in the sentence

He	is a	good	tennis player	He	plays tennis	well
		bad	teacher		teaches	badly
She			swimmer	She	swims	
			driver		drives	

i) Make pairs of sentences from the tables above.
   Example: 'She's a bad driver. She drives badly.'
ii) Make pairs of sentences in the same way with these prompts:
   Example: French speaker = 'He's a good French speaker. He speaks French well.'
   piano-player: builder: singer: cook: typist.

2 Notice how we form adverbs from adjectives. There are three main types:
   i) Adverbs made from an adjective + *ly* or *ily*:
   quick – quickly   angry – angrily
   careful – carefully   noisy – noisily
   dangerous – dangerously easy – easily
   ii) Adverbs which have the same form as the adjective:
   hard – hard   fast – fast
   iii) Adverbs which are completely different from the adjective:
                   good – well
   Ask another student about himself, his (or her) friends or relatives using some of the adverbs above.
   Example: Does your father work very hard?
            Do you drive very carefully?

3

A	B	C	D
He	drove so dangerously	that	he lost his job

i) Think of words to replace 'drove' and 'dangerously' in box B.
ii) Now, with another student, ask and answer questions like this:
   Question: How dangerously did he drive?
   Answer: So dangerously that he lost his job.

4

A	B	C
He doesn't work	as hard as	he used to

i) Think of words to replace 'hard' in box B.
ii) Now write four sentences using this structure.

FORMATION AND MANIPULATION

Unit 7 b

Pronunciation, Stress and Intonation

Note: The emphasis in this Unit is to give students a clear grasp of the formation of different types (regular and irregular) of adverbs of manner (those that answer the question *How?*), and a clear understanding of the discrimination between adjectives and adverbs and how they are used.

As an initial discrimination exercise, write these two sentences on the board.

         1   2
   He's a worker   *He works*

Then give a number of words (adjectives and adverbs mixed) – 'good/dangerous/well/carefully/dangerously/careful/slow/quickly/quick/slowly' – and ask students to say whether the word goes with 1 or 2. Ask them then to make the sentence, i.e. add the word you have given to sentence 1 or 2:

For example: T: careful
               S: He's a careful worker.
               T: slowly
               S: He works slowly.

This exercise should be done at a good pace.

Additional Paired Practice Phase

Give this short conversation (orally or on the board) –
      S.1: Is she a very good singer?
      S.2: Yes, she sings very well.

– and then ask students to work in pairs making the same type of conversations from these prompts (to replace 'good singer'):

  i) hard worker   iv) bad tennis player
 ii) careful driver   v) fast worker
iii) good typist   vi) good swimmer

Note: point out that we use *the* with instruments in English. Give this short Substitution Drill: HE PLAYS THE TRUMPET VERY WELL.
  1. piano   5. Does he
  2. She   6. guitar
  3. violin   7. piano
  4. He   8. saxophone

Fluency Practice for 3. and 4.

HE DROVE SO DANGEROUSLY THAT HE LOST HIS JOB. (Point out the unstressed [ðət].)
  1. carelessly   6. spoke
  2. worked   7. quickly
  3. She   8. drove
  4. typed   9. He
  5. badly   10. fast

HE DOESN'T WORK AS HARD AS HE USED TO. (Point out the unstressed [əz] in 'as . . . as'.)
  1. She   6. I
  2. well   7. carefully
  3. They   8. She
  4. He   9. He
  5. fast   10. well

Note: It is extremely important that the class be given only as much practice with the drills above as is warranted by their attention and speed of response. If they start slowing down through lack of interest, do not use all the prompts. Stop, and go on to a new activity – perhaps even ask them to write down some of the sentences.

N.B. ARE THE STUDENTS STILL LEARNING THE PAST FORMS OF THE VERBS?

Unit 7
c
EXPLOITATION OF THE EPISODE

Key Structures and Vocabulary	Suggested Explanations
a) in a terrible state (1)	Very dirty, and perhaps wet, too.
b) Just about your *size* (4) and his clothes *fit* you (7)	If a person has small feet, he needs small shoes. If he puts on very big shoes, they won't fit him because they are the wrong size.
c) They're no good to him (5)	He can't use them now.
d) Wasn't he *the fellow* who . . .? (15)	*Fellow* is another word for a *man;* we use the word in conversation: 'He's a nice/clever etc. fellow'.
e) make contact with (24)	The police want to catch him before he has time *to meet, telephone or talk to* any of his friends.
f) It's very kind of you to . . . (32)	This is a polite way of saying 'Thank you for . . . You're very kind.'

Section 1
1. Sample questions
a) What sort of state were Coke's clothes in?
b) When did the old lady's husband die?
c) Where are all the clothes of the old lady's husband?
d) What clothes did Coke find upstairs?
2. Extra activity–Completion Exercise (student books closed)
   T: 'You know, your clothes are in a . . .' (pause for response)
   S: 'terrible state' etc. etc.
3. Optional fluency practice
   THEY'RE NO GOOD TO HIM (Use intonation pattern on the tape)
a) me
b) them
c) him
d) her
e) you
f) us
g) He
h) them

Section 2
1. Read the text (or play the tape). Then ask students to read it silently themselves.
2. Question phase as before.
3. Fluency practice
   WHAT DO YOU KNOW ABOUT COKE?
a) we
b) her
c) she
d) him
e) the accident
f) the film
g) he
h) us
4. Revision of items practised in previous units: 'very little', 'I'm afraid', 'in fact', 'Yes, that's right', 'someone else' and 'have to'.

Section 3
1. Sample questions
a) How quickly did Coke put the clothes on?
b) Were the clothes new and clean?
c) Where was the old lady when Coke came downstairs?
d) Did Coke want to stay?
e) What happened just after the old lady said 'Just like my husband'?
2. Fluency practice
   IT'S VERY KIND OF YOU
a) good
b) That's
c) them
d) her
e) It's
f) nice
g) him
h) good
i) you
3. Focus students' attention on the sentences in which the following words or phrases occur and (perhaps after drilling) ask them to write true sentences of their own using the words or phrases:
a) as quickly as I could
b) at least
c) look just like
d) very kind

THE MAN WHO ESCAPED
Episode 7

Unit 7

C

SYNOPSIS: *Coke found food in a small house in the country. Baxter arrived at a small station. Another detective met him there and asked Baxter why Scotland Yard was so interested in Coke. A sergeant in a police station not far from the house Coke was in sent a young policeman to the house to tell the old lady in it about Coke.*

1 "You know, your clothes are in a terrible state," the old lady said after the meal. "You ruined them when you had the accident!"
"That's all right. They're just my work-clothes," Coke answered.
"My husband was just about your size. A little heavier perhaps. All his clothes are upstairs. They're no good to him. He died two years ago." She pointed up to the room above them.
"Why don't you see if any of his clothes fit you. You can bring them back tomorrow."
"Nobody can be this lucky!" Coke thought to himself. He went upstairs and turned the light on. It was clear that the old lady was almost in another world. She trusted everybody. He found a heavy jacket, a woollen shirt and some trousers hanging in the room.

2 "What do you know about Coke?" Baxter asked Halls. They were in the car now. "Very little, I'm afraid. In fact, I don't think I know anything about him at all. Wasn't he the fellow who was in that spy case about four years ago?"
"Yes, that's right. Coke always said it wasn't him . . . that it was someone else."
"That's what they all say. But what's so special about him?"
"Coke was in Army Intelligence. He knew important secrets. We could never understand why he sold them. There wasn't a real motive. Some said he did it for money. We couldn't prove it, but if he was a spy, he still knows too much. We could never find out who he sold the secrets to. That's why we have to catch him before he makes contact with any of his old friends!"

3 Coke put the clothes on as quickly as he could. They were old and shabby, but at least they were warm. When he came downstairs, the old lady was still in front of the fire. She smiled when she looked at him. "You know, you look just like my husband in those clothes . . . when he was much younger, of course."
Coke tried to be polite. He wanted to leave quickly.
"I can't thank you enough. It's very kind of you to do all this for me."
The old lady did not seem to hear him.
"Just like my husband," she said again. Just then, there was a knock on the door.

Unit 7 d

FURTHER PRACTICE

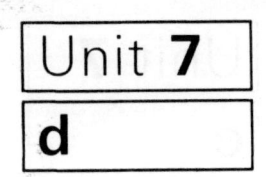

1. Invention Exercise

1) Make your own sentences with the pattern: So good/bad, etc. that
   MODEL: The film was so bad that they walked out in the middle.

   Example:
   PROMPT: film/interesting/twice
   RESPONSE: The film was so interesting that I saw it twice.

   Prompts:
   a) weather/cold/two sweaters
   b) football match/bad/in the middle
   c) music/loud/a headache
   d) service in the restaurant/slow/out
   e) lecture/uninteresting/out
   f) book/good/3 times

2) Now make sentences with the pattern: So well/badly, etc. that
   MODEL: The short man played so badly that he lost the match.

   Example:
   PROMPT: Fred/dangerously/his job
   RESPONSE: Fred drove so dangerously that he lost his job.

   Prompts:
   a) orchestra/badly/out
   b) she/piano/well/a prize
   c) man/carelessly/3 accidents in a week
   d) athlete/slowly/the race
   e) Flash/house/badly/down
   f) boss/hard/ill

2. Conversation

Susan used the car today. She drove Tom to college this morning and then went to her mother's house. She is driving Tom back from the college now.

TOM: Why are you driving so slowly?
SUSAN: I'm going as fast as the speed-limit.
TOM: You can forget the speed-limit. Nobody drives that slowly!
SUSAN: Well, I want to drive carefully. The roads are crowded.
TOM: But they were just as crowded this morning. You drove a lot faster then!
SUSAN: That's just it. I drove too fast.
TOM: What? You mean something happened after you left me?
SUSAN: (nervously) It was in the centre of town. I was in a hurry, and . . .
TOM: Yes? Go on! What happened?
SUSAN: A child ran out in front of me.
TOM: You mean . . . you mean . . .
SUSAN: Wait! Listen! The girl was a good distance away so I didn't slow down.
TOM: (relieved) Well, what's so terrible about that?
SUSAN: Just a second. There's more. The child fell down.
TOM: Fell down? You mean you hit her?
SUSAN: No, but I almost did. I braked as hard as I could. I stopped, but only just in time.
TOM: Well, at least you didn't have an accident!
SUSAN: No, but that isn't the only reason I'm driving so carefully.
TOM: Oh, no! Did something else happen?
SUSAN: No, but there's a police car behind us. It's following us, so we can't forget the speed-limit, can we?

Correct the statements

'The roads were not as crowded this morning.'
'No, the roads were just as crowded this morning.'
1) Susan is driving very fast now.
2) She drove very slowly this morning.
3) A dog ran out in front of Susan.
4) The child was not very far away.
5) Nothing happened when the child ran across the road.
6) When the child fell, Susan did not do anything.
7) Susan is driving slowly and carefully only because she wants to.

FURTHER PRACTICE

Unit 7
d

1. Invention Exercise

a) Follow the technique of doing this exercise suggested in earlier Units.

b) Notice that the first exercise practises the pattern *so + adjective + that* and the second the pattern *so + adverb + that*. (Both exercises also once again give more practice with regular and irregular Simple Past forms.) After the class has done each exercise individually, they could be given the prompts again, this time with books closed and the prompts taken at random from both exercises. This would then act as a discrimination exercise at the same time.

c) Once again, the prompts call for a variety of verbs. In Exercise 1, the verb *was* occurs in each item, followed by another, thus:
for a) *was/bought, put on* or *wore;* for b) *was/walked out* or *left;* for c) *was/got* or *had;* for d) *was/walked out;* for e) *was/walked out;* for f) *was/read it.*
For Exercise 2, the verbs which could be used in the items are:
for a) *played/walked out;* for b) *played/won;* for c) *drove* or *worked/had;* for d) *ran/lost;* for e) *built/fell;* for f) *worked/was* or *became* or *fell.*

2. Conversation

Key Points
1. Practice with the intonation of questions in the conversation
2. Meaning and intonation of 'Yes? Go on!' when encouraging someone to explain
3. Meaning and use of 'speed-limit'
4. Meaning and intonation of 'Nobody drives that slowly!'
5. Practice with the unstressed forms of:
   a) *are* [ə] in 'The roads are crowded'
   b) *as* [əz] in 'just as crowded' and 'as hard as I could'
   c) *at* [ət] in 'at least you didn't . . .'
   d) *of* [əv] in 'the centre of town' and 'in front of me'

Presentation Notes
1. Follow the initial presentation procedure as for the previous conversations (outlined on Teacher Page 6).
2. Choral repetition after parts of the conversation, concentrating on, and using, the intonation patterns on the tape.
3. *Simple Substitution Drill:*
   WELL, WHAT'S SO TERRIBLE ABOUT THAT?
   (Prompts to replace *terrible*.)
   a) wonderful   d) bad
   b) good   e) hard
   c) interesting   f) easy
4. Get students to work in pairs practising this part of the conversation, using other words in the place of *roads* and *crowded*.
   Model: A. The roads are crowded today.
            B. They were just as crowded yesterday, too.
   Example: Prompts: shop/busy
            S.1: The shop's busy today.
            S.2: It was just as busy yesterday.
   Prompts:
   a) traffic/heavy
   b) TV programmes/good
   c) weather/nice
   d) train/late
   e) restaurant/crowded
5. Focus students' attention on the phrase 'No, but I almost did!' after a sentence like 'You mean you hit her?' Give other sentences orally to the class for them to answer 'No, but I almost did!': for example –
   'You mean you got on the wrong bus?'/'You mean you missed the train?' etc.
6. With student books closed, use the following prompt words and phrases as a Recall exercise for some of the key sentences and questions:
   a) Why/slowly?
   b) that slowly!
   c) good distance/slow down
   d) at least/accident!
   e) police car

Unit 7
e/f

e Summary

1
Many students learn to form adverbs ending in -*ly* and then proceed to use the adverb in place of the adjective – 'She's a terribly singer', for example. In the same way, although they can form adverbs, they will often use the adjective after the verb – 'I saw it very clear', for example. In order to help students master the distinction between the distinct uses of the two forms (for example, *angry* and *angrily*), it may be necessary to return to the Formation and Manipulation page (page 40) again and to do once again the discrimination exercise and the Paired Practice. In order that students do not begin to feel bored with repeating the same material, however, it would be advisable at this stage to add other adjectives which students might frequently meet or need to use, for example, *accidental/accidentally, stupid/stupidly, loud/loudly*.

2, 3 and 4
Here, the important point to make is that, like learning the various forms of irregular verbs, students are probably best advised to learn new adverbs as and when they meet them. One good reason for saying this is that, although there are *rules* for the formation of adverbs in English (particularly with regard to the problems of spelling), such rules are often taken to apply to all adverbs of manner, and students often produce such sentences as 'He ran fastly' instead of 'He ran fast'.

f Exercises for homework

2
Situation 5 (page 39) uses the phrase 'He doesn't work quite as hard as he used to'. The exercise might well be supplemented by asking students to use the same original sentences and asking them to transform them into negative sentences: For example: He doesn't work quite as hard as his father did.

3
The Guided Composition in this Unit is once again fairly rigidly controlled, and it might be advisable to add a further writing exercise of a less controlled nature. For example, read the conversation with the class again (page 42) and then ask them to write a letter from Tom to a friend telling the friend about Susan's *near-accident*: they might begin something like this:

'Dear John,
   You know that Susan drives our car now. She is quite a good driver, but one day last week . . .'

4
We have only asked students to write true sentences using two of the structures practised in this Unit. A useful testing and transfer phase is to take other patterns which have occurred in the Unit and ask them to write true sentences using those, too.

Unit 7
e/f

e Summary

Focal points in this Unit.

1. Adjectives (*good, bad, careful, noisy*) are used with nouns and come before the noun: 'He's *a good worker*'/'She's *a careful driver*'. Adverbs (*well, badly, carefully, noisily*) are used after the verb and answer the question '*How* does he work?': 'He *works carefully*'.

2. Most adverbs are formed by adding *-ly* to the adjective. Notice how certain things change in the spelling:
   a) quick – quickly   (adjective – *ly*)
   b) careful – carefully ('l' – *lly*)
   c) terrible – terribly ('ble' – *bly*)
   d) angry – angrily   ('y' – *ily*)

3. Some adverbs have exactly the same form as the adjective:
   hard; fast; early; late.

4. Remember particularly the irregular *good – well*.

5. Use the pattern 'He . . . so (*badly/carelessly* etc.) that he . . .' when you want to show the result of an action:
   'He drove carelessly. + He lost his job.'
   = 'He drove *so carelessly that* he lost his job.'

6. Use the pattern *as . . . as* to compare how two people do (or did) the same thing:
   'He doesn't work quite *as hard as* his father did.'

f Exercises for homework

1. Do all the exercises and questions on pages 39 and 40.

2. **Transformation Exercise**

   Example:

   He works hard. His father worked hard, too.
   You write:
   He works as hard as his father did.
   a) The new girl types well. The old secretary typed well, too.
   b) You speak French fluently. Your teacher spoke fluently, too.
   c) He works fast. His father worked fast, too.
   d) That boy writes carefully. His brother wrote carefully, too.
   e) He talks loudly. The other teacher talked loudly, too.

3. **Guided Composition**

   Read situation 4 on page 39 again carefully, and then write about this person:
   Mary/shorthand-typist/American firm/any more//badly/carelessly/at least 10 mistakes/every letter//worst/30 mistakes/letter for the boss//lost/job//

4. **Transfer Exercise**

   Write 5 true sentences about yourself, relatives or friends using the patterns '*so . . . that*' and '*as . . . as*':

   Example:

   My father speaks French so well that people sometimes think he is French.
   My friend works as quickly as I do.

Unit 8
a Comparison of adverbs

1 
(a) Which man/harder?
(b) man with shovel/more money/tractor driver?

2 
(a) How/both drivers?
(b) How/driver number 3/drive?
(c) Who/win?

3 
(a) Who/best job?
(b) Who/hardest?
(c) Who/most money?

4 
(a) How/ski?
(b) Who/worse?
(c) What/the man?
(d) both beginners?

5 
(a) What/both men?
(b) evening?
(c) Why/more clearly?

6 
(a) How/when younger?
(b) What/one day?
(c) What/old lady?
(d) How/Tom/now?

Main Teaching-Points
1. Formation and use of comparative adverbs
   a) regular – 'more carefully' etc.
   b) irregular – better/worse/harder/faster.
2. Use of *more/less* + *than*.
3. Superlative forms 'the best', 'the worst', 'the most', 'the least'.
4. Importance of unstressed pronunciation of [ðən] after comparisons.

Extra Points and Activities
1. Use and pronunciation of '(exactly) the same as'.
2. The use of 'neither . . . (nor)'.
3. The use of 'neither of them', 'both of them' and 'one of them'.
4. Meaning and use of 'manage to do'.
5. Meaning and use of 'at least'.
6. The use of *rather* and *a bit* as modifiers of adjectives and adverbs; and *much* with comparatives.

44

| Do something { BETTER/WORSE/HARDER / MORE DANGEROUSLY/MORE CLEARLY etc. } than..... | Unit 8 |
| MORE and LESS THAN   THE BEST and THE WORST | a |

1

One of these men is a tractor driver. The man with the shovel is an ordinary worker. They both have to work hard, but one of them has to work a bit harder than the other. Which of them do you think it is? The man with the shovel, by the way, earns less money than the tractor driver.

1. Correct the statements!
    a) Only one of the men has to work hard.
    b) The tractor driver earns less than the other man does.
2. Ask and answer the questions!
    a) tractor driver/hard?
    b) as hard as the other man?

2

Both these drivers are good. Both have fast cars but one of them is driving a bit better and faster than the other is. We cannot be sure which of them is going to win the race, but it looks as if number three is going to.

1. Ask and answer the questions!
    a) both/good   b) both/well
2. What can you say about one of them?
3. Correct the statements!
    a) The driver of three is not driving as well or as fast as seven is.
    b) We can be sure that three is going to win the race.

3

The man with the watch never has to work as hard as the other two do. He has the best job of the three. He earns the most money and does the least work. The man with the shovel has the worst job. He works the hardest but earns the least.

1. Correct the statements!
    a) The man with the watch has to work harder than the other two do.
    b) He earns the least money and does the most work.
2. Who do you think has the worst job? Why?

4

Neither Tom nor Susan can ski very well. They are both ski-ing very badly at the moment, but she is ski-ing even worse than he is. At least he is managing to keep his balance. It is hard for both of them. They are both beginners.

1. Correct the statements!
    a) Both Tom and Susan can ski well.
    b) She is ski-ing a bit better than he is.
2. Why can we say Tom is ski-ing better?
3. Why is it hard for both of them?

5

Both of these men are looking at the moon but neither of them can see it very clearly. It is a rather cloudy evening. One of the men can see the moon just a bit more clearly than the other can because he has a much bigger telescope.

1. Ask and answer!
    a) What/looking at?   b) clear evening?
    c) very clearly?   d) Which man/more clearly?
2. Ask why one can see it more clearly than the other! (and answer)

6

Tom drives a lot more carefully than he did when he was younger. He almost ran over an old lady one day. He just missed her. She managed to get out of the way just in time. He drives much more carefully now than he used to.

1. Correct the statements!
    a) Tom ran over an old lady one day.
    b) She did not get out of the way.
    c) Tom still drives very dangerously.

Unit 8 b

FORMATION AND MANIPULATION

1 Pronunciation

REMEMBER: *than is pronounced* [ðən]

Example: Planes now fly faster [ðən] they used to

2 He drives dangerously, but . . .

A	B	C	D	E
she drives	more	dangerously	than	he does

i) Put the words 'careful', 'quick', 'slow' in their correct forms into box C.
ii) Make sentences beginning 'He drives dangerously, but . . .' (Remember you can also put other words into box E in place of *he*)

3 He works well/fast/hard/badly, but . . .
(Make sentences)

she works you work they work	better faster harder	*than* [ðən]	he does
	worse		

4

That man has	the best the worst	job
He does	the least the most	work

Make sentences with: job, house, car, *and* money, time, fun

5 These words are like dangerously, carefully, etc. (See **2** above) – clearly, loudly, weakly, heavily.

FORMATION AND MANIPULATION

Unit 8 b

Note: The emphasis in this Unit is not on quantity but on quality. Students must grasp the essentials of the formation of comparative adverbs. It is not necessary for them to learn long lists of adverbs at this stage. Students should be aware that the comparative form of some adverbs is formed by using *more,* of others by adding *er* (fast–faster) and of others by using a different word (good–better).

1.

Insist AT ALL TIMES on the use of the weak (unstressed) form of *than* which is [ðən]. Correct the students every time [ðən] is not used until the use of the weak form becomes automatic.

2, 3 and **4.**

Use the tables for both written and oral practice. Vary these activities. Insert a short writing phase (4 or 5 minutes) into the oral practice (e.g. 'Now write down 4 or 5 of the sentences you have just made.').

Fluency Practice

HE DRIVES MORE CARELESSLY THAN I DO. [ðən]
1. than you do
2. works
3. quickly
4. slowly
5. eats
6. faster
7. She drinks
8. plays
9. He plays
10. better

THEY WORK HARDER THAN I DO. [ðən]
1. Does she . . .?
2. He doesn't
3. than Mary
4. faster
5. drive
6. more carelessly
7. Does he . . .?
8. They work
9. quickly
10. quietly

REMEMBER: The past forms of verbs. Now is a good time to revise and test all the verb-forms learnt so far.

Unit 8 C

EXPLOITATION OF THE EPISODE

Key Structures and Vocabulary	Suggested Explanations
a) There was a *poker* lying in the fireplace (16)	A poker is a long metal bar or rod which we use to stir an open fire with. (Point out the structure 'There was . . . . - - -ing', too.)
b) he got away (39)	He escaped.

Section 1
1. Sample questions
a) Did the old lady hear the knock?
b) Why not?
c) How did the person outside know there was someone inside?
d) What did Coke say to the old lady?
e) Did Coke speak softly to the old lady?
f) Where did Coke go when the old lady left the room?
2. Ask special 'How . . .?' questions to elicit short adverb-of-manner answers:
a) How did Coke's heart begin to pound?
b) How did he have to decide what to do? etc.
(Note: Ask the same type of questions with **2** and **3**, too.)
3. Fluency practice
HE HAD TO DECIDE WHAT TO DO
a) We
b) where to go
c) when
d) I
e) who to ask
f) She
g) He
h) how to get there

Section 2
1. Sample questions after listening to the teacher (or tape)
a) Who was at the door when Mrs. Hartley answered it?
b) What did the policeman say? (police station. sergeant. something.)
c) What was there lying in the fireplace? Why didn't he pick it up?
d) Why couldn't the policeman see Coke?
e) What did Coke say to the policeman? How did he speak?
f) When Coke hit the policeman, what did the policeman do?– and what did Mrs. Hartley do?
2. Fluency practice
I'VE GOT SOMETHING TO TELL YOU
a) to ask
b) her
c) to give
d) him
e) them
f) to send
HE COULD SEE HER QUITE CLEARLY
a) I
b) We
c) him
d) hear
e) them
f) I
g) well
h) He

Section 3
1. Silent reading phase followed by questions:
a) How much later did the phone ring at the police headquarters?
b) Who answered the phone?
c) How did Coke get away from the policeman?
2. Focus students' attention on the phrasal verbs 'put . . . on', 'put . . . down', 'turn to (somebody)'.
3. Focus *special attention* on line 29: 'What? Coke? Where? When?'. First of all, ask students to repeat what Halls said very carefully, concentrating on the intonation (as on the tape).
Then ask them if they can say what was possibly said at the other end of the telephone to make Halls ask the simple questions.

THE MAN WHO ESCAPED
Episode 8

Unit 8

C

SYNOPSIS: *After Coke escaped from prison, he found a small house several miles away from the nearest village. The old lady in the house gave him food and clothes. She was deaf. A policeman came out to her house to tell her to look out for Coke.*

1 The deaf old lady did not hear the knock, but Coke did. His heart began to pound wildly. Whoever it was obviously knew there was someone inside because there was a light on and smoke coming from the chimney. He had to decide what to do, and quickly.
"There's someone at the door", he said loudly, but the old lady did not understand.
"There's someone at the door", he said again, this time even more loudly than before. She went out of the room and Coke quickly stepped back into the shadows of the front room.

2 The old lady opened the front door. Coke could see her quite clearly, but nothing else. He listened carefully.
"Hello, Mrs Hartley. I'm from the village police station. The sergeant sent me. I've got something to tell you."
Then Coke saw the policeman very clearly. Coke looked around quickly. There was a poker lying in the fireplace. He almost went to get it and then stopped.
"No!" he thought "That's too dangerous. They already think I'm a spy. Whatever I have to do I can do just as well with my fists." He stepped back and waited. The old lady and the policeman came through the door into the sitting-room. Coke was still behind the door, so the policeman could not see him.
"Good evening officer. Can I help you?" Coke said very loudly and clearly. The policeman turned around and looked at Coke. He was very surprised. Then Coke hit him as hard as he could in the stomach and he fell to the floor heavily. The old lady screamed. The policeman tried to get up, but fell back weakly. Coke ran out of the room.

3 The phone rang about five minutes later at the local police headquarters. Halls answered it.
"What? Coke? Where? When?"
Baxter stood up as soon as he heard Coke's name. He quickly put his hat and coat on. Halls listened carefully to the voice on the other end and quickly made a few notes. Then he put the phone down and turned to Baxter.
"Well, we know where Coke is now. A policeman almost caught him only five minutes ago."
"What do you mean, 'he almost caught him'? Did he catch him or didn't he?"
"No, he got away. He stole the policeman's bike."

Unit 8 d

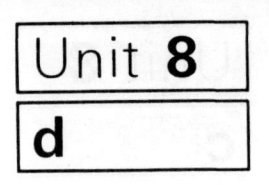

FURTHER PRACTICE

1. For Comprehension

Read this short report, and then answer the questions.

A British university is now doing research into the difference between men and women drivers. It seems that women often drive more carefully than men. The research suggests that men drive faster and more recklessly, but that they also react a bit faster in emergencies. This is perhaps because it seems they concentrate more when they are driving.

Correct these statements (Notice the use of *less* here!):

a) It seems that men drive more slowly than women do.
b) Men drive less recklessly than women do.
c) Men react more slowly than women do in emergencies.
d) Men concentrate less when driving than women do.

Now give full answers to these questions:

e) What is the university mentioned doing research into?
f) What does the research suggest is the difference in the way men and women drive?
g) What does it suggest is the difference in emergencies?
h) Why is this?

2. Conversation

Tom and Susan spent a few days in London last month. They left their car at home and stayed in a good hotel in the centre of town. They spent a lot of money. This is what happened the day they went home.

SUSAN: Why do we have to walk to the station? And where is it?
TOM: It's just down that road . . . I think.
SUSAN: Look! There's a policeman! Ask him the way.
TOM: All right. Excuse me. Can you tell me the way to Waterloo Station?
POLICEMAN: Yes. Walk down this road, take the first turning on the left. Then walk until you come to the river and . . .
TOM: The river?
POLICEMAN: Yes. You can't see it very clearly from here. When you come to it, there's a bridge. Just walk across it. Follow the signs that say 'To Waterloo Station'. You can't miss it.
TOM: And is it very far? I mean, how long does it take to walk there?
POLICEMAN: About fifteen minutes, if you walk quickly.
TOM: I see. Thank you very much.
POLICEMAN: Not at all.
SUSAN: Fifteen minutes! And with these heavy suitcases, too! I think we ought to take a taxi.
TOM: Not at this hour. Look at the traffic. It's moving very slowly. We can get there just as quickly on foot.
SUSAN: Well, I can't possibly carry this case any farther.
TOM: All right. Let me take it, then.
SUSAN: Don't be silly. You can't carry your case and mine as well!
TOM: Yes, I can. The cases aren't that heavy . . . hmm!
SUSAN: You see! They're heavier than you thought!
TOM: Perhaps it's not such a bad idea after all.
SUSAN: What isn't such a bad idea? What do you mean?
TOM: Taxi! Taxi!

Questions

1. What is the first thing Tom asks the policeman?
2. What exactly are the policeman's instructions?
3. How long does he say it takes?
4. What does Susan think they ought to do and why?
5. Why doesn't Tom want to do this?
6. What does Tom find out when he lifts the case?
7. What does he say then and what does he do?

Practice

Practise the pattern CAN YOU TELL ME THE WAY TO . . .? with someone else. Think of places you both know. Ask the other person questions with the pattern. Then the other person must tell you how to get there, using such phrases as 'Walk down/up . . .', 'Walk until you come to a . . .' and 'Take the first/the second/the third turning on the . . .' (Notice that you say *Drive* if you are talking to someone in a car)

FURTHER PRACTICE

Unit 8
d

1. For Comprehension

a) Ask students to turn their books face down, and then read the text aloud.

b) After the first reading, it might well be advisable to ask a number of short-answer questions:
  i) Is the University American? Is it British?
  ii) Is it doing experiments? Is it doing research?
  iii) Do women drive more carefully than men?
  etc.

c) Text completion – students still have books face down:
T: 'A British (pause for completion: – Ss: 'University') . . . is now doing (pause: Ss: 'research') . . . into the difference . . . (pause: Ss: 'between'). etc.

d) Ask students now to look at the report and read it silently.

e) Use the questions under the report orally. Set them later as homework.

f) Get students to ask each other general questions like the following:
Do you think women talk more than men?/ Do you think women work more efficiently than men?/Do you think teachers work harder than builders? etc.

2. Conversation

Key Points
1. Choral repetition practice with question intonation patterns in the conversation
2. Intonation of '. . . I think' expressing doubt or uncertainty
3. Practice with 'Excuse me. Can you tell me the way to . . .?'
4. Use and intonation of 'Not at all' after the phrase 'Thank you'
5. Fluency practice with these patterns:
   'How long does it take to . . .?'
   'We can get there just as quickly . . .'
   and 'I can't possibly (do) . . .'
6. Preview of *let* in 'Let me take it'
7. Meaning and use of *that* in 'The cases aren't that heavy!' (see p. 42 Notes to Conversation, Unit 7 – 'that slowly')
8. Meaning, use and intonation of 'You see!' (= I told you so) and 'I see' (= I understand)

Presentation Notes
1. Follow the same initial procedure as outlined previously.
2. Choral repetition of the conversation (the class perhaps divided into two 'choruses' – one repeating Tom's part, the other Susan's part) focusing students' attention on the intonation patterns and pronunciation on the tape.
3. *Fluency practice with two patterns:*
   a) HOW LONG DOES IT TAKE TO WALK THERE?
      i) get there   iv) get there by bus
      ii) fly to Paris   v) read that book
      iii) drive to London   vi) start your car
   b) WE CAN GET THERE JUST AS QUICKLY ON FOOT.
      i) by bus   v) He
      ii) by car   vi) on foot
      iii) you   vii) by bicycle
      iv) by train
   Note: At this point, ask students to work in pairs and make short dialogues using both the patterns above:
   For example:
   S.1: How long does it take to get there by bus?
   S.2: About half an hour . . . I think.
   S.1: Oh, we can get there just as quickly on foot, then.
4. Try and get students to recall some of the sentences from the conversation, using the following prompts, and concentrating on the intonation:
   a) way to Waterloo Station?
   b) very far?
   c) take a taxi.
   d) possibly/case any farther.

Unit 8
e/f

e Summary

1
The point about the unstressed [ðən] should have been part of the practice constantly throughout this Unit. If, however, a number of the students are still giving the strong form of *than*, then, as a final reminder, they should practise once again the Substitution Drills on Teacher page 46. This point can further be reinforced by special note of it when doing some of the Exercises for Homework orally.

2 and 3
We have concentrated on the formation and use of Comparative Adverbs. At the same time we have asked students to use three or four superlative forms of both adjectives and adverbs. It will probably be necessary quickly to revise the Comparative and Superlative forms of Adjectives, particularly the problems of 'slow/slower' vs. 'interesting/more interesting' and 'the slowest' vs. 'the most interesting'.

4
To remind students of these modifiers, refer them to the various examples throughout the Unit.
At the same time, remind them of certain other structures used in the Unit, particularly *one of them/both of them/neither of them*; *manage to do*; *I've got something to tell you*; *Can you tell me the way to . . .*; and *How long does it take to . . .?*

f Exercises for homework

2
This exercise tests the control of both adjectives and adverbs, and since the number of items is small, it could be supplemented by changing some of the sentences (during an oral preparation phase) so that another form is necessary. For example, question a) demands *better*. If it were changed to 'He plays the violin very . . . and so does John' (good), it would demand *well*. Or, again, if it were changed to 'He is a . . . violinist, but John is much . . .' (good), then it would demand *good* and *better*. By doing this, the teacher can increase the usefulness of the exercise.

3
It is important that students use the modifier *much* for extra practice. Students could also be asked to form the sentences again, but this time using a different modifier – *a bit, far* or *rather*.

4
This Guided Composition is, like that in Unit 7, fairly rigidly controlled. Students could be asked to write another conversation of the same kind i.e. asking the way, but this time without referring to an original.

5
Remember once again that students can write *true* sentences with other patterns practised in the Unit, too.

Unit 8

e/f

e Summary

Focal points in this Unit.

1. Remember that *than* is pronounced [ðen].

2. Remember the way we form and use adverbs when comparing things:
   a) 'He drives *more carefully than* you do.'
   b) 'She works *faster than* he does.'
   c) 'He plays tennis *worse/better than* I do.'

3. Remember the Superlative forms we have used in this Unit:
   a) 'He gets *the most* money and works *the least*.'
   b) 'He has *the best/the worst* house.'

4. We can add the words *a bit, much, rather* or *far* to a Comparative:
   a) 'They react *a bit faster* in emergencies.'
   b) 'He drives *much more carefully* now than he used to.'

f Exercises for homework

1. Do all the exercises on pages 45 and 48.

2. Fill in the correct form of the word in brackets in these sentences:

   Example:

   Maria sings . . . than Julia does. (good)
   You write: *better*, because this is the form of the word needed here.

   a) He plays the violin much . . . than John does. (good)
   b) Margaret types . . . than Mary does. (fast)
   c) He's a . . . driver. He had another accident last week. (careless)
   d) This case is . . . than I thought. (heavy)
   e) This new chair is extremely . . . (comfortable)
   f) Haven't you got a . . . book than that. (interesting)
   g) I can't see it very . . . . (clear)
   h) You're walking very . . . today! (slow)
   i) They say that men drive . . . and . . . than women do. (fast) (reckless)

3. Use the model and write more sentences of your own using the prompts:

   MODEL: He drives *much more carefully* now than he used to.
   PROMPTS: sing/good
   You write: *She sings much better now than she used to.*

   Prompts:
   a) play/good   f) work/hard
   b) eat/slow   g) drive/careless
   c) speak English/fluent h) dance/bad
   d) work/careful   i) go to bed/late
   e) speak/clear

4. **Guided Composition**

   Read the conversation between Tom and Susan again (page 48), and then write a conversation between a man who is lost and a policeman, using the prompts:

   MAN: Excuse//way/the Central Hotel?//
   POLICEMAN: Pardon?
   MAN: way/Central Hotel?//stranger here//
   POLICEMAN: Yes.//that road/second turning/right//Then until/traffic lights . . .
   MAN: Traffic lights?
   POLICEMAN: Yes.//not very clearly//When/first turning/right//not miss//
   MAN: very far?//how long/walk there?//
   POLICEMAN: 10 minutes/quickly//
   MAN: see//Thank you//

5. **Transfer Exercise**

   Now write some true sentences about yourself or your relations or friends.
   Use this model:

   I . . . much more . . . ly than I used to.
   He . . . far . . . er than he used to.

   Examples:

   My brother writes much better than he used to.
   I drive far more carefully than I used to.
   My sister types much faster than she used to.

Unit 9
a
Going to do

1 
(a) When/land/ on the moon?
(b) stay/long?
(c) When/take off?
(d) astronauts/ inside?
(e) walk on the moon?

2 
(a) What/Fred/a few seconds?
(b) When/wife?
(c) Where/wife/ now?
(d) Fred's wife/ do?

3 
(a) What/Julia and boyfriend?
(b) What/fastest way?
(c) When/train?
(d) What/Julia/ think?

4 
(a) What/Tom and Susan?
(b) When/start?
(c) When/guests?
(d) What/Tom want to know?

5 
(a) Where/Arthur and Deborah?
(b) When/curtain?
(c) What/ Deborah/say?

6 
(a) Why/Julia/ get wet?
(b) What/driver?

Main Teaching-Points
1. The formation and use of 'going to do' in statements, questions and negatives, together with short answers to 'going to' questions.
2. The use of certain time-pointers with 'going to': for example – 'soon', 'in 24 hours', 'in a few seconds', 'any second'.
3. The use of 'very long' and 'very much' in negative sentences: 'It's *not* going to be there *very long*'/'We *aren't* going to see *very much* . . .'.

Extra Points and Activities
1. Meaning and use of *obviously*.
2. The use of *get* in 'get a nasty shock' and 'get wet'.
3. *if* + Present Simple after 'going to'.
4. Meaning and use of 'to offer somebody a lift'.

| I am
He/she is
We/you/they are } GOING TO DO/GO/COME (etc.) if { DOES
DOESN'T DO | Unit 9
a |

1

The spacecraft is going to land on the moon in a few seconds. It is not going to stay there very long. It is going to take off again in 24 hours. Are the astronauts going to stay inside the spacecraft? Or are they going to walk on the moon?

1. Give short answers with 'is/isn't' or 'are/ aren't'.
   a) Is the spacecraft going to take off now?
   b) Is it going to land soon?
   c) Is it going to stay there very long?
2. Ask questions about the astronauts
   a) inside   b) on the moon

2

Fred Collins is going to get a very nasty shock in a few seconds. He does not know that his wife came in only a few seconds ago and is standing behind him. What is she going to do? What do you think the girl with Fred is going to do?

1. What kind of shock is Fred going to get?
2. Ask why (and answer)!
3. Ask a question about Fred's wife with 'When'!
4. Ask and answer a question with 'going to' about the girl!

3

Julia and her boyfriend saw a film in the centre of London this evening. The fastest way home is the train but they are obviously going to miss it. It is going to leave any second. "I'm going to find a boyfriend with a car!" Julia is thinking to herself.

Ask and answer the questions!
1. What/this evening
2. What/fastest way home
3. catch or miss
4. When/leave

4

Tom and Susan are going to give a party this evening. A lot of people are going to come. The party is going to start at 8.30 so the first guests are going to come any minute. "When are you going to take off that apron?" Tom wants to know. "In a minute," is Susan's answer.

1. Ask and answer the questions!
   a) When/a party
   b) start
   c) the guests
2. What is Susan doing and what is she going to do?

5

Arthur and Deborah are at the opera again. The curtain is going to rise and the opera is going to begin in a few seconds. "I hope that woman is going to take off her hat!" Deborah is saying loudly. "We aren't going to see very much if she keeps it on!"

1. Ask and answer the questions!
   a) When/the curtain
   b) the opera/soon
2. What does Deborah hope the woman in front is going to do and why?

6

It is going to rain and Julia hasn't got an umbrella. "I'm going to get very wet if that bus doesn't come soon!" she is saying to herself. She does not know it but the driver of that car is going to stop and he is going to offer her a lift.

1. Ask and answer the questions!
   a) raining now   b) soon
2. What is going to happen if the bus doesn't come soon?
3. What is it that Julia doesn't know?

Unit 9 b

FORMATION AND MANIPULATION

1 Pronunciation

REMEMBER: the word *to* is often pronounced [tə].
For example: The rocket is going [tə] land on the moon. (Page 51 situation 1)

2

A	B	C	D
He's	going to	come in	soon

i) Think of words to replace 'He's' in box A.
ii) Think of words to replace 'come in' in box C.
iii) Now write five sentences using the words you have for boxes A and C.

3 Very often when we use 'going to' we also say the time. Look at the situations on page 51 and find other time expressions to replace those in **2** box D.

4 Now look at this sentence:

A	B	C	D	E
I'm	not going to	see	him	today

Here are some more time expressions that we use with 'going to':
NOW   TOMORROW   NEXT WEEK   NEXT MONTH.
i) Think of words to replace those in boxes A, C, D and E.
ii) Say and write as many sentences as you can using all the words you have for exercise i and Part **3**.

5 Now, make questions (and answer them) using the correct parts of the table above and question words like Where . . .? When . . .? Why . . .? and How . . .?
Example: 'When are you going to meet him?' 'As soon as possible.'

6 *It's going to* (page 51 situation 6)
We talk about what the weather (and other things) are going to do like this:
(Make sentences)

	rain snow stop thunder	soon in a minute in a little while tomorrow
It's going to		

7 Notice this structure from page 51 situation 6 –
(Make sentences)

I'm He's She's	going to	get wet be tired be late	if	the bus the train	doesn't	arrive come soon get here

52

FORMATION AND MANIPULATION

Unit 9 b

1.

Insist on the weak (unstressed) form of to [tə] whenever it precedes a consonant sound. (Don't bother to labour the difference between consonants and vowels if the students don't immediately grasp the difference.) Use this simple discrimination drill as well as, or instead of, the simple explanation.

Give the root form of the following verbs and ask the students to give you *to* (in weak or strong form, as appropriate) followed by the verb just given. Introduce the drill this way:

Teacher: I say 'come', you say 'tə come'
I say 'open', you say 'tuː open'

Verbs: live play answer stay use remember rain snow boil ask dance watch introduce step earn escape get have eat lie think drink understand take teach interview

(All these verbs have already occurred in this book.)

2.

Make quite sure that the students can use both full and short forms of 'he is/he's' but concentrate on the spoken (short) form in all oral situations. Also let the students see that the root form of the verb never changes after 'going to'.

4. and 5.

Vary the use of the table so that students get a chance to both speak and write some examples. Insert a writing phase in the oral classwork.

6.

Make the sentences about the weather a little more realistic by asking the students to give 'mini weather-forecasts' about the weather this afternoon/evening/tomorrow/next week etc. Then get students to ask each other, and answer, questions about the weather, e.g.

S.1: Is it going to snow tomorrow?
S.2: Yes, it is/No, it isn't.

Extend the drill if you think it suitable to cover such things as:

The kettle's very hot! Yes, it's going to boil in a minute.
The car's very noisy! Yes, it's going to break down in a minute.

7.

Drill also the negative version of this structure (page 51 situation **5**). Write this table on the board while the students are writing sentences from table 7, student page 52.

I'm You're We're	not going to	get see have	very much	if she	waits much longer comes late misses the bus

N.B. Test the past forms of verbs.

Unit 9
C EXPLOITATION OF THE EPISODE

Key Structures and Vocabulary	*Suggested Explanations*
a) was right behind him (1)	he was very close behind him, he was the person following.
b) two-way radio (9)	a radio for listening to and talking to other people.
c) take half an hour to get to the phone (10–11)	he cannot get to a phone in under half an hour.
d) get away (20)	escape.
e) headlights (22)	the biggest, most powerful lights on the front of a car.
f) almost lost his balance (25–26)	he nearly began to fall over but didn't.

Section 1
1. Listening phase followed by special questions listed below for short-answer practice.
   a) Who got into the car first? (Baxter did.)
   b) Who was right behind him? (Halls was.)
   c) Who knew the area better? (Halls did.)
   d) Who escaped on a bike? (Coke did.)
   e) Who didn't realise policemen have two-way radios? (Coke didn't.)
   f) Who thought he could get pretty far in half an hour? (Coke did.)
2. Completion practice: (books open once, then closed)
   T: Baxter got into the car . . .
   Ss: first
   T: Halls was . . .
   Ss: right behind him etc. etc.
3. Point out the word *really* is used in questions when there is doubt in the mind of the questioner e.g. 'Is it really going to rain?' 'Do you really think I'm going to pay for it?' 'Are you really going to come?'

Section 2
1. Listening phase followed by choral reading and questions.
2. Optional fluency practice
   LOOK! THERE'S SOMEONE ON A BIKE!
   (Prompts to replace 'on a bike'.)
   a) over there
   b) in that car
   c) coming in
   d) watching T.V.
   e) having a sandwich
   f) in the garden
3. Baxter shouted: 'He isn't going to get away this time!' Ask students to say some of the things Coke thinks he is *not* going to do. Give these prompts on the blackboard.
   a) stay on my bike (I'm not going to stay on my bike)
   b) wait for Halls (I'm not going to wait for Halls)
   c) go back to prison (I'm not going to go back to prison)
   d) ride slowly (I'm not going to ride slowly)
   Now get students to ask and answer questions about these things e.g.:
   S.1: Are you going to stay on your bike?
   S.2: No, I'm not going to.
4. Written practice
   Get students to write sentences about what Coke is going to do. Give these prompts:
   a) off his bike (e.g. He's going to get off his bike)
   b) drop his bike
   c) run into the trees at the side of the road
   d) get away

Section 3
1. Ask students to read the text silently, then ask comprehension questions. Sample questions:
   a) What helped Coke now?
   b) Where was Baxter when Coke suddenly turned etc. etc.
2. Now, read the text or play the tape.
3. Use the sentence completion technique e.g.
   T: All Coke's . . .
   Ss: . . . training . . .
   T: . . . as a soldier . . .
   Ss: . . . helped . . . etc.
4. Get students to ask each other questions about the text using these prompts (written on blackboard)
   a) training/help him?
   b) Baxter/lose balance?
   c) Coke/him on chin?
   d) Baxter fall down?
   e) Halls jump Coke?
   f) Coke/him over back?
   g) Coke run towards road?
   h) Halls/pain in ribs?
   i) headlights?
   j) one of doors open?
   k) jump in?
   l) Halls/try/run after car?

THE MAN WHO ESCAPED
Episode 9

Unit 9

C

SYNOPSIS: *Coke found food and clothes in a cottage several miles away from the nearest village. However, a policeman came to tell the old lady in the cottage to watch out for Coke. Coke knocked the policeman down and stole his bike.*

1 Baxter got into the car first. Halls was right behind him. "You drive. You know the area better than I do," Baxter said. They raced out of the town and into the dark countryside.
"It's ridiculous," Halls said. "Does he really think he's going to get away from us on a bike?"
"Coke isn't a fool," Baxter answered. "He probably doesn't realise we already know what happened in the old lady's house."
"You mean he doesn't know that even village policemen have small two-way radios these days?"
"That's right. He probably thinks it's going to take that policeman at least half an hour to get to the nearest phone. He thinks he can get pretty far in that time."

2 Ten minutes later, about three miles from the old lady's house, Baxter suddenly saw someone on the dark road ahead.
"Look! There!" he shouted. "There's someone on a bike! And look! He's going to get off!"
Halls saw the man quite clearly, but only for a second. As soon as the man saw they were in a police car, he dropped his bike and ran into the trees at the side of the road.
"That's Coke!" Baxter shouted. "He isn't going to get away this time!" Baxter jumped out of the car even before Halls stopped it, and ran after Coke. Halls jumped out, too. He did not even switch off the headlights.

3 All Coke's training as a soldier helped him now. Baxter was just behind him when Coke suddenly turned. Baxter tried to grab him but almost lost his balance. Then Coke hit him on the chin as hard as he could. Baxter fell to the ground heavily. At that moment, Halls jumped on Coke from behind but Coke threw him over his back and against a tree, and then ran back towards the road before Halls could get up. Even when he did, he fell back to the ground again. There was a terrible pain in his ribs. Coke saw the police car very clearly. The headlights were still on, and one of the doors was open. Coke jumped in.
It took Baxter several seconds to realise where he was. At first, all he could feel was a terrible pain in his jaw. Then he heard the sound of a car engine starting. He looked up and saw Halls pointing to it. Suddenly Baxter realised everything. Halls tried to run after the car but it was too late. Coke was gone and so was their car!

Unit 9 d

FURTHER PRACTICE

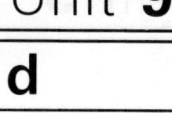

1. Invention Exercise

Ask questions with Are(n't) you, is(n't) he, etc. going to (do).

Example:

PROMPT: Mary/tonight?
RESPONSE: Are you going to see Mary tonight?
    or: Isn't he going to take Mary out tonight?
    or: Aren't you going to phone Mary tonight?

Prompts:

a) a car/next week   e) married/later
b) the train/soon   f) in England/this summer
c) television/tonight g) that letter/soon
d) a taxi   h) a drink for me

2. Conversation

Two years ago, before he married Susan, Tom taught English in Paris. He taught at an institute for adult students. One evening he went to another institute to give some oral examinations.

TOM: You speak English very well. I'm going to give you a very good mark. Don't worry.
STUDENT (Girl): Thank you very much.
TOM: Not at all. Oh, when you go out, please tell the next student to come in.
STUDENT: Certainly. Good bye (Goes out, closing door. Short pause. Another person comes in).
WOMAN: Excuse me. Are you Mr Atkins?
TOM: Yes. You don't know me, of course. I don't teach here. I just give oral examinations here now and then. Don't be nervous.
WOMAN: Nervous? Who? Me?
TOM: Now, sit down please. I'm going to ask you a few questions. Then we're going to have a short conversation in English. Do you understand?
WOMAN: Yes, of course I do. But may I ask *you* something first?
TOM: After the examination, please. Just concentrate on *my* questions for the moment. First of all, why are you learning English?
WOMAN: Why am I learning English?
TOM: Yes. I mean, what are you going to do with it? Are you going to be a teacher of English, or what?
WOMAN: Please stop just a second. I really *must* ask you something first.
TOM: (irritated) Very well. If you insist.
WOMAN: Would you like a cup of coffee?
TOM: Pardon? What did you say?
WOMAN: You see, I'm English, too. I'm one of the teachers here. I came to ask you if you would like a cup of coffee?

Questions

1. Why did Tom go to the institute that evening?
2. Who did he think the woman was?
3. Who was the woman really?
4. Ask and answer why she came in!

Recall

Without looking at the text, try to remember what Tom and the woman said with these words:

TOM: sit. worry. a few questions. Then/a short conversation. first. why/English? do with it? in your job? a teacher?
WOMAN: stop. something first. teacher here. come/coffee.

FURTHER PRACTICE

Unit 9 d

1. Invention Exercise

a) Follow the technique of doing this exercise suggested in earlier Units.

b) The prompts call for a variety of verbs as well as for the use of 'going to' in questions. The verbs which could be used are: for a) *buy* or *borrow*; for b) *get* or *catch*; for c) *watch*; for d) *be* or *get*; for e) *get* married; for f) *stay* or *have (spend) a holiday*; for g) *write* or *read*; and for h) *get, fetch, make* or *buy*.

c) Ask students to work in pairs, one student asking the questions from the prompts, the other giving short answers.
For example:
  S.1: Are you going to buy a car next week?
  S.2: No, I'm not.
OR S.1: Is your brother going to buy a car next week?
  S.2: Yes, he is.

EXTRA ACTIVITY: Practice Situations to be done orally: teacher gives the situation, students give a 'going to' response.
For example:
Situation: Tom is sitting on a bus and is taking a newspaper out of his pocket.
Response: He's going to read it./He's going to look at it.
Situations:
 i) There is a large rain-cloud in the sky.
 ii) Julia is sitting at her desk. The telephone is ringing.
 iii) Frank has a lighter in his hand and a cigarette in his mouth.
 iv) The French lesson starts at 11. It's 10.55 and the students are walking into the classroom.

2. Conversation

Key Points
1. Meaning and use of 'concentrate on'
2. Meaning, use and intonation of–'Not at all'/'Certainly'/'Excuse me'/'Yes, of course I do'/'Very well. If you insist',/ 'Pardon? What did you say?'

3. Practice (especially intonation) with this part of the conversation:
   T: 'First of all, why are you learning English?'
   W: 'Why am I learning English?'
4. Practice with the unstressed forms of:
   a) *of* [əv] in 'of course', 'first of all', 'cup of coffee' and 'one of the teachers'
   b) *and* [ən] in 'now and then'
   c) *to* [tə] in 'going to do' etc.
   d) *for* [fə] in 'for the moment'

Presentation Notes
1. Follow the initial presentation procedure as for previous conversations.
2. Choral repetition after parts of the conversation, concentrating on, and using, the intonation patterns on the tape.
3. *Paired practice work with*
   a) Model: 'First of all, why are you learning English?' 'Why am I learning English?'
      Example: 'What/doing here?' =
      S.1: 'First of all, what are you doing here?'
      S.2: 'What am I doing here?'
       i) why/worry?
       ii) who/waiting for?
       iii) what/talking about?
       iv) why/laughing?
      and
   b) Model: 'Would you like a cup of coffee?' 'Pardon? What did you say?'
      Example: a glass of beer =
      S.1: 'Would you like a glass of beer?'
      S.2: 'Pardon? What did you say?'
       i) my pen
       ii) some chocolate
       iii) a magazine to read
       iv) a holiday today
       v) a job in our firm.
4. *Fluency practice phases (Substitution Drills) with*
   '*May* I *ask you* something?' and '*When* you *go out, please tell* the next student *to come* in.'

Unit 9
e/f

e Summary

1 and 2

The most important thing in this Unit has been to give students manipulative oral practice with 'going to do' in statements, negatives and questions, and some clear indication of the other linguistic *pointer* words which we often use with 'going to'—'very soon', 'next Monday', 'in a second' etc. The phrases that we have used are naturally far from exhaustive, so the teacher could well add others in examples to give students a wider knowledge of such words and phrases. Such phrases might be *as soon as I can* (e.g. 'I'm going to buy one as soon as I can.') and *as soon as possible* (e.g. 'She's going to change her job as soon as possible.')

Much in the same way, we have introduced the extra element of an *if*-clause after 'going to' (situations 5 and 6, page 51), and students could be given more practice with this type of sentence—especially since it forces the use of (and reinforces the practice of) the Present Simple, particularly the 3rd person *s*:

'We aren't going to see very much if she keeps her hat on.'
'We aren't going to hear very much if she talks a lot.'
'We aren't going to understand very much if she speaks French.'

It would be well to refer students back to the Formation and Manipulation page and to do another Substitution Drill with this pattern.

f Exercises for homework

2

Although this is primarily a written exercise, it can be prepared orally in the classroom.
For classroom use, too, it can be adapted.
a) Pair students to ask questions to elicit the sentences in the exercises:
　For example:
　　S.1: Did Julia catch the 7.45 train yesterday?
　　S.2: Yes, she did, but she isn't going to catch it tomorrow.
　OR: S.1: Did you see the film last month?
　　S.2: No, I didn't, but I'm going to see it next month.
b) Ask students for examples of their own (–true, if possible–):
　For example: I played football last Saturday, but I'm not going to play next Saturday. We went to Paris last Easter, and we're going to go there again this Easter.

3

Unlike most of the Guided Compositions up to this point, this exercise allows the student considerably more freedom (and use of imagination) whilst it is nevertheless based upon two of the pieces of material in the Unit.
a) To help students to prepare to write the conversation, ask them first of all to ask (orally or written) some of the questions they would ask if they were invited to a party:
　For example: How many people are going to be there?/What are we going to drink?/Is there going to be dancing?/How long is it going to last?
b) Then focus their attention on some of the phrases in the Conversation (page 54) which Tom or Bill might use during their conversation:
　For example: Don't worry./Not at all. (–in reply to 'Thank you for the invitation')/Certainly. (–in reply to 'Can I bring a friend?)/But may I . . .?/I mean, . . ./Stop just a second./Very well. If you insist.

Unit 9
e/f

e Summary

Focal points in this Unit.

1. Remember how we use 'going to' to talk about things in the future:

   a) They're going to give a party
   b) We aren't going to watch it
   c) Are you going to tell him?

   + in a few seconds /in a minute
   today (=later today)
   this evening
   next week
   now
   (very) soon

2. Remember the form of the verb after *if* in sentences like:
   'We aren't going to see very much *if she keeps* her hat on.'
   'I'm going to get very wet *if the bus doesn't come* soon.'

f Exercises for homework

1. Do all the exercises on pages 51, 52 and 54.

2. Complete these sentences, using 'going to' or 'not going to':

   Example:
   I watched *Panorama* last week, but . . . (not/next week).

   You write:
   I watched *Panorama* last week, but I'm not going to watch it next week.

   a) Julia caught the 7.45 train yesterday, but . . . (not/tomorrow).
   b) I didn't see the film last month, but . . . (next month).
   c) She bought some meat in that shop last Monday, but . . . (next time).
   d) I didn't travel by air the last time, but . . . (next time).
   e) We stayed at home last night, but . . . (not/tonight).
   f) I spent £20 on Christmas presents last year, but . . . (not/so much this year).
   g) They broadcast the Prime Minister's speech yesterday, and . . . (again tomorrow).
   h) We didn't plan our holidays last summer, but . . . (this summer).
   i) I visited Bill in hospital this morning, but . . . (not/again today).
   j) I didn't pay the bill when it came, but . . . (very soon).

3. **Guided Composition**

   Read situation 4 on page 51 again carefully. Then write a telephone conversation between Tom and one of his friends, Bill, which took place a week before the party. Try to use some of the phrases from the Conversation on page 54, too. Begin like this:

   TOM: Hello, Bill! This is Tom Atkins here.
   BILL: Hello, Tom! How are you?
   TOM: Very well, thanks. Look, we're going to give a party next week. Would you like to come?
   BILL: Certainly! Who else are you going to invite?

   (Note: Use these phrases and words in the conversation: You're not going to . . ., are you?/What time . . .?/20 guests/pop records/bring anything/plenty to eat and drink/first of all/If you insist.)

4. **Transfer Exercise**

   Look at your own diary, agenda or school timetable and write 5 true sentences about things you are going to do tomorrow, the next day or next week.

Unit 10 a

Requests and offers and Take/get/bring/show someone something

1
(a) How/Deborah feel?
(b) What/maid/ say?
(c) What/Deborah want?
(d) What/maid?

2
(a) What sort of service/ waiters?
(b) What/Arthur order?
(c) What/ head waiter?

3
(a) What/Tom?
(b) How/last teacher/room?
(c) What/student?
(d) Tom saying?

4
(a) When/Peter/ from Canada?
(b) When/plane/ land?
(c) What/Peter/ to customs man?
(d) customs man saying?

5
(a) Who/new boyfriend?
(b) Where/now?
(c) His question?
(d) Julia's answer

6
(a) What/later?
(b) the men/ask a moment ago?
(c) head waiter saying

Main Teaching-Points
1. Meaning and use of 'Shall I . . .?' when offering to do something, and 'Would you . . .?' when making a request.
2. Use and practice of the verbs *take, bring, get* and *show* in the *take him some champagne* and *take it to him* patterns.

Extra Points and Activities
1. Meaning and use of *instead* in 'No, do that instead'.
2. Practice with the verb *help* in 'help someone do something'.
3. Preview of *should*.
4. Meaning and use of 'anything to declare'.
5. Use of *none* in 'none of the men'.

Take ⎫		Shall I?	**Unit 10**
Get ⎬ someone something.	Would you?	
Bring⎪			**a**
Show ⎭			

1

Deborah feels terrible this morning. "Shall I bring you some tea now?" her maid asked her a few seconds ago. "No, bring me an aspirin instead," Deborah told her. The maid is going to get her the aspirin now.

1. Ask how Deborah feels this morning!
2. What exactly did the maid ask her?
3. What exactly did Deborah tell her?
4. What is the maid going to do?

2

Arthur often eats here. The waiters always give him the best service. The head waiter spoke to Arthur only a minute ago. "Bring me a bottle of your best champagne, please!" Arthur told him. The head waiter is talking to another waiter now. "Take him this champagne!" he is saying. "Take it to him now!"

1. Ask what the waiters always do and why!
2. What did the head waiter do and when?
3. Ask what Arthur told him (and answer)!
4. What is the head waiter saying now?

3

Tom is going to give his class a lesson here, but the last teacher left the room in a terrible mess. A student is going to help him tidy it up. "Would you close the window, please?" Tom is saying. Someone should clean the board and pick the books and chairs up, too.

1. What is Tom going to do?
2. What did the last teacher do?
3. What is that student going to do?
4. What is Tom saying?
5. What else could he say with "Would . . .?"?

4

Tom's younger brother, Peter, flew back from Canada today. His plane landed only a few minutes ago. When the customs officer asked him if he had anything to declare, he told him he hadn't. The customs officer does not believe him. "Would you show me what's in that suitcase?" he is asking.

1. What did Peter do today and when did his plane land?
2. Where is he now?
3. What did the customs officer ask him and what did Peter tell him?
4. What is the customs officer saying now?

5

This is Julia's new boyfriend. He is the one who offered her a lift a few days ago. They are at the cinema now. "Shall I get you some chocolates?" he is asking. "Thank you very much. That's very kind of you," is Julia's answer.

1. Who is the man with Julia and what did he do a few days ago?
2. What is he offering to get her now?
3. What exactly is he saying and what is Julia's answer?

6

There is going to be a party in this room later. A few moments ago, none of the men knew what to do. "Where shall we put the piano?" "What shall I do with the flowers?" they asked. The head waiter is telling them now. "Bring the flowers here and take the piano over there!" he is saying.

1. What is going to happen here later?
2. What questions did the men ask a moment ago and why?
3. What is the head waiter saying now?

Unit 10 b

FORMATION AND MANIPULATION

1 Pronunciation

Shall is often pronounced [ʃəl] (the weak or unstressed form). Notice the way the teacher says *shall*. Now, read the following sentences aloud until you can say *shall* in its weak form correctly and without hesitation.

i) Shall I type those letters now?
ii) When shall I phone you?
iii) Shall I get more flowers?
iv) Where shall I put the flowers?
v) What shall I do with the milk?
vi) Shall I answer the phone for you?

2

A	B	C
Would you	open the door,	please?

i) What other word can you put in box A to replace 'Would'?
ii) Look at the situations on page 57; there are many phrases there which you can put in box B.
iii) Now say and/or write ten sentences beginning 'Would/Could you . . .?'

3

A	B	C	D	E
Would you	give	me	a book,	please?

i) Look at these words: GET   BUY   BRING   SEND
   Which box can you put them in? A, B, or C?
ii) Think of some other words to replace 'me' in box C.
iii) Now, think of five things which you can put in box D.
iv) Now write or say some sentences beginning with 'Would/Could you . . .?'

4

A	B	C
Shall I	come in	now?

i) Look at the situations on page 57. How many words can you find to replace 'come in' in box B?
   Example: 'turn off the light'.
ii) Here are some more time expressions which you can use in box C:
    SOON   TOMORROW   AT ONCE   IMMEDIATELY
iii) Make questions using the words that can go in boxes A, B and C.

5

Ask the person sitting next to you questions with 'Would/Could you . . .?' and 'Shall I . . .?' using the following prompts:

open the window. show me/him the book. phone me/you later. give me/her a drink of water. switch on the radio. ask them to come in. make me/them a cake. get me/her a newspaper.
The answers to these questions can be:
'Yes, of course' or 'Certainly' or 'I'm sorry but I can't at the moment.'

FORMATION AND MANIPULATION

Unit 10 b

1.
Insist on the weak (unstressed) form of *shall* [ə]. Use choral repetition and individual repetition of the six sentences until the students use the weak form without hesitation.

Note: Avoid any use of or reference to the 'shall we' form at this stage unless you feel that the students will be able to grasp and operate the difference between the 'Shall we leave you now?' (request for permission) and 'Shall we go to the cinema tonight?' (suggestion).

2.

Impress on students the use of *please* after requests with 'would you' and 'could you'. Tell them that if they don't use *please* they are not being polite and that *please* is very rarely omitted (refer them to situation number **4** page 57 where the customs officer is not trying to be polite). Point out that 'could you' is slightly more polite than the 'would you' form which seems to suggest that the answer should be *yes*.

3.

a) Forming sentences from table **3**. Make sure that students both notice and use the correct form of the pronoun after *give, get,* etc. Use a simple discrimination drill to check students on this. e.g. put *I* and *me* on the board, label them *a* and *b* and then ask students to tell you whether the words you use are like *a* or *b,* for example: I, you, us, we, them, him, her, she, etc.
b) Remember to include a writing phase when using the substitution tables. Ask the students to write 6–10 sentences from the tables.

When students have mastered the formation of the three structures practised, use the following substitution drill to build up oral fluency. (Write the model on the blackboard, but give the prompts orally.)
N.B. Insist on the weak (unstressed) form of *shall*.

SHALL I COME IN NOW?	
1. later	11. get
2. soon	12. me a book
3. do it	13. buy
4. at once	14. him
5. Would you	15. next week
6. see him	16. some socks
7. ask him	17. clothes
8. them	18. us
9. Could	19. send
10. immediately	20. her

N.B. Check on the learning of the past forms of verbs.

Unit 10 c

EXPLOITATION OF THE EPISODE

Key Structures and Vocabulary	Suggested Explanations
a) the road ahead (10)	on the road in front of him at a distance.
b) get by (11)	pass.
c) could you give me a light (15)	I have a cigarette but I haven't any matches or a lighter, so I say to my friend who has matches or a lighter, 'Could you give me a light?'
d) his tenth cigarette that night (15–16)	He had a packet of ten cigarettes when he arrived that night, now it is empty.
e) a straight road (20)	a road with no curves.
f) two-tone sound (25)	the warning signal given by a police car in a hurry.
g) shot through (35)	went through very quickly (like a bullet from a gun)

Section 1
1. Listening phase followed by short-answer questions:
   a) How long did Coke drive for?
   b) How did he feel in the police car?
   c) What did he remember about the new pocket radios?
   d) Where did the policemen put them?
   e) What did he wonder?
   f) Why did they probably not have them?
   g) Was the road blocked?
   h) By what?
2. Choral repetition, followed by completion exercise:
   T: 'Coke drove for . . .
   Ss: about twenty minutes.'
   T: 'He felt . . .
   Ss: nervous
   T: in the . . .
   Ss: police car.' etc.

Section 2
1. Silent reading phase followed by correct my statements phase:
   T: The three policemen were happy . . .
   Ss: No, the two policemen were bored.
   T: It was a crowded spot . . . there was a lot of traffic . . . 'Could you give me a drink?' . . . It was his first cigarette . . . They both looked down . . . and saw a bicycle coming towards them . . . 'It's a bus . . . perhaps they're bringing us some money . . . or something to drink . . .' They listened to the car . . . as it went away. It was a short curved road . . . and the bus was very near . . . 'Is it going to start?' . . . 'It looks like it' . . . Shall I stop it? . . . Our orders are to let every car through . . . Just then they heard the three tone sound of the engine . . . was in plenty of time . . .
2. Fluency practice
   COULD YOU GIVE ME A LIGHT?
   a) a drink
   b) a cigarette
   c) some coffee
   d) pass me
   c) get me
   f) a cake
   SHALL I STOP IT?
   a) him
   b) tell
   c) ask
   d) get
   e) bring
   f) show

Section 3
1. Comprehension phase after listening to the teacher or the tape.
   a) What did the policemen do for a second? (They hesitated)
   b) What did one ask the other?
   c) What was his name?
   d) Did they think Coke was in the police car?
   e) How far did he move the car back?
   f) Was the gap wide enough for another car to get through?
   g) Did Coke drive through slowly?
   h) In which direction did he race?

THE MAN WHO ESCAPED
Episode 10

Unit **10**

c

SYNOPSIS: *When Coke saw Baxter and Halls in a police car, he jumped off his bike and ran into the trees at the side of the road. Baxter and Halls ran after him. Coke managed to get away from both of them and to steal their car.*

1 Coke drove for about twenty minutes. He felt nervous in the police car but he knew it was his only chance.
"I wonder how that policeman managed to contact police-headquarters so quickly?" he asked himself. Then he remembered a newspaper article about the new pocket radios all policemen had. They were small things which they put in their pockets.
"Of course! That's it!" he thought. Then he wondered if detectives like Halls and Baxter also had them. He knew they probably did not, because they already had radios in their cars. Suddenly, however, something on the road ahead interrupted his thoughts. Two police cars were there, side by side, blocking the road. Nothing could get by them!

2 The two policemen at the road block were bored. It was a lonely spot between two hills and there was very little traffic.
"Could you give me a light, Tom?" one of them said. It was his tenth cigarette that night. Just then, they both looked up and saw a car coming towards them.
"It's a police car," the other one said. "Perhaps they're bringing us some hot coffee, or something to eat."
They both watched the car as it came closer. It was a long, straight road and the car was still a good distance away.
"Isn't it going to stop?"
"It doesn't look like it."
"Shall we stop it? Our orders are to stop every car."
Just then, they heard the two-tone sound of the horn. It was obvious that whoever was in the car was in a great hurry.

3 The two policemen hesitated for a second. Then one of them turned to the other. "Would you move the car out of the way, Bob, or shall I?"
"But our orders were to . . ."
"Look! That's a police car, can't you see? You don't think Coke's going to come through here in a police car, do you?"
The other policeman got into the car and moved it back a few inches; the gap was just wide enough for another car to get through now.
"Aren't you going to move back some more?" the other shouted.
Before he could do so, Coke shot through the narrow gap and raced down the road, in the direction of London.

Unit 10 d

FURTHER PRACTICE

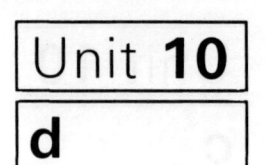

1. Invention Exercise

Ask questions with 'Shall I . . .?' or 'Would you . . .?' using the prompts. Make 2 sentences from the prompts when you can.

Example:

PROMPT: those books
RESPONSE: Shall I carry those books for you?
   or: Would you carry those books for me?

Prompts:

a) the windows
b) that letter
c) the grass
d) a cup of tea
e) your breakfast
f) your suitcase
g) the light
h) the radio
i) time
j) more clearly/slowly

2. Conversation

Arthur often travels abroad. This is a typical conversation at the reception desk in a hotel.

RECEPTIONIST: Good evening, sir.
ARTHUR: Good evening. My name's Tigers. I believe you have a room reserved for me.
RECEPTIONIST: Just a moment, Mr Tigers. Let's see . . . Tigers . . . yes, Mr Tigers, Room 204. Would you fill in this form, please?
ARTHUR: Certainly. Er . . . I can't find my pen and there isn't one on the desk.
RECEPTIONIST: Isn't there? How strange.
ARTHUR: Perhaps someone walked off with it. Could you lend me yours?
RECEPTIONIST: Of course. Here you are. How long do you intend to stay, Mr Tigers?
ARTHUR: I'm not sure. It all depends. But I'm probably going to leave on Thursday.
RECEPTIONIST: On Thursday. I see. Would you tell us as soon as you know?
ARTHUR: Yes, of course. Where shall I put the number of my passport?
RECEPTIONIST: Just at the bottom. That's right. Thank you.
ARTHUR: Oh, would you wake me up at 7 tomorrow?
RECEPTIONIST: At 7. Certainly. Porter! Take Mr Tigers' suitcase to his room. Just follow the porter, Mr Tigers.
ARTHUR: Thank you. Good bye.
RECEPTIONIST: Good bye. Oh! Mr Tigers. My pen!
ARTHUR: Your pen?
RECEPTIONIST: Yes. I lent it to you a moment ago. You remember?
ARTHUR: Oh yes, of course you did. I put it in my pocket by mistake. Here you are. I'm very sorry.
RECEPTIONIST: That's quite all right.

Questions

1. What is the first thing Arthur says when he goes into the hotel?
2. What is the next thing Arthur has to do?
3. How exactly does the receptionist ask him to do this?
4. What does the receptionist do when Arthur tells her there isn't a pen on the desk?
5. How does Arthur ask her to do this?
6. What does Arthur say when the receptionist asks how long he intends to stay?
7. When does Arthur want to get up and what does he say about this?

Correct the statements

1. Arthur lent the receptionist his pen.
2. He is sure he is going to leave on Thursday.
3. Arthur intended to put the pen in his pocket.

Practice

Listen to the tape. Practise the intonation of 'Would you . . .?', 'Certainly' and 'Don't you remember?'

FURTHER PRACTICE

Unit 10
d

1. Invention Exercise

a) Follow the technique of doing this exercise suggested earlier.

b) First ask students to give sentences beginning 'Shall I . . .?' for each of the prompts. The verbs which can reasonably be used are:
for a) *close, shut* or *open;* for b) *post, put a stamp on, type* or *take . . . to the Post Office;* for c) *cut* or *mow;* for d) *get, bring* or *make;* for e) *cook, make* or *get . . . ready;* for f) *carry, take, bring* or *pack;* for g) and h) *put on, switch on, turn on, put off, switch off* or *turn off;* for i) *tell;* and j) *speak* or *talk* or *explain.*

c) Now ask students to use the same prompts for requests beginning 'Would you . . .?' The verbs will once again be the same as those listed in b) above.

d) Ask the class to work in pairs, asking 'Shall I' or 'Would you' questions, and giving a short answer. Here are two examples:
S.1: Shall I open the window?
S.2: Yes, please.
S.1: Would you carry this for me, please?
S.2: Certainly.

2. Conversation

Key Points
1. Use and intonation of social formulae 'Good morning/evening/afternoon'
2. Meaning of *reserved*
3. Use and intonation of exclamations like 'How strange'
4. Meaning of 'walk off with' as in 'Perhaps someone walked off with it'
5. Revision and practice with 'lend'
6. Use and intonation of 'Here you are' (when handing someone something)
7. Meaning and use of *intend* + to do
8. Meaning and use of 'It all depends'
9. Meaning and use of 'by mistake'

Presentation Notes
1. Follow the initial presentation procedure as for earlier Units.
2. Practise with 'There isn't a pen on the desk.' 'Isn't there? How strange.'
   Give other negative sentences like these—
   'There isn't any sugar in my tea./There isn't any chalk here./There aren't any cigarettes left./There isn't any coffee in the machine.' etc.
   —and get students to answer (individually or in chorus) with—
   'Isn't (Aren't) there? How strange/unusual/odd.'
3. Give the class individual words from the conversation. See if they can remember the full sentences these words occurred in. Test in particular
   a) form   c) bottom
   b) room   d) mistake
4. Ask the class to form more sentences with 'by mistake'. If you want to, give them an invention exercise for this. Here are some prompts:
   a) the wrong bus
   b) somebody else's room
   c) the wrong homework exercise
   d) your umbrella
   e) the letter away
   f) the wrong office.
5. If you are using the tape recorder, let the class hear the tape once or twice. Then ask them to give the response to what the receptionist says. Simply pause the tape after she has said something and before Arthur speaks. Then let the class hear what Arthur says again to check their own responses. If necessary, occasionally give prompts, such as 'pen', 'off with', 'sure', 'depends', 'on Thursday', etc.

Unit 10 e/f

e Summary

1

This Unit has aimed at teaching students to ask other people to do things in a polite manner acceptable in the majority of English situations by using 'Would you . . .' or 'Could you . . .'. At this stage, there is no need to teach other complex ways of asking people to do things (e.g. 'I wonder if you'd mind . . .'), as they are taught later. Two points *are* worth emphasising, however. The first is the intonation we use in English with such utterances as 'Would you open the window, please?'; and the second is quite simply to focus students' attention on the word *please*.

1 and 2

Ask students if they have noticed the 'for you/for him/for us', etc. phrases and where we put them in a sentence like – 'Shall I carry that suitcase for you?'

3

This Unit concentrates on the use of the verbs *get, bring, take* and *show* as used in the pattern *He brought me some cigarettes*. One or two points should be cleared before going on to the next Unit:
a) Students should already have some insight into the distinction in English between *bring* and *take*.
b) They should be proficient in the manipulation of the past form of the verbs: for example 'Shall I *take* her some flowers?'/'He *took* them a present.'
c) Their attention should be focused on the form of the words after verbs like *take, bring, get, send* etc. – *me/you/him/her*.
d) They should notice what happens when we use 2 pronouns, as in situation 2 (page 57): – 'Take him this champagne!' '*Take it to him now!*' – but there is no need at this stage to go into a great deal of detail or intensive practice on the point.

f Exercises for homework

2

This exercise is obviously a test of students' ability to recognise and use the correct form of the personal pronouns. Some of these sentences could well be expanded into Substitution Drills during the oral preparation phase for homework: for example: SHALL I POST THAT LETTER FOR YOU?
Prompts:
a) him   d) her
b) do the work   e) them
c) get the tickets

4

Once again we have set a less controlled writing exercise (– it is still *guided*–), but this time we have introduced a new element, letter writing. One of the main reasons for this is that, of all the types of extended writing done by students while learning a foreign language, letter writing seems to be the most practical and transferable. Few students will need to write compositions later; they may need and will probably want to write letters. Since the book in no way sets out to teach letter writing systematically, we have left it to the teacher to tell students –
a) how we write the address and date at the head of an English letter;
b) the various forms of address we can use in English ('Dear . . .', 'My dear . . .' etc.); and
c) the various endings one can use in an English letter – 'Yours faithfully', 'Yours sincerely', etc.

As for the preparation in the classroom of this particular letter, we suggest that the teacher writes on the blackboard a model letter made from question and answer and suggestions from the various members of the class. In this way, the students as a group will be involved in 'creating language', whilst benefiting from immediate correction (by the teacher) instead of committing to paper a number of errors while writing at home.

Unit 10
e/f

e Summary

Focal points in this Unit.

1. Remember the polite way we ask other people to do things for us:

    Would you
    Could you   open the window, please?

2. Remember how we offer to do something:

    Shall I carry that for you?
    Shall I get you some chocolate?

3. With words like *bring, take, get, show, send* and *lend* in the table below use this word order:

1	2	3
Shall I send Could you give	him her them	some tea? the books? the letter?

Notice particularly the form of the words in column 2.

f Exercises for homework

1. Do all the questions and exercises on pages 57 and 60.

2. Choose the correct form:
    a) Shall I post that letter ...? (your/you/for you)
    b) Would you send ... the book, please? (to me/me/I)
    c) Could you lend ... some money? (him/he/to him)
    d) Shall I take ... some fruit when I go and see her? (she/to her/her)
    e) Would you give ... these letters, please? (them/to them/they)

3. Put the words in their correct order to make sentences:

    Example:

    to give/Tom/a lesson/going/is
    Answer: Tom is going to give a lesson.

    a) bring/I/you/a cup of tea/shall?
    b) that phone/you/could/for me/answer?
    c) a light/me/could/give/you?
    d) me/yesterday/sent/a parcel/my parents.
    e) five shillings/them/last night/lent/he.

4. **Guided Composition**

    You arrived back from holiday yesterday. Before you went on holiday, you left a book at a friend's house, and you want him (or her) to bring it back as soon as possible. Write a letter asking for it. Begin your letter like this:

    'Dear ...,
    I flew back from France last night after a wonderful holiday. When I came through the Customs ...'

    Now continue the letter using as many of the following prompt words and phrases as you can, and any other words and phrases from this Unit (particularly pages 57 and 60):

    Customs officer/anything to declare// 'show/suitcase'//no money/people/offer/ lift//kind of them//more about holiday/ see you//remember/book/your house?// bring/tomorrow?//

5. **Transfer Exercise**

    a) Write down what you say if you want someone i) to give you a light for your cigarette, ii) to tell you the time, iii) to carry something for you, iv) to answer the phone (or front door), and v) to send you a particular book.

    b) Write down what you say when you offer i) to open a window, ii) to close a door, iii) to help someone, iv) to put something somewhere, and v) to sign a document (hotel register, cheque, letter etc.).

Unit 11 a Present perfect with 'For' and 'Since'

1
(a) When/boy friend?
(b) When/Julia?
(c) What time/now?
(d) Julia/ask?
(e) Why/he/angry?

2
(a) How long/Tom and Susan?
(b) How long/house?
(c) How long/the Barclay's?
(d) How long/their house?

3
(a) How long/Peter/in England?
(b) When/woman?
(c) How long/Peter/wait?
(d) How long/woman/talk?

4
(a) How long/Julia/office?
(b) How long/others/work?
(c) What/typists?

5
(a) How long/match?
(b) When/match/start?
(c) What/police?
(d) What/TV cameras?
(e) Why/Tom/better view?

Main Teaching-Points
1. Present Perfect Simple 'has/have been' and 'has/have had', statements, negatives and questions.
2. Present Perfect Continuous, 'has/have been doing', statements, negatives and questions.
3. The discrimination between *for* and *since*.

Extra Points and Activities
1. Use of 'How long have you . . .?' and 'Have you . . . very long?' questions.
2. Short answers with 'Yes, I have/No, I haven't' etc.
3. Use of *either* in negative sentences.
4. Meaning and use of *neither* in 'Neither have the others'.
5. Use of *try + to do*.
6. Meaning and use of 'to keep order', 'in front of' and 'get a better view'.

HAS/HAVE HAD		10 minutes		9 o'clock
HAS/HAVE BEEN	FOR	6 months	SINCE	1970
HAS/HAVE BEEN DOING		3 years		last Friday, etc.

Unit 11

a

1

Julia had a date with her new boyfriend in this restaurant at 8. He came on time but she did not. She came in only a moment ago. It is 9. "Have you been waiting long?" she asked him when she came in. "Yes, I have," he is saying. He is rather angry because he has been waiting for an hour.

1. Ask when he came! Ask about Julia, too!
2. What exactly is her question?
3. What exactly is his answer?
4. Why is he angry?

2

Tom and Susan have been married a very short time. They haven't had that house very long, either. The couple next door, the Barclays, have been married a very long time. They have been living in the same house all that time!

1. Ask questions with 'very long' on the end!
    a) Tom and Susan/married
    b) the Barclays/married
    c) Tom and Susan/that house

3

Tom's brother, Peter, has been back in England for only half an hour. He is waiting to phone Tom, but the woman got to the phone box just a few seconds before he did. That was ten minutes ago. She has been talking for ten minutes and Peter has been waiting that long, too.

1. Ask and answer questions with 'How long'!
    a) Peter/back in England
    b) woman/in the phone box
    c) Peter/outside
    d) talk
    e) wait

4

Julia has not been in the office very long. Neither have the others. They have been working for less than ten minutes. They have been working since 9 o'clock. Actually one man has just been standing by the window for the last ten minutes. The two typists have not been doing very much, either. They have been talking.

1. Say what each person is doing now!
2. Now ask questions with 'How long'!
3. Make sentences with 'since' and 'for'!

5

This match has been going on for half an hour. The teams have been playing only since 2.30 and there is trouble already. In the very first minute, some of the crowd began to throw things and fight. The police have been trying to keep order and have been arresting people. The TV cameras have been filming everything. There is a very tall man in front of Tom. Tom has been trying to get a better view for some time, but it is impossible.

1. Ask and answer questions with 'How long'!
    a) the match   b) the teams
    c) some of the crowd d) the police
    e) the cameras   f) Tom/a better view
2. Make sentences with 'since' and 'for' about all the things you see in the picture!

Unit 11 b

FORMATION AND MANIPULATION

1 Pronunciation
   a) *I've* is more frequent than *I have* in spoken English, so say *I've* (You've, he's, she's, it's, we've).
   b) *for* is almost always pronounced [fə(r)].

2

A	B	C
I've	been living in London	for ages

   i) Think of all the other words that can replace 'I've' in box A.
   ii) Now look at the situations on page 63 and find words to replace 'been living in London' in box B.
   iii) Look at the situations on page 63 again. This time find all the time expressions that can replace 'for ages' in box C.
   v) Now, write or say ten sentences using the words that can go in boxes A, B and C.
   vi) The word *had* can also go in box B if you put words like 'a car', 'a big house' after it.
   vii) Make five sentences with 'I've (etc.) had a . . .'

3

A	B	C	D
How long	has he	been living	in London?

   i) Think of all the words which can replace 'has he' in box B.
   ii) Now replace boxes C and D (refer to the situations on page 63).
   iii) Look at these time expressions, some you know, some are new:
   FOR AGES   SINCE LAST SUMMER   FOR A WEEK   SINCE CHRISTMAS   FOR A VERY LONG TIME
   SINCE YESTERDAY   FOR YEARS AND YEARS   SINCE 1968   FOR A MOMENT
   SINCE HE ARRIVED.
   iv) Use the expressions in exercise iii to answer questions beginning with 'How long'. Ask and answer these questions with the person sitting next to you.
   Example: A: How long have you been living here?
   B: Since last summer.

4

A	B	C
Have you	been in England	very long?

   i) Look at these words – they can replace 'been in England' in box B.
   'known him'   'had a cold'   'been waiting for them'
   ii) With the person sitting next to you, ask and answer 'very long' questions. For positive answers use 'Yes' plus the time expression in Part 3, exercise iii. For negative answers use the 'No, not very long' or 'No, I haven't' forms.

FORMATION AND MANIPULATION

Unit 11 b

1.

a) Insist on the use of *'ve* for *have* in all positive statements. (And also *haven't* for **4** ii.)
b) Teach the difference in the pronunciation of *for* before vowels and consonants.
e.g. [fə] two years
but [fər] ages

2.

Establish the difference between a point in time and a period of time by using the following technique.

Write | since – yesterday
      | for   – a week | on the blackboard.

Ask students to say *since* or *for* for each of the following: a long time, yesterday, 1970, the war, a week, several weeks, last summer, Christmas, you came in, he arrived, a short while, years and years, my birthday.

3.

a) Teach the weak (unstressed) forms of *have* and *has* [həv] [həz] and [əv] [əz] after 'how long'. If students have difficulty in producing the aspirated *h* a second time (i.e. after 'how long') teach only the [əv] [əz] forms.
b) Extension of Exercise. This is the natural place for the teacher to extend the scope of the exercise to ask students questions about their own experiences. Cover such areas as: learning English, in this room, studying this book, had a car, those shoes, etc. Students can also use the prompts to ask each other similar questions.

4.

Remember that *have* in 'Have you . . .' questions is pronounced [həv] when it comes at the beginning of a sentence, not [əv]. Avoid teaching the difference in meaning between the unstressed and stressed forms of *have* unless the students seem able to grasp and use the difference.
i.e. Have [həv] you known him very long? (No particular meaning implied.)
Have [hæv] you known him very long? (I didn't think you knew him at all.)

Extra Fluency Practice

I'VE BEEN HERE SINCE CHRISTMAS
1. She's
2. yesterday
3. ages
4. waiting
5. half an hour
6. They
7. swimming
8. learning French
9. since they were children
10. seven years

N.B. Check on the learning of the past forms of verbs. Give a test revising all forms so far learnt. (Select 10 or 20 from the total.)

Unit 11
C EXPLOITATION OF THE EPISODE

Key Structures and Vocabulary	Suggested Explanations
a) It must be ... (5)	I think it is certainly ...
b) ten minutes away ... (7)	It takes ten minutes to get there (see Teacher page for Episode 9 Key Structures and Vocabulary, item c).
c) jaw ... (8)	Show the students where your jaw is.
d) get rid of ... (15)	to throw away–to make oneself free of–give a few examples in sentences. e.g. 'I want to get rid of this old table, old car, old book' etc.
e) roar ... (32)	a lion roars.

Section 1
1. Listening phase followed by special questions listed below for short answers:
   a) Were Halls and Baxter in a town? (No, they weren't)
   b) Was the night dark? (Yes, it was)
   c) Could they see anything? (No, they couldn't)
   d) How long had they been walking? (For twenty minutes)
   e) Did Halls say it was 20 minutes away? (No, he didn't)
   f) How many minutes did he say? (Ten)
   g) What sort of man was the Chief Inspector? (Sarcastic)
2. Completion practice: (books open once, then closed)
   T: How much ...
   Ss: farther
   T: is it to the ...
   Ss: nearest village. etc. etc.
3. Optional, if you think the students can learn to use the 'shall we' (line 13) form as a suggestion then use the following prompts to form the basis of an oral drill.
   a) go to the cinema
   b) stay at home tonight
   c) have a meal
   d) see you later
   e) watch television
   f) wait for him
   g) give him a lift (explain)
   h) go in now

Section 2
1. Listening phase followed by choral reading and questions.
2. Correct my statements phase. 'Baxter turned off the main road ... He wanted to keep the police car ... The army never used the area ... Coke remembered it from the hours when ... he used to be a sailor ... He knew there was a town ... down a main road ... Just after he got to it ... he stopped and left the bus in a road ... Then he ran into the village itself ...'
3. Imagine Coke was nervous. Ask students to make sentences about what he asked himself before he made any decisions. Use the 'Shall I ...?' form and give these prompts:–
   For example:
   turn off the main road =
   Shall I turn off the main road?
   get rid of the police car
   stop outside the village
   leave the car in a field
   walk into the village

Section 3
1. Silent reading phase. Then ask students to close books and answer simple comprehension questions. Sample questions:
   a) Where was the village?
   b) What did he find?
2. Now read the text or play the tape.
3. Question phase: get students to ask each other questions (and answer them) based on the text. e.g. Q: Where was the village? A: almost 200 miles away.

THE MAN WHO ESCAPED
Episode 11

Unit 11

C

SYNOPSIS: *Halls and Baxter tried to catch Coke when they saw him on a road in the countryside late at night. Coke, however, got away from them and stole their car. He also got through a police road block.*

1 "How much farther is it to the nearest village?" Baxter asked.
He and Halls were in the middle of the countryside. The night was very dark and there was no traffic on the roads. They could not see a house or even a public phone box anywhere.
"It must be on the other side of that hill" Halls answered.
"I hope so! We've been walking for twenty minutes now! When we started, you said it was only ten minutes away!" Baxter said angrily. He was tired and his jaw hurt. He could already imagine the Chief Inspector's comments at their next interview. The Chief Inspector was a very sarcastic man. "Well, Baxter, perhaps you would explain all this to me. It seems you had a car when you saw Coke and that he had it after he saw you. Very interesting. How shall we explain all this to the papers? Shall we say something like 'The police are always ready to help'?"

2 Coke turned off the main road. He wanted to get rid of the police car as soon as possible. The army often used the area for manoeuvres and Coke remembered it from the days when he was a soldier. He knew there was a village down a side road. Just before he got to it, he stopped and left the car in a field. Then he walked into the village itself. He wanted something and he was sure he could find it here.

In his apartment in London, a well-dressed man named Eric Masters turned on the radio and listened. The news was still bad. Coke was still free, the announcer said. Masters looked very frightened. He turned off the radio suddenly and picked up the phone.

3 In a village almost 200 miles away, Coke found what he wanted.
"People in villages like this always trust their neighbours. How lucky!" he thought when he saw the motorbike. It was in a garage at the edge of the village. The garage was not even locked and there was a leather motorcycle suit on a nail. There were also a pair of gloves and a helmet. Everyone in the village was asleep. Coke worked silently. He pushed the bike down the road. When he was far enough away from the village he started the engine. It roared loudly. He got on the motorbike and raced towards London.

Unit 11 d

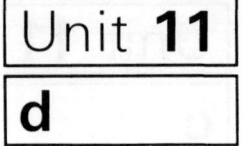

FURTHER PRACTICE

1. Conversation for Paired Practice

Read the Model conversation, and use the prompts to make others like it.

MODEL: A: Are you still living in London?
         B: Yes, I've been living there for 3 years now.

Prompts:

1) A: working for them
   B: two years
2) A: those French cigarettes
   B: a couple of months
3) A: studying English
   B: eighteen months
4) A: reading that book
   B: 6 weeks
5) A: writing that letter
   B: half an hour
6) A: waiting to see the boss
   B: ages

2. Conversation

Two months ago Julia bought a pullover from a large department store. The pullover is worn out already. Julia took the pullover back during the lunch hour today. She went there with a friend, Mary, who works in the same office. This is what happened.

MARY: It's certainly very busy here today, isn't it?
JULIA: Yes, and there aren't enough salesgirls. We've been standing here for at least five minutes!
MARY: Quick. Catch that salesgirl's eye! She's just finishing with a customer.
JULIA: Miss! Miss! Excuse me. I think I'm next and I haven't very much time.
SALESGIRL: Yes, madam. How can I help you?
JULIA: I'm afraid I have a complaint. It's this pullover. I've only had it for two months and it's already worn out.
SALESGIRL: Worn out? May I see it?
JULIA: Yes, here you are. Look at the sleeves. They're the worst part. Do you see? They've worn very badly.
SALESGIRL: And how long do you say you've had it?
JULIA: For only two months. Since Christmas, in fact. Look, here's the receipt.
SALESGIRL: Thank you. This is very strange. We've been selling this particular make for years and we haven't had any complaints in all that time.
JULIA: Well, I'm sorry. I'm sure it isn't my fault it's already worn out.
SALESGIRL: One moment, please. Let me call the manager. Mr Simons! Mr Simons!
MR SIMONS: Yes?
SALESGIRL: It's this lady. She's had this pullover for two months and it's already worn out.
MR SIMONS: Really? Let me see, please. Hmmm ... yes ...
JULIA: I've been wearing it at the week-ends; that's all.
MR SIMONS: Yes, well ... make out a credit-slip for the lady, would you, Miss Smith?
JULIA: A credit-slip?
MR SIMONS: Yes. You can buy anything you like with it in the store.
JULIA: I'd rather have my money back, if you don't mind.
MR SIMONS: I see. Well, I suppose we can arrange that.
JULIA: Thank you.

Correct the statements

1. There are not many people in the shop today.
2. Julia has a lot of time.
3. She has been standing there for an hour.
4. She has had the sweater for a year.
5. The shop hasn't been selling that particular make for long.
6. Julia has been wearing the sweater at work.
7. Julia wants a credit-slip for the sweater.

Answer these questions

1. Ask and answer how long Julia has been standing there!
2. Ask why!
3. Why is she not satisfied with the pullover?
4. What exactly does she say when the manager offers her a credit-slip?

Practice

Think of some more sentences of your own using the pattern 'I'd rather ..., if you don't mind'. Describe the situations we can use these sentences in.

FURTHER PRACTICE

Unit 11 d

1. Conversation
for Paired Practice

a) Read the Model conversation and ask class as a whole group to repeat in chorus, paying particular attention to the use of *still,* the intonation used in the question and the answer, and the unstressed form of *for* [fə]. (Student books should be face down.)

b) Divide the class into half, and ask them once again to repeat the conversation in chorus, one half repeating A, the other B. Do this once again giving the prompt words only – 'living in London?' and '3 years'.

c) Take another pair of prompts and follow a) and b) as above, before allowing the class to work in pairs using all the prompts given. While you are walking around listening to them, make certain that all students have the opportunity both to ask and answer questions.

d) After students have practised the conversations in pairs using *for,* get them to work in pairs again, this time using *since.* Give the prompts –
  i) 1967   iv) the day before yesterday
  ii) last July   v) 6.30
  iii) last Christmas vi) lunchtime.

2. Conversation

Key Points
1. Meaning and use of certain vocabulary items: 'catch someone's eye', 'worn out', 'receipt', '(this particular) make', 'complaint' and 'credit-slip'
2. Intonation of the pattern 'It's certainly . . ., isn't it'
3. Use of *enough* with nouns as in 'There aren't enough salesgirls'
4. Use of 'Excuse me' when interrupting or getting someone's attention
5. Meaning and use of 'It isn't my fault . . .'
6. Preview of *let* as in 'Let me call the manager' and 'Let me see'
7. The use (and intonation) of *Really?* when expressing surprise
8. Meaning and use of the pattern 'I'd rather . . ., if you don't mind'
9. Use and intonation of 'would you' as a tag after an imperative, as in 'Make out . . ., would you?'

Presentation Notes
1. Follow the initial presentation procedure as for the previous conversations.
2. Choral repetition of parts of the conversation (whole class or groups), concentrating on, and using, the intonation patterns on the tape.
3. Use the three exercises on the student page (Correct my statements, Answer these questions, and Practice).
4. For Practice with 'I'd rather stay at home, if you don't mind'/'I'd rather have beer, if you don't mind' etc. – give prompts 'at home' and 'beer' for students to reproduce the examples. Then give more prompts, as with an Invention exercise, for students to give more examples: e.g. the cinema/by car/steak/ television etc.
5. After phases dealing with the Key Points (above), give the following words and phrases for recall of certain sentences:
   a) very busy
   b) at least five minutes
   c) this particular make
   d) fault
   e) this pullover
   f) credit-slip (for the lady)
   g) anything you like
   h) money back.

Unit 11
e/f

e Summary

1
If this Summary is used in class, ask students to go back to specific pieces of material in the Unit – the Presentation situations (page 64) or the Conversation (page 67) – and to do the same sort of thing. For example, take situation 3: 'The woman is talking. She started talking ten minutes ago. She has been talking for ten minutes.'

2
Once again, while summarising how we ask questions with 'How long . . .?', get students to ask each other questions beginning 'How long . . .?' This will also lead to a final consolidation of *for* vs. *since* if they have to answer as well.

3 and 4
Give another short discrimination exercise, this time making students add *since* or *for* to a phrase they hear. For example:
T: 6 o'clock   Ss: since 6 o'clock
T: 3 days   Ss: for 3 days   – and so on.
Focus students' attention at this point on the two unstressed forms of *for* – [fə] as in '[fə] two days', and [fər] as in '[fər] a week'.

f Exercises for homework

2
Prepare this exercise in class as other Invention Exercises in previous Units. You may then like to extend the range of activity by asking the students to use the prompts for a short paired dialogue phase, thus also bringing in once again practice with 'How long . . .?'

Here is an example:
Prompt: wait/bus/ten minutes
S.1:   How long have you been waiting for the bus?
S.2:   For ten minutes.
This type of dialogue can be extended further to the following:
S.1:   What's he doing?
S.2:   He's waiting for a bus.
S.1:   How long has he been doing that?

3
In the last Unit we asked students to write a personal letter. The Conversation on page 67 provides admirable basic material, we feel, for a letter from an individual (in this case, a customer) to a firm (in this case, a shop). To this extent, therefore, it is not a pure 'business letter', although students should be told to write the address of the shop they are writing to above the form of address ('Dear Sir,').
As for the preparation of the letter, the same technique could be used as in the last Unit OR a sample letter could be given (– used as an aural comprehension passage or a dictation –) including other model sentences such as 'When I got home, I found that . . .'; 'I'd like to make a serious complaint . . .'; and 'I'd rather *not* have another pullover; if you don't mind. I'd rather have my money back.'

Unit 11
e/f

e Summary

Focal points in this Unit.

1. a) Look at the ideas which are expressed in a 'have been' sentence:
   I am in London.   I have been in
   I came here 3   London for
   years ago.   3 years.
   b) Now look at a 'have had' sentence:
   I have a car.   I have had a car
   I bought it 6   for 6 months.
   months ago.
   c) Now look at a 'have been (do)ing' sentence:
   It is snowing.   It has been snow-
   It started snowing   ing for an hour.
   an hour ago.

2. To ask questions about a period of time we use the form:

   How long + have been doing . . .?
              have had . . .?

   Example:
   How long have you been learning French?
   How long have you had that hat?

3. Remember that *since* is used with times that we can point to on a calendar or clock.

   since + 6 o'clock/yesterday/
           last Monday/last January/
           15th March/1966/Easter

   since is also used with phrases to which the speaker can put a definite time or date.

   since + the end of the war/I was 6/
           I left school/she got married/
           his last birthday/
           the last office party

4. Remember that *for* is used with periods of time.

   for + half an hour/45 minutes/
         3 hours/2 days/6 weeks/
         a fortnight/18 months/
         25 years/ages and ages/
         a week or so

f Exercises for homework

1. Do all the exercises and questions on pages 63, 64 and 66.

2. **Invention Exercise**
   With 'has/have been doing . . . for/since'
   Examples:
   a) PROMPT: work/Bristol/2 years.
      RESPONSE: I've been working in Bristol for 2 years.
   b) PROMPT: live/London/1965.
      RESPONSE: She's been living in London since 1965.

   Prompts:
   a) wait/bus/10 minutes
   b) learn/English/6 months
   c) work/garden/1 o'clock
   d) smoke/heavily/2 years
   e) drive/that car/3 years
   f) live/a flat/last July
   g) build/that house/March
   h) look for/prisoner/he escaped
   i) ring/bell/5 minutes

3. **Guided Composition**
   Write a letter of complaint to a shop about a woollen pullover you bought while you were on holiday in England about a month ago. You want to complain because it has worn very badly. Read the Conversation on page 66 again, and try and use as many of the words, phrases and patterns as you can in your letter: these patterns are particularly useful – 'I'm afraid I have a complaint'/'. . . it's already worn badly'/'it isn't my fault . . .'/'I'd rather . . ., if you don't mind.' Begin your letter like this:

   'Dear Sir,
       While I was on holiday in your town about a month ago, I bought a green pullover in your shop. I'm afraid . . .'

4. **Transfer Exercise**
   Write 10 true sentences about yourself or friends using 'have done', 'have been' or 'have been doing' + *since* or *for*:
   For example: 'I've had this car for 3 years'/ 'I've been learning English since 1969'.

Unit 12 a

Have been doing/have just done/ haven't done yet/had better do

1
(a) How long/they/club?
(b) What time?
(c) good time?
(d) What/Deborah/say?
(e) Where/other people?

2
(a) Fred/good time?
(b) Where/his wife?
(c) Why/quiet?

3
(a) Where/Julia?
(b) How long/bus?
(c) What/round corner?

4
(a) What/Peter?
(b) How long?
(c) What/operator?
(d) Why/Peter/hang up?

5
(a) Who/Peter/stay with?
(b) How long/job?
(c) What/Tom/tell/Peter?

6
(a) How/Frank/lately?
(b) Why/overtime?
(c) What/doctor/say?

Main Teaching-Points
1. More practice with Present Perfect Continuous and Present Perfect Simple.
2. Present Perfect Simple with *just* (as in 'He has just come home') and *yet* in questions and negatives.
3. 'Had better' (as in 'She had better take it') and 'had better not' (as in 'You had better not work so hard'). Intensive practice with unstressed forms 'I'd better'/'You'd better' etc. . . ..

Extra Points and Activities
1. Discrimination between *been* and *gone*.
2. Meaning and use of *Look* and *hang up* in situation 4.
4. Meaning of *lately* and its use with Present Perfect tenses.
4. Meaning of *overtime, examine* and *take things easy* in situation 6.
5. Overall concentration on unstressed forms.

PRESENT PERFECT CONTINUOUS (continued practice)
PRESENT PERFECT + 'JUST' and 'YET'
HAD BETTER DO and HAD BETTER NOT DO

Unit 12
a

1
Arthur and Deborah have been in a night-club since 8 p.m. It is 2 in the morning now. They have been having a very good time. "I really think we had better leave now" Deborah is telling Arthur. "Everybody else has gone home except the waiter and the band."

1. Ask and answer the questions!
   a) Where/now   b) How long
   c) What time/now   d) a good time
2. What is Deborah telling Arthur?
3. Do you agree? Why?

2
Fred Collins has been having a good time, too. He has just come home. His wife is asleep upstairs. He had better be very quiet. He had better look where he is going. His wife is going to be very angry if he wakes her up.

1. What has Fred been doing?
2. What has he just done?
3. What is going to happen if he is not careful?
4. Make some sentences about him with 'had better' and 'had better not'!

3
Julia is going to meet her boyfriend. She has been waiting for the bus for some time but it has not come yet. She is going to be late again if it does not come soon. A taxi has just come round the corner. Perhaps she had better take it.

1. What is Julia going to do?
2. What is she doing now? Ask 'how long'!
3. What is going to happen if the bus does not come soon?
4. What has just happened?
5. What had she better do?

4
Peter is making a long-distance call to Canada. He has been talking for six minutes and the operator has just asked him to put some more money in. He has not got any. "Look," he is saying to the person in Canada, "I think I'd better hang up now."

1. What is Peter doing?
2. Ask how long (and answer)!
3. What has the operator just asked him to do?
4. What is he saying?

5
Peter came back to England a month ago. He has been staying with Tom and Susan since then. He has been looking for a job for a month but has not found one yet. "Some employers don't like people with long hair," Tom is telling him. "Perhaps you'd better get a hair cut!"

1. Ask and answer questions about Peter!
   a) When/back to England
   b) How long/with Tom and Susan
   c) How long/a job
   d) one yet
2. What is Tom telling him?

6
Frank Martin has not been feeling very well lately. He has been working a lot of overtime because he wants to buy a new car. The doctor has been examining him. "You've been working too hard, that's all," he is saying. "You'd better take things easy for a while. You'd better not work so hard."

1. What has the doctor been doing?
2. What had Frank better do and why?
3. Ask and answer the questions!
   a) very well lately
   b) Why/so much overtime lately

Unit 12 b

FORMATION AND MANIPULATION

1

A	B	C
He's been	having a good time	

i) Find other words to replace 'He's been' in box A.
ii) Look at the situations on page 69 and find things to put in box B.
iii) Box C is empty. Words like *recently* and *lately* can go here, so can expressions of time with the words *since* and *for*. Think of as many as you can. If you can't think of many, look at the Formation and Manipulation page of Unit 11.
iv) With the person sitting next to you, ask and answer questions like this:
Question: What's he been doing recently?
Answer: Having a good time, *or* He's been having a good time.
v) Now make questions starting 'Have you . . .?' (answer, 'Yes, I have' or 'No, I haven't').
Example: Question: Have you been having a good time recently?
Answer: Yes, I have.

2 Look at these words: LOOKING   FEELING   EATING
i) Now look at the first sentence of situation 6, page 69.
ii) Find other words to replace 'Frank Martin', 'feeling' and 'lately'.
iii) With the person sitting next to you, ask and answer questions like this:
Question: What's the matter with Frank Martin?
Answer: Oh, he hasn't been feeling very well lately.
and like this:
Question: What's the matter?
Answer: Well, actually, I haven't been feeling very well lately.

3

A	B	C	D	E
Has he	come in	yet?	Yes, he's just	come in

i) Think of words to replace 'he' in boxes A and D.
ii) Now, think of words to replace 'come in' in boxes B and E.
iii) Now say or write five sentences using the new words you have.

4 i) Make sentences from the table.   ii) Make sentences from the table.

You'd better	get a meal
We'd better	go now
I'd better	find a taxi

You'd better not	work so hard
He'd better not	eat so much
They'd better not	smoke so much

NOTE: 'We'd' is the short form of 'We had' but we always say and write '*d*. For example: 'You'd better get a haircut' Page 69, situation 5.

FORMATION AND MANIPULATION

Unit 12 b

General note on pronunciation. There shouldn't be any great problems with the production of the spoken forms of the verb *have* since written short forms are in everyday use. However it will be necessary to insist on their use at all times because many students will still show a certain resistance to using them.

1. Give students the following prompts to elicit 'have been doing' responses.
    i) You look very tired.
    ii) She looks very happy.
    iii) They look very well.
    iv) They look very pleased.
    e.g. T: They look very happy. Ss: Yes, they've been having a good time lately.

2. Tell students that there is very little difference in meaning between *lately* and *recently*. Encourage them to use other expressions which frequently occur in this structure:
    in the last few days, in recent months, for ages, since last year etc. etc.

Extra Fluency Practice

SHE HASN'T BEEN FEELING TOO WELL LATELY
1. happy   5. very
2. I   6. They
3. recently   7. for ages
4. John   8. looking

3. The following structures are often used together because the use of one very frequently leads to the other as an answer. For example: Have you read that book yet?
    Yes, I've just read it.
    or: No, I haven't read it.
Use these prompts to get first positive answers then negative answers.
    i) Have you read that book yet?
    ii) Have you seen that film yet?
    iii) Have you met my father yet?
    iv) Have you been to Paris yet?
    v) Have you driven that new car yet?
    vi) Have you answered his letter yet?
    vii) Have you heard that pop song yet?
    viii) Have you started the washing-up yet?
    ix) Have you introduced him yet?
    x) Have you discussed it yet?

4. Many students have only heard the spoken form of 'you*'d* better.' It is a common misconception that the *'d* is the short form of *would*. Write 'We had better go' on the blackboard and tell students that we say (and usually write) 'We*'d* better go'.
Use the following drill for fluency practice.
    i) T: It's raining. Go indoors. Ss: We'd better go indoors.
    ii) It's cold. (put on coat).
    iii) I'm thirsty. (get a drink).
    iv) I'm tired. (sit down).
    v) The train is going now. (say goodbye).
    vi) The pub's closing. (go home).

N.B. Check on the learning of verb-forms.

Unit 12

c

EXPLOITATION OF THE EPISODE

Key Structures and Vocabulary	*Suggested Explanations*
a) dialled (4)	selected (chose) the number.
b) at least twelve times (5)	not less than twelve and probably more.
c) What the devil (6–7)	what on earth (i.e. it's not a serious oath).
d) a cold edge (9)	like a knife (cutting).
e) at the other end (11)	answering the telephone.
f) helmet and goggles (32–33)	protective coverings for the head and eyes.

Section 1
1. Listening phase followed by special questions listed below for short-answer practice. (books closed)
   a) Who lived comfortably and ate well? (Masters did)
   b) Did he usually worry about the future? (No, he didn't)
   c) Was he worried now? (Yes, he was)
   d) What did he do nervously? (He dialled)
   e) Did anybody answer immediately? (No, they didn't)
   f) How many times did the phone ring? (At least twelve)
   g) What sort of voice answered. (A sleepy voice/A sleepy one)
   h) What was the first thing said? (Who is it?)
   i) Was it a woman's voice? (No, it wasn't)
   j) Was it a kind voice? (No, it wasn't)
2. Completion practice: books open once, then closed.
   T: Eric Masters had the face of a man who lived
      . . . and ate . . .
   Ss: comfortably   well etc.

Section 2
1. Listening phase (books closed) followed by choral repetition (after teacher or tape, books still closed).
2. Silent reading phase.
3. Divide the class into two sections. One section to read the part of Masters, the other section to read the part of Hugo, teacher reads the part of the narrator.
4. Optional fluency practice:
   I'VE BEEN THINKING ABOUT COKE ALL EVENING
   a) all day
   b) her
   c) them
   d) She's
   e) him
   f) wondering
5. Writing phase. Get students to write sentences about what Masters *has just done*. Give these prompts on the blackboard:
   telephone Hugo/wake Hugo up/make Hugo angry/tell him Coke free ask him/what is he going to do.

Section 3
1. Ask students to read the text silently, then ask comprehension questions. Sample questions:
   a) Was the motorbike slow?
   b) How did Coke drive?
   Stop these questions at lines 27–28 (. . . lights in his mirror).
2. Now make use of a correct my statements phase.
3. Finally read the text of the last paragraph or play the tape.

THE MAN WHO ESCAPED
Episode 12

Unit 12

c

SYNOPSIS: *Coke knew it was dangerous to stay in the police car, so he stole a motorbike from a small village.*

1 Eric Masters had the face of a man who lived comfortably and ate well. It was the face of a man who usually did not worry about the future. All this was gone now. He was very worried indeed when he picked up the phone and dialled nervously. At first, nobody answered at the other end. The phone rang at least twelve times but Masters did not hang up. Finally a sleepy voice answered angrily, "Who is it? What the devil do you want at this hour?"
It was a man's voice, and it was educated and smooth, but it had a cruel, cold edge.

2 "Is that you, Hugo? This is Eric," Masters said quickly.
The man at the other end became even angrier.
"And why are you ringing at this hour? I've been in bed for an hour!"
"But, haven't you heard the news, Hugo? Coke's still free!"
"Of course I've heard. So have my friends," the man answered coldly.
"I can't sleep. I've been thinking about Coke all evening!"
"Perhaps you'd better take a sleeping pill!"
Masters almost screamed the next question into the phone. "What are you going to do, Hugo? What are you going to do?"
The man at the other end answered just as coldly and as calmly as before, "Do? We're going to kill Coke! That's what we're going to do. That is, if he is stupid enough to come to London!"

3 The motorbike was fast but the roads were icy. Coke drove dangerously. He knew he had to. He had very little time.
"I'd better keep to the side roads," he thought, but he did not because the main road was much faster, and he had very little time. A police car went by in the opposite direction. He began to feel a little safer. Then, around 2 o'clock in the morning, he suddenly saw lights in his mirror. They were the headlights of another police car, and this time it was just behind him. It came closer and closer and then suddenly speeded up. For several seconds, Coke and the car raced along side by side. Coke looked up. The two policemen in the car were looking at him but they could not see his face clearly. He was wearing a helmet and goggles. Coke raised his hand and waved casually. The driver was already looking at the road again, but the other still had his eyes on Coke. Then, the car speeded up again. In a few seconds it was far ahead of him. Coke raced towards London. He knew exactly where he wanted to go.

Unit 12 d

FURTHER PRACTICE

1. Invention Exercise

Make sentences with 'had better do' using the prompts.

Examples:

1) PROMPT: those shoes.
   RESPONSE: You'd (He'd/I'd, etc.) better clean those shoes.
2) PROMPT: up early tomorrow
   RESPONSE: I'd better get up early tomorrow.

Prompts:

a) a haircut
b) very quiet
c) that old car
d) the bank
e) less beer
f) bed early tonight
g) that letter now
h) a new car
i) the office earlier
j) more slowly
k) faster
l) a phone call

Describe the situations in which the sentences are used.

2. Conversation

Frank Martin went to see his doctor last week, but he was not satisfied with what the doctor told him. He asked to see a specialist. Like everybody else in Great Britain, Frank can insist on this. He does not have to pay for this or any other medical treatment. This is what happened when he saw Dr Scott, the specialist.

DR SCOTT: Now, Mr Martin. I've just been reading what your own doctor says. I gather you haven't been feeling very well lately? Is that right?
FRANK: It's . . . it's my leg, doctor. My right leg. I keep getting a strange pain in it.
DR SCOTT: Could you describe this pain to me?
FRANK: It's like . . . like boiling water running down my leg. It's been getting worse lately, too. I've been losing sleep.
DR SCOTT: You mean the pain's been keeping you awake?
FRANK: Yes, that's right. It's been keeping me awake.
DR SCOTT: Now, tell me, how long have you had this trouble?
FRANK: The pain? For about a year now.
DR SCOTT: Hmmm . . . Have you been getting tired lately after you've been for a walk? For instance, have you been getting a bit short of breath, perhaps?
FRANK: Why, yes! Yes, I have, doctor!
DR SCOTT: Hmmm . . . I think we'd better give you a few tests here in hospital.
FRANK: Do you think it's serious, doctor?
DR SCOTT: Probably not.
FRANK: But . . . Doctor Cooke, my local doctor, thinks it's only that I've been working too hard lately.
DR SCOTT: That could be the reason. Don't worry. We'll soon find out.

Correct the statements

1. Frank has been getting a strange pain in his arm.
2. It has been getting better lately.
3. Frank's own doctor thinks he has been eating too much lately.
4. The specialist thinks what the other doctor says is impossible.

Questions

1. What has the pain been doing to Frank?
2. What has been happening to Frank after he has been for a walk?
3. What does the specialist think they had better do?

Ask and answer the questions about Frank

1. How long/this trouble?
2. pain/better or worse lately?

FURTHER PRACTICE

Unit 12 d

1. Invention Exercise

a) Follow the presentation procedure used in previous Units.

b) Some students may find it difficult to describe in simple language the situations in which the sentences they produce might be used. In this case, both in order to make students aware of the situations, and to produce an extra activity, prepare them to work in pairs by suggesting simple dialogues from the prompts:
For example:
Prompt: the bank =
    S.1: I haven't got any money.
    S.2: You'd better go to the bank, then.
Prompt: more slowly =
    S.1: The traffic's heavy today.
    S.2: You'd better drive more slowly, then.
Other types of dialogue can also be composed, using the prompt in the stimulus, for example:—
S.1: You'd better type that letter now.
S.2: Why?
S.1: Because I want to post it early.

c) Finally ask students to give you advice about certain things: for example:
T: I've got a terrible cold.
Ss: You'd better stay at home/go to bed/take some medicine, then.
T: My car is very old now.
Ss: You'd better sell it/get another/buy a new one, then.

d) Another phase (as c)), this time asking students to use 'You'd better not . . ., then'– for example:
T: I've got a bad cough (demonstrate and give prompt *smoke*).
Ss: You'd better not smoke so much, then.

2. Conversation

Key Points
1. Vocabulary items: 'satisfied with', 'specialist', 'insist on', 'medical treatment', 'lose sleep', 'keep (someone) awake', and 'short of breath'
2. Meaning and use of 'I gather . . .'
3. Practice with *lately*
4. Meaning and use of 'It's like . . . - - -ing'
5. Practice with the pattern 'Could you describe . . . to me?'
6. Meaning and use of *could* as in 'That could be the reason'

Presentation Notes
1. Follow the presentation procedure used in previous Units.
2. If you are using a tape recorder, and the students have heard the conversation once or twice, play it again, and stop it at certain points, asking them *either* to finish a sentence (e.g. 'I gather you . . .' Ss: 'haven't been feeling very well lately'.) *or* to give the next response (e.g. 'Do you think it's serious, doctor? . . .' Ss: 'Probably not'.).
3. *Fluency Practice*
COULD YOU DESCRIBE THIS PAIN TO ME?
(Prompts to replace 'this pain' and 'me'.)
  a) to him   f) the car
  b) the coat   g) your office
  c) your umbrella h) the room
  d) to her   i) to us
  e) the film   j) the treatment
4. To practise '*I gather* he has/you haven't (etc.) been . . .', give some sentences for students to repeat, sentences to which we would naturally add 'I gather':
For example:
T: He's been working very hard lately.
Ss: I gather he's been working very hard lately.
5. As a *final Recall phase*, give the following prompts for recall of certain sentences from the Conversation: insist on the intonation they have heard on the tape:
  a) gather/very well
  b) strange pain
  c) worse lately
  d) short of breath, perhaps?
  e) a few tests
  f) worry. find out

Unit 12
e/f

e Summary

1

The two new elements in this Unit with the Present Perfect Simple are *just* and *yet*. It is naturally important to consolidate at this point the use of these two elements, in particular the meaning of *just* (= a few moments or seconds ago) and its position in the sentence, – and the meaning of *yet* as used in negative statements and questions, and its position in the sentence, too.
Both (*just* and *yet*) might well warrant extra drilling for final consolidation.

2

Make a particular point of focusing students' attention on the unstressed forms of *had* [(hə)d] used in conversation with all persons. Focus their attention, too, on the negative form and the form of the verb after 'had better'.
Although we have not asked students in this Unit to use the question 'Had(n't) I better do . . .?', certain groups of students could well be taught this at this stage, even if only through one or two Substitution Drills. For example:
HADN'T YOU BETTER DO IT NOW?
a) phone her   d) type that letter
b) see them   e) describe it to me
c) order it

f Exercises for homework

2

To prepare this orally in the class for a written homework, do the exercise with student books closed. If one student gives a sentence in the first person, ask another to give the same sentence with *he* or *we* etc. As an extra activity, pair the students for dialogue practice using the prompts as given, and this Model conversation (on the blackboard, if necessary):
S.1: Have you found a job yet?
S.2: No, I haven't. I've been looking for a good job for three weeks, but I haven't found one yet.

3

This is the third letter we have suggested as a Guided Composition. Students should be reminded of the requirements in format of an English letter (personal). Because this letter is considerably less controlled than any previous Guided Compositions – students are only instructed to use vocabulary and patterns from two sources in the Unit, and are only given the beginning of the letter – it is important that by question and answer work the teacher should try to elicit some of the sentences etc. they will need or ought to use. The following are the main items which should be included:
I haven't been feeling very well lately./a lot of overtime/doctor/examine/working too hard/take things easy/I'd better . . ./so I'd better not . . ./strange pain/it's like . . ./get better/short of breath

Unit 12

e/f

e Summary

Focal points in this Unit.

1. Remember how we use the words *just* and *yet* with the Present Perfect Simple:

   a) 'He has *just* come home'. 'A taxi has *just* come round the corner'. '. . . the operator has *just* asked him to put some more money in'.

   b) 'The bus has not come *yet*'. 'He has not found a job *yet*'.

   Notice particularly where we put them in a sentence.

2. Remember how we use 'had better' to give advice to other people—'You *had better not work* so hard'.—and to suggest that it is a good idea to do something—'We *had better leave* now'./'I *had better not tell* them'.
   Notice particularly the form of the verb after 'had better', and the position of *not* in a negative sentence.

f Exercises for homework

1. Do all the questions and exercises on pages 69 and 72.

2. **Invention Exercise**

   Write sentences using the prompts:

   MODEL: I've been . . . $\genfrac{}{}{0pt}{}{for}{since}$ . . ., but I haven't . . . yet.

   Examples:

   a) PROMPT: job/three weeks
      RESPONSE: I've been looking for a job for three weeks, but I haven't found one yet.
   b) PROMPT: the bus/9 o'clock
      RESPONSE: I've been waiting for the bus since 9 o'clock, but it hasn't come yet.
   a) my homework/half an hour
   b) the train/twenty minutes
   c) the concert/7.30
   d) a car/20 years
   e) the postman/8 o'clock
   f) this book/2 weeks
   g) English/18 months
   h) this letter/6 o'clock
   i) a sports car/last Christmas
   j) pop records/20 minutes

3. **Guided Composition**

   Using some of the vocabulary and sentence patterns from situation 6 (page 69) and from the Conversation (page 72), write a short letter to a friend politely refusing an invitation to go on a long walk in the country. Begin your letter like this:

   'Dear . . .,
   Thank you very much for your invitation to go on a long walk next week-end. It was very nice of you to think of me, but I'm afraid . . .'

4. **Transfer Exercise**

   Write at least 5 sentences about yourself using this pattern:

   I haven't done the job yet, so I'd better do it as soon as I can.
   I haven't booked the tickets for the concert yet, so I'd better book them this afternoon.

Unit 13
a Past continuous and past simple

1
(a) What/people/doing?
(b) first time?
(c) What/director?
(d) What/all the different people?
(e) When/'cut'/last time?
(f) What/the different people/then?

2
(a) What/all the people/Charles jumped?
(ask two questions about each person)

3
(a) What/in a few seconds?
(b) What/Frank/now?
(c) some of the men?
(d) old man?
(e) manager?
(f) What/manager/bell rings?

4
(a) What/old lady?
(b) What/two old men?
(c) What/young man?
(d) What/children?
(e) What/young couple?

Main Teaching-Points
1. I/he/she/it was
   We/you/they were   doing ... when ... did.
   Fluency practice with Past Continuous concentrating on unstressed [wəz] and [wə].
2. I/he/she etc. did ... when ... did.
3. Discrimination between use and meaning of **1.** and **2.** Examples:
   a) They *were fighting* when he shouted 'Cut!'
   b) They *stopped* when he shouted 'Cut!'

Extra Points and Activities
1. Practice with *This is the first/second/third* etc. *time I have done* ...
2. Meaning of *shout* vs. *cry*.
3. Revision of 'as ... as' in 'as fast as they could' (situation 4).
4. Prepositional uses, such as 'playing *on* the swings', 'working *at* his machine', etc.

He/she	WAS DOING
We/you/they	WERE DOING
He (etc.)	DID

.... when .... DID

Unit 13

a

1

These people are making a film. This is the second time they have filmed this scene. The director is going to shout "cut" in a second. Two men are fighting. The King is talking to the Queen. She is listening. A beautiful girl is crying. Two other men are watching the fight. One of them is laughing. The director shouted "cut" at exactly this point before. They were all doing the same thing when he did this. They all stopped and had a short rest when he shouted "cut".

1. Ask what these people are doing now and answer:
   a) the two men   b) the King
   c) the Queen   d) the beautiful girl
   e) the two other men
2. Now say what all these people were doing when the director shouted "cut" at this point before. Make at least five different sentences!
3. What did they all do when the director shouted "cut" last time? (short rest)

3

This is where Frank works. You can see exactly the same thing every day at this time. A bell is going to ring in a few seconds and everybody is going to rush out, as they always do. Frank is working at his machine. Some of the men are watching the clock. An old man is sweeping the floor and the factory manager is standing in front of his office. He is looking at his watch and at the men. He always goes back into his office when the bell rings. This is exactly what was happening when the bell rang yesterday, too.

1. Notice the question "Was Frank working when the bell rang yesterday?"
   Notice the short answer using the same model: "Yes, he was"/"No, he wasn't"!
   a) Frank/the clock?
   b) manager/his watch?
   c) old man/the floor?
   d) some of the men/clock? etc.
2. Now ask what these people did when the bell rang (and answer)!

2

This is a scene from one of Charles Kay's very old films. It was called "Terror in the Castle". Charles played a monster, half-man, half-gorilla. Everybody was having dinner when he jumped down. A girl was playing the lyre. The King was drinking wine. The Queen was laughing and the King's brother was smiling at her. The King's son was kissing one of the Queen's maids. A second later, the monster jumped down and they all ran away.

1. Ask what each person was doing in this old film when Charles jumped down. Give full answers! Then say what each person did when he jumped down!

4

These two pictures show both what was happening and what happened in a park yesterday when it suddenly began to rain. An old lady was feeding some pigeons. Two old men were sitting on a park bench and talking. A young man was looking at the flowers. A young couple were walking hand in hand. Some children were playing on the swings. When it began to rain the two old men got up and stood under a tree. The old woman put a newspaper over her head and the young man put his umbrella up. The young couple and the children began to run as fast as they could.

1. What do these two pictures show? What happened suddenly?
2. Ask questions about these people with "What was/were ... ing when it began to rain?"
3. Now ask "What did ... do when it began to rain?"

Unit 13 b — FORMATION AND MANIPULATION

1 Pronunciation
was and *were* are words that have weak or unstressed forms which are used very frequently in spoken English.
We write: *I was there*   and *We were there*.
BUT WE SAY: I [wəz] there and We [wə] there.

2

A	B	C	D	E
She	was working	when	he	arrived

i) Think of other words to replace 'she' and 'he' in boxes A and D. Don't forget that you can also use names in these boxes.

ii) Read the situation on page 75 again and look for verbs to replace 'work' and 'arrive' in boxes B and E.

iii) Now write or say ten sentences using the new words you have for the boxes.

iv) Here are some more words which you can use to make sentences like 'She was working when he arrived.'

B
- eating breakfast
- having a bath
- doing the washing-up
- writing a letter
- making tea
- watching television
- washing the children

D and E
- the phone rang.
- Joe arrived.
- the light went out.
- someone knocked at the door.
- the man left.
- the clock stopped.
- the news started.
- the house caught fire.
- the baby was sick.

v) Now, with the words in the boxes in exercise iv, ask and answer questions like this:
Question: What were you doing when the phone rang?
Answer: (I was) watching television.

3

A	B	C	D	E
I	stood up	when	Bill	came in.

i) Look at situations 2 and 4 on page 75, you will find many verbs to replace those in boxes B and E.

ii) Use those and these below to make ten new sentences like: 'I stood up when Bill came in.'

B
- stood up
- stopped talking
- went away
- sat down
- opened the door
- smiled

E
- Bill came in.
- the policeman left.
- the film-star came in.
- the music stopped.

iii) Now, with the person sitting next to you, ask questions using the items in box E and answer them with the items in box B:
Example: Question: What did you do when the policeman left?
                Answer: (I) sat down.

FORMATION AND MANIPULATION

Unit 13 b

1. Pronunciation

Insist on the use of the weak (unstressed) forms of *was* and *were* in spoken work. If the students seem to grasp the use of the weak forms without too much difficulty, they should be told about the use of the strong (stressed) forms of *was* and *were*. Tell the students that we only use the strong forms of *was* and *were* to emphasise a thing or things really were so or really did happen;

For example: A: I know you didn't see me at the cinema, but I *was* there.
           B: *Were* you?
           A: Yes, I *was*.
For example: A: They were [wə] going to the cinema when it started to rain.
           B: *Were* they?
           A: Yes, they *were*.
Remember: It was [wəz] raining when I left home. *Was* it?
and They were [wə] going to Rome when the car crashed. *Were* they?

2. and 3.

A note on word order. It is possible to start a sentence with either of the two components which make up the structures under study at the moment. So, it is possible to say
   'She was working when he arrived.'
and 'When he arrived, she was working.'
              AND
   'She stopped when he arrived.'
and 'When he arrived, she stopped.'
The difference is only one of style. However, since students will frequently meet both forms, both should be practised.

2.

Use fast oral practice with individual students, like this:
   T: What was happening when the phone rang?
   S: When the phone rang, he was eating breakfast.
(base the questions and answers on exercise **2** iv)

3.

Once again, use a similar technique for exercising the reversed order of the structure in part **3**, exercise ii.
For example: T: What happened when the policeman left?
             S: When the policeman left, she sat down.

Extra Fluency Practice

i) for WAS DOING WHEN DID. Give students these prompts for oral response: television/phone: newspaper/letter arrived: cutting grass/hurt hand: wife sleeping/Fred home: bus/taxi around corner: typing letter/man arrived.

ii) for DID WHEN DID. Give students these prompts for oral response: stood up/phone rang: indoors/rain started: read it/letter came: made tea/water boiled: cooked meal/husband home: opened door/dog barked.

Unit 13

C EXPLOITATION OF THE EPISODE

Key Structures and Vocabulary	Suggested Explanations
a) ground floor flat (4)	a flat at street level.
b) tapped softly (5)	made a little noise on the window with his finger-tips.
c) haven't got any right to ... (11)	there is no good reason why you should help me.
d) after all (18)	even though you did try (after all your trouble).
e) stared (19)	looked at him with eyes wide open.
f) against the law (27)	not permitted in this country.

Section 1
1. Listening phase followed by a re-creation from prompts phase. e.g.
   T: Coke/London/6.
   Ss: Coke reached London just before 6.
   Use these prompts: Coke/London/6 ... city/wake up ... streets/dark ... drove/block/flats ... far/river/ south east ... light/one/ground floor ... shining/kitchen ... window/tapped ... still standing/back door ... looked up/woman/there ... hesitated/saw ... almost/back/shadows ... she/him calmly ... in/expecting ... softly ... towards her/ stood/open doorway ... haven't/right/ask/help ... said/pause ... nobody else/can go ... is? ... better/in/calmly.
2. Fluency practice
   He *was* still stand*ing* at the window *when* the back door open*ed*.
   Give the following prompts to elicit similar structures from the students:
   I/bus stop/start to rain. She/in bed/letter arrive. He/television/ I arrive. They/talk/concert start. He/work/I go home. They/dance/music stop. He/eat/she leave restaurant. I/cough/doctor arrive. She/cook/guests come.

Section 2
1. Listening phase followed by comprehension questions. e.g.
   a) Who caught an early train? (Baxter did)
   b) Where to? (London)
   c) Who was waiting for him? (The Chief Inspector (was))
   d) What was he looking at? (a photograph) (mention the frequently used form *photo*)
   e) Who did the Chief Inspector look at? (Baxter) etc.
2. Writing phase (lines 14–19 only)
   Ask students to write the account of what happened from Baxter's point of view. Tell them to use exactly the same structures and vocabulary, only to change the necessary pronouns etc. e.g. 'I caught a very early train to ...' etc.

Section 3
1. Silent reading phase for three or four minutes, then ask students to close their books and ask questions to which the following are the answers. e.g.
   T: 'You really shouldn't help me'
   Ss: What did Coke say?
   'In her kitchen' 'Eating breakfast' 'She didn't say anything' 'That Coke was a spy' 'No, she didn't' 'Silently' 'Kate was' 'He wanted help' 'To find the real spies'
2. Choral reading phase.

THE MAN WHO ESCAPED
Episode 13

Unit 13

C

SYNOPSIS: *Eric Masters, a man who knew Coke before Coke went to prison, phoned a man called Hugo. Masters was terribly worried. For some reason, he was very afraid of Coke.*

1 Coke reached London just before 6. The huge city was just beginning to wake up but the streets were still dark. He drove to a block of small flats not far from the river in the south east. There was a light on in one of the ground floor flats. It was shining in the kitchen. He went to the window and tapped softly. He was still standing at the window when the back door opened. When he looked up, a woman was standing there. He hesitated when he saw her and almost went back into the shadows again, but she looked at him calmly. "Come in, Ted. I've been expecting you," she said very softly. He walked towards her and stood in the open doorway.
"I haven't got any right to ask for your help," he said after a pause. "But there's nobody else you can go to, is there? You'd better come in," she answered calmly.

2 Baxter caught a very early train to London. When he got to Scotland Yard, the Chief Inspector was waiting for him. When Baxter went into his office, he was sitting at his desk and looking at a photograph. The Inspector looked at Baxter quickly, then back at the photo. "Perhaps it was a good thing you didn't catch Coke after all," he said suddenly. Baxter stared at him in surprise.
"What do you mean, sir? I don't understand."
"I have a picture here of a man who knew Coke in the army. He was also a witness at Coke's trial. I've been interested in the man for some time now. Perhaps we'll be able to find out more about him now that Coke's free," the Inspector said, and gave Baxter the photograph.
"This is the man. Watch him. Follow him everywhere!"
Baxter looked at the man in the photo carefully. It was Eric Masters.

3 "You really shouldn't help me, Kate. It's against the law," Coke said. He and the young woman were sitting in her kitchen. He was eating breakfast hungrily. Kate did not say anything.
"I mean, everybody thinks I'm a spy," he went on.
"But I don't think so," she finally said. Coke finished his breakfast silently. Then he said, "You were the only person who ever believed I was innocent. That's why I came to you. Who else will help me?"
"Help you to do what, Ted?" Kate asked.
"Help me to find the real spies," he answered slowly.

Unit 13 d

FURTHER PRACTICE

1. Practice Situations

Make 2 sentences for each of these situations, one with 'was doing ... when ... did' and one with 'did ... when ... did'.

Example Situation:

Robert drove to Southampton yesterday. Halfway there the car broke down. Robert walked to a garage to get a mechanic.

Example Sentences:

1) Robert *was driving* to Southampton yesterday *when* his car *broke down*.
2) *When* his car *broke down*, Robert *walked* to a garage to get a mechanic.

Situations:

a) Julia watched television last night. The phone rang in the middle of the programme. She answered it.
b) Arthur played golf yesterday afternoon. Halfway round the course he received a telegram. He left immediately.
c) Deborah went to the cinema yesterday afternoon. During the performance the film broke down. She then went home.
d) The policeman walked down the High Street yesterday morning. A man asked him the time. The policeman told him.

2. Conversation

Tom Atkins saw an accident between two cars last month. He is a witness in court today. You are going to hear the lawyer for one of the drivers, then Tom, and then the lawyer for the other driver.

1ST LAWYER: Mr Atkins, would you please tell the court what you were doing when the accident happened and what you saw?
TOM: Yes, I was driving home from work. It was about 5.15, and there was a blue car in front of me. We were both driving along Harbour Road when a small white Ford suddenly shot out of a side road. It shot right in front of the blue car. The driver tried to stop, but it was impossible. He ran into the white Ford.
1ST LAWYER: I see. Now, how fast was the car in front of you going when the accident happened?
TOM: The blue car? 30 miles an hour. Certainly no more than that.
1ST LAWYER: And the white Ford shot out without any warning?
TOM: Yes, that's right.
1ST LAWYER: Thank you, Mr Atkins.
2ND LAWYER: Mr Atkins! How can you be sure the blue car was only doing 30?
TOM: Because I was only doing 30, and the blue car wasn't going any faster than I was.
2ND LAWYER: Are you sure of that? Absolutely positive?
TOM: Yes, I am. I'm positive!
2ND LAWYER: Positive? How can you be so positive, Mr Atkins? Were you looking at your speedometer when the accident happened?
TOM: Of course not. I was looking at the road ahead. That's how I managed to see the accident!
2ND LAWYER: Well, if you weren't looking at your speedometer how can you possibly be sure how fast you were going?
TOM: Because I never go faster than 30 on that road. It's against the law, that's why!

Correct the statements

1. Tom was driving in front of the blue car.
2. The white Ford shot right in front of him.
3. The blue car was doing about 50 miles an hour.
4. The blue car was going faster than Tom was.
5. Tom was looking at the speedometer when the accident happened.

Questions

1. Whose fault do you think the accident was? Say why?
2. Do you think the blue car was driving dangerously at all? Give reasons.
3. Ask and answer these questions about Tom when the accident happened:
   a) how fast?   c) from work or to work?
   b) looking at?
4. How does Tom know what speed he was doing when the accident happened?
5. Who do you think the first lawyer is defending? Who do you think the second lawyer is defending? Give reasons!

FURTHER PRACTICE

Unit 13
d

1. Practice Situations

a) This exercise is designed not only to allow students another opportunity of practising the focal point of the Unit ('was doing'/'did'), but also to give them more insight into the significant features of the type of situation which calls for the use of 'was doing . . . when . . . did' on the one hand, and 'did . . . when . . . did' on the other.

b) Give the situations orally and *ask questions about the situation itself* before actually asking students to tell you about the situation using the two sentence models they are given in the example. The questions for situation a) might be:
   Who watched television?
   When did she watch television? Did she forget it?–or did she answer it?
   When did the phone ring?
Remember that you only want short answers–'Julia did', 'Last night', etc.

c) Here are four more situations for oral practice:
 i) Julia took a shower this morning. During her shower the water suddenly went very cold. She got out quickly.
 ii) Tom took his wife to a party and they danced together. Tom stepped on his wife's foot and she screamed.
 iii) John listened to the radio last night. In the middle of the programme a friend came to see him. He turned the radio off.
 iv) Mary rode her bicycle yesterday. Halfway down the hill, the front wheel fell off. She got very angry.

2. Conversation

Key Points
1. Meaning and use of vocabulary items 'witness', 'lawyer', 'court', 'shoot out of a side road', 'run into', 'speedometer' and 'against the law'
2. Revision of 'Would you . . .' as in 'Would you please tell the court . . .?'
3. Use and position of *both* as in 'We were both driving . . .'
4. Revision of 'I see' = 'I understand'
5. Meaning and use of the verbs *go* and *do* with speeds, as in 'How fast was it going?' and 'It was doing 30 (m.p.h.)'
6. Meaning and use (+ intonation) of the pattern 'How can you possibly be sure . . .?'
7. Meaning and use (+ intonation) of 'Absolutely positive?'
8. Revision of 'faster than', concentrating on the unstressed [ðən]

Presentation Notes
1. Follow the same initial procedure as outlined previously.
2. After the class has heard the tape or read the conversation (much of it in chorus) two or three times, split the class into groups of three and get them to act out the conversation. They could either use the language exactly as in the original Conversation, or they could make up the dialogue, relying on prompts given to them:
   e.g. tell the court what/accident/saw?
     home from work/5.15/blue car/
     –and so on.
3. Use the material under the Conversation on the student page (Correct my statements, and Answer the questions) orally with the class–student books face down–and then get students to use the same material working in pairs.
4. Play the tape (or read the Conversation) once again, and use the following words and phrases to get students to reproduce some of the sentences from the Conversation. Concentrate on the intonation as well as the correct structure:
 a) Harbour Road/white Ford
 b) how fast/car in front?
 c) sure?/positive?
 d) speedometer/accident?

Unit 13
e/f

e Summary

1

An important point to remind students of here is the unstressed forms of *was* [wəz] and *were* [wə] in normal spoken English. Give students at this point a final repetition phase, so that they get used to [wəz] and [wə] in statements and questions. (The pronunciation of *was* and *were* is markedly more stressed in negatives.) Here are some sentences for simple repetition by students at normal speaking pace:
I was driving home.
How fast was it going?
He was drinking wine.
What was he doing?
They were sitting in the park.
Where were they sitting?

2

Remind students once again of the very important difference between 'was doing/did' and 'did/did' –
a) Work through one or two of the situations on pages 75 and 78 again; and
b) Ask students questions like this about their own experiences –
   T: What time did you get to work/school/college this morning?
   What was the boss/your teacher/the lecturer doing when you walked in?
   What did he/she do when you walked in?

f Exercises for homework

2

Whilst doing the exercise orally, different students giving the responses, get another student to ask a question; thus for Prompt a) –
S.1: I was having breakfast when the telephone rang.
S.2: What did you do when the telephone rang?

3

This exercise can be set as a written homework, and need not necessarily be prepared in the classroom. Students should be aware, however, that the exercise demands completion with a 'was/were doing' or 'did' form.

4

As this composition is based very closely upon the first two situations on page 75, thorough question and answer work might be sufficient preparation. One way of helping students to prepare this sort of work, however, is to ask a number of questions, to which the answers themselves begin to form a composition. Here are some such questions:
Were they making a horror film? – or a love story? – or a war film? – or a comedy?
Were they taking it easy or working hard? Tell me what they were wearing!
Tell me what the director was doing! (Was he walking around or sitting still?)
Were all the actors acting or were some of them drinking coffee? – and so on.

Unit 13
e/f

e Summary

Focal points in this Unit.

1. Note the formation of the Past Continuous Tense:
   a) I, he, she, it was/we, you they were + doing.
   b) Questions and negatives are formed like this:

   He wasn't/we weren't doing . . .
   Was he/were they doing . . . ?

2. Remember that there is an important difference between two sentences like this:
   He was crossing the road when he saw me.
   and this:
   He stopped when he saw me.
   In these sentences, 'he was crossing' is a background idea, 'he stopped' is a simple action.

f Exercises for homework

1. Do all the exercises and questions on pages 75 and 78.

2. **Invention Exercise**

   Example:

   PROMPTS: to work this morning/an accident
   RESPONSE: I was walking to work this morning when I saw an accident.
   or: John was riding to work this morning when he had an accident.

   Prompts:
   a) breakfast/the telephone
   b) lesson/bell
   c) my shirt/a button (off)
   d) along the road/a banana skin
   e) the guitar/a string
   f) newspaper/bus
   g) in the park/a friend
   h) tennis/rain
   i) homework/noise outside

3. **Complete these sentences** (using 'was/were doing' or 'did')
   a) I was walking through the park yesterday when . . .
   b) When I opened the door . . .
   c) It was snowing when . . .
   d) I was ringing the doorbell when . . .
   e) When I got to the lesson, . . .

4. **Guided Composition**

   Read situations 1 and 2 on page 75 again very carefully. Then write about a short visit to a film studio. Begin like this
   'The other day I went to visit a film studio. When I got there, a friend met me, and we went straight to where they were shooting a scene for . . .'.
   Say what sort of film they were making, and describe what the different people were doing when you got there. Describe, too, what they all did when they stopped for the lunch break. Finally, describe what some of the people were doing when you left later in the afternoon.

5. **Transfer Exercise**

   Write 5 sentences about yourself which are true. Use the tenses we have practised in this Unit.
   If you write this as an example: *I was driving to London last week-end when my car broke down.*
   then add another sentence, perhaps: *When my car broke down, I phoned a garage.*
   Or if you write this as an example: *I got out of bed this morning when my alarm rang.*
   then add another sentence, perhaps: *I was sleeping when my alarm-clock began to ring.*
   or: *When I got out of bed, the sun was shining through the window.*

Unit 14 a

The simple future used in requests, offers, and of 'Must' and 'Can'

1
(a) When/Fred/army?
(b) What/doctor/going to do?
(c) Fred ask?
(d) doctor answer?

2
(a) What/Susan ask Tom?
(b) Where/Peter?
(c) What/Peter/say?

3
(a) What can't/old lady?
(b) What must/do?
(c) Where/to?
(d) What/there?

4
(a) What/Tom a moment ago?
(b) How/offer?
(c) How/old lady/thank him?

5
(a) What/Tom doing?
(b) What/Peter/say?
(c) serious?

6
(a) How/Frank?
(b) What/doctor/say?
(for a week)
(every six hours)
(c) What/Frank/tomorrow?

Main Teaching-Points
1. *Will* in statements and questions, and *won't* in negative sentences.
2. 'Will you . . .' in requests, and 'I'll' in offers of help.
3. Revision of *must* and *can*; and the future forms 'will/won't have to' and 'will/won't be able to'.
4. Reflexive pronouns (*myself, yourself, ourselves*, etc.) used emphatically, as in 'Perhaps we can do it ourselves!'

Extra Points and Activities
1. Meaning and use of *at all* and *even* with *won't*: 'It *won't* hurt *at all*' and 'You *won't even* feel it'.
2. Use of *possibly* with *can't*, as in '*I can't possibly* carry it myself'. (See also page 48, Unit 8.)
3. Revision of Positive + *too*, and Negative + *either* (situation 3).

"WILL YOU . . . . ?" in requests/"I'LL" used in offers of help
Future of MUST and CAN
Reflexive Pronouns used emphatically as in "I can't do this myself"

Unit 14
a

1

Fred Collins joined the army a few days ago. A doctor is going to give him an injection in the arm.

"Will it hurt?" Fred wants to know.
"No, don't worry. It won't hurt at all. You won't even feel it." the doctor is saying.

1. What is the doctor going to do?
2. What exactly is Fred's question?
3. What is the exact answer?
4. Ask the questions with 'Will'. Give short answers with 'Yes, it/he will' or 'No, it/he won't'
   a) hurt
   b) Fred feel it
   c) be very pleasant

2

Susan wrote a letter and asked Tom to post it only a second ago. She said "Will you post this for me, Tom? It must catch the next post."

Peter is going out for a walk. "I'll post it for you. I'm going out for a walk anyway," he is saying.

1. What did Susan ask Tom to do a second ago?
2. How exactly did she ask him to do this?
3. Why has Peter got his coat on?
4. What is he saying?

3

The old lady cannot carry her case herself. "I can't possibly carry this myself. I must find a porter!" she is thinking. She is in Manchester now. She is going to catch a train to London. She will have to find a porter there, too. She won't be able to carry that case then, either.

1. Where is the old lady now?
2. What must she do now and why?
3. Where is she going?
4. What will she have to do there and why?

4

Tom is going to catch the same train. He noticed the old lady a moment ago and offered to help.

"I'll carry that case for you. You can't possibly carry it yourself," he said. The old lady is thanking him. "Thank you. That's very kind of you."

1. When did Tom notice her and what did he offer to do?
2. What exactly did he say?
3. What is the old lady doing now?
4. What exactly is she saying?

5

Tom is looking at the engine of his car. There is something wrong with it and he does not think he can possibly repair it himself. "I'll help you. Perhaps we can do it ourselves!" Peter is saying. Actually it is something very serious. Tom and Peter cannot possibly repair it themselves. They will have to get a mechanic.

1. What is Tom looking at and why?
2. Ask and answer the questions
   a) Tom/repair it himself
   b) Peter think/themselves
3. What exactly is Peter saying?
4. What will they have to do and why?

6

Frank Martin is very ill. The doctor is talking to him.

"You'll have to stay in bed for a week and you'll have to take this medicine every six hours."

Frank has a ticket for a big football match tomorrow. He won't be able to use it.

1. Why is the doctor there?
2. Ask questions about Frank with "Will he have to . . . ?" or "Will he be able to . . . ?" Answer "Yes, he will" or "No, he won't"!
   a) in bed very long
   b) medicine very often
   c) that ticket
   d) the match tomorrow
   e) on television

Unit 14 b

FORMATION AND MANIPULATION

1 Use this table to ask someone else to do something for you. Imitate Susan's intonation in situation 2.

Will you	post this letter carry this bag give Mr. Kent this message play that record sing that song again	for	them her me him us	?

2 With another person, make a conversation using this table. Imitate Tom's intonation in situation 4.

A:	I'll	carry that bag answer the phone do the dishes post the letter close the window	for you.	B:	Thank you.	That's very	nice kind good helpful	of you!

3 How many sentences can you make from this table? Make at least twelve orally.

You	will/won't	have to be able to	work late see the boss go to that film take the test post the letter	tomorrow some other time later next week

Notice the question forms and the short answers

Will you	be able to have to	come again?	Yes, I will/No, I won't.

Ask someone else questions with these prompts: see me this evening. play golf tomorrow.
(Tell that person to give short answers.) work late this evening. give me an answer soon.
  repair the car yourself. take it to a mechanic.

4 i) Look at and repeat these words aloud: myself   himself   herself   itself   yourself
  ourselves   yourselves   themselves

  ii) Now make sentences with those words and 3. Tom and Peter/all that work
    these prompts: 4. Susan/all the dirty dishes
  Example: little girl/that heavy bag. (That little 5. Arthur/all that champagne
  girl cannot carry that heavy bag herself.) 6. I/this difficult question
   1. little girl/all that ice-cream 7. We/all these books
   2. We/all this work 8. Tom/that broken chair
  iii) Notice that when we are speaking directly to *more than one person,* we use 'yourse*lves*'.
    Example: 'All right, children. You'll have to clean up the room yourselves!'

82

FORMATION AND MANIPULATION

Unit 14 b

General Note:
There is a lot of work involved in this unit, so it may be necessary to spend more time than usual on the Formation and Manipulation pages.

1.

Remind students that the word *please* is very frequently used with this structure as a standard form of politeness. Don't forget to insist on the polite intonation pattern as used by Susan in situation 2.

Fluency Practice

WILL YOU OPEN THE DOOR FOR ME, PLEASE?
1. them
2. close
3. window
4. us
5. switch on the light
6. the T.V.
7. off
8. the radio
9. carry

2.

Insist on the use of the weak (unstressed) forms of *for* and *of* in the tables, i.e. for [fə] you and of [əv] you.

Extra Oral Practice

Give these prompts orally for students to use as in table **2.A**:
see him; tell them; answer it; get some; buy one; ask her; write it; sell them; change it.

3.

Remember the weak (unstressed) form of *to* [tə]. Tell students that 'I won't be able to . . .' is frequently preceded by 'I'm very sorry, but . . .' and 'I'm terribly sorry, but . . .' as a polite way of introducing an apology. Ask students to apologise for not being able to do the following things:
help you after all/buy that car from you/come to your party/go on holiday with you/write to you/take you out for a meal/invite you in for coffee.

4.

Point out that 'She can't do it herself' and 'She can't do it *by* herself' have the same meaning. Practise 4 ii) both with and without *by*.

N.B. HOW ARE YOUR STUDENTS GETTING ON WITH LEARNING THE VERB-FORMS?

Unit 14
c

EXPLOITATION OF THE EPISODE

Note: This Episode previews *might* which is dealt with in Unit 15. Do not draw attention to it if possible.

Key Structures and Vocabulary	*Suggested Explanations*
a) small parts (3)	not starring parts or roles, but supporting parts.
b) Just then (4)	at that particular moment.
c) looked up (12)	looked from the photo to the Chief Inspector.
d) quite by accident (15)	we had not planned it.
e) chance we'll have to take (26)	a risk we'll have to accept.
f) bundle (30)	an irregular package tied together in some way.
g) try . . . on (33)	put on clothes (etc.) to see if they are the correct size.
h) unwillingly (36)	he didn't want to do it.

Section 1
1. Listening phase followed by short-answer questions (books closed)
a) What was Kate?
b) What seemed to surprise her?
c) What did she seem ready for?
d) Why was this?
e) Did she work on television?
f) Was her life dull?
g) Was she working just then?
h) Did she hesitate when Coke asked for help?
i) Who did Coke want to find?
j) What did she say?
2. Oral practice (books closed). What did Kate say? Use these prompts:
a) help you
b) start right now
c) you find out/I back
d) get some things now
3. Silent reading phase.

Section 2
1. Choral reading phase followed by:
2. Completion phase (books closed, if possible) e.g.
T: Not very far . . .
Ss: away
T: Baxter was still . . .
Ss: sitting etc.
3. Fluency practice
THAT'S A CHANCE WE'LL HAVE TO TAKE
a) you
b) he
c) they
d) to accept
e) This is
f) a risk
g) to consider
h) to remember
i) to think about

Section 3
1. Listening phase
2. Correct my statements.
Time passed quickly . . . for Kate . . . that day . . . He slept a lot . . . but sat down . . . and ran about . . . the house . . . calmly. It was morning . . . before Kate left . . . The summer sun . . . was just rising . . . when she came through the window . . . She was carrying a small box . . . and nothing else.

THE MAN WHO ESCAPED
Episode 14

Unit 14

C

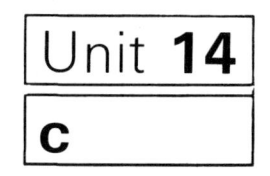

SYNOPSIS: *(Note: The synopsis now uses all tenses previously introduced) Baxter caught the train back to London early this morning. He is now in the Chief Inspector's office. The Chief Inspector has just told him to follow Masters everywhere. Meanwhile, Coke is hiding in Kate's flat.*

1 Kate was what the Americans call 'a cool character'; nothing seemed to surprise her very much. She seemed ready for anything. Perhaps this was because she was an actress. She played small parts in films and on television. Her life was full of surprises. Just then she was not working at all. Perhaps that was why she did not hesitate even for a second when Coke said he wanted her help to find the real spies.
"All right," she said. "I'll help you and I'll start right now. Wait here!"
"What do you mean? Where are you going?" Coke asked.
"You'll find out when I come back. I'll have to get some things now!"
Before Coke could ask her anything more, she was gone.

2 Not very far away, Baxter was still sitting in the Chief Inspector's Office. He was still looking at Masters' photograph. He looked up. "What's so interesting about him? Why do you want me to follow him?" he asked.
"A few days ago, quite by accident we learned a few things about him. Coke might . . . notice I say 'might' . . . be innocent after all. It's only a possibility. We want to see what Masters does if Coke contacts him," the Chief Inspector answered. Baxter was even more surprised now. "I don't understand, sir? What do you think Masters might do?" he said.
"Masters might try to kill him if he's really afraid of him."
"But surely that's dangerous, sir. I mean, if Coke is innocent, Masters might kill him . . . and if he isn't innocent, we're letting him go free. After all, Coke might kill Masters . . . or someone else!"
The Chief Inspector looked very serious.
"That's a chance we'll have to take, Baxter!" he said.

3 Time passed very slowly for Coke that morning and afternoon. He slept a bit but then got up and walked about the flat nervously. It was evening before Kate came back. The winter sun was just setting when she came through the door. She was carrying a large bundle and a lot of other things.
"Where have you been? You've been gone for hours!" he said.
"Yes, I've been busy. Here. Try these things on," she answered. She unwrapped the bundle quickly and showed him a suit, shoes and shirt. There was also a coat with an expensive fur collar, the sort millionaires wear in films. Coke put the clothes on unwillingly. "I'll have to change my appearance more than this!" he said.
"Of course you will," she answered. "And I've got just the things you'll need!"

Unit 14 d

FURTHER PRACTICE

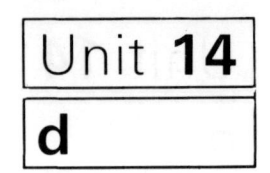

1. Practice Situations

Make 2 sentences for each situation, one with 'He'll/she'll/they'll have to . . .' and one with 'He/she/they won't be able to . . .'

Example Situation:

Julia usually catches the 8.15 bus. The next one is at 8.40. It is 8.20 now, and she is running out of the house.

Example Sentences:

1) She won't be able to catch the 8.15 bus.
2) She'll have to catch the 8.40.

Situations:

a) Bob has just broken his leg. He wanted to play football this evening.
b) Tom likes to put cream in his coffee, but they've only got tinned milk.
c) Frank wanted to leave work early today. He wanted to see a football match. The boss asked all the men to do overtime.
d) Deborah and Arthur wanted to drive to France, but the car broke down yesterday. Deborah has just booked 2 plane tickets, instead.

2. Conversation

Mr Kent, Julia's boss, is talking to Julia on the office phone.

MR KENT: Do you think you could possibly work late this evening, Miss Frost? I'm afraid there's some work we really must finish this evening. I can't possibly do it myself.
JULIA: Work late? I . . . I suppose so, if you really think it's necessary.
MR KENT: Thank you. We'll have to work about an hour's overtime. That's all. (hangs up)
JULIA: (to herself, while dialling) Oh, dear. Now I'll have to ring Jim and tell him. He won't like it.
JIM: Hello? 26721.
JULIA: Is that you, Jim? This is Julia. Look . . . I'm afraid I won't be able to meet you at 7 this evening. I'll have to come later.
JIM: What? You mean you're going to be late again?
JULIA: Now listen, Jim, please. It isn't my fault. I'll have to work late this evening and then I'll have to go home. I can't possibly go to the restaurant straight from work!
JIM: It's always something, isn't it? When will you be able to come, then?
JULIA: Don't worry. You won't have to wait long. I'll be there at 8.
JIM: At 8? But we're going to a film after dinner. Remember?
JULIA: I know . . . and it starts at 8.30. We'll just have to miss it this evening, that's all. We'll be able to see it some other time.
JIM: Oh, no we won't! Tonight's the last night!
JULIA: Oh, dear . . . I suppose I'll just have to come straight from work, that's all.
JIM: Yes, you will. Meet me at the restaurant at 7!
JULIA: All right, Jim. I'll be there.

Questions

1. What does Mr Kent ask Julia to do?
2. How exactly does he ask her to work late?
3. Where is Julia going to meet Jim?
4. What does she want to do before she meets him?
5. What are her exact words when she tells Jim this?
6. What does she say when Jim tells her about the film at 8.30?
7. Ask if they will be able to see the film tomorrow! (and answer)
8. What does Julia finally decide she'll have to do?

FURTHER PRACTICE

Unit 14
d

1. Practice Situations

a) Use the same procedure for these situations as outlined in Unit 13. Remember to ask short-answer questions about the situations themselves before asking for the 'will have to' and 'won't be able to' responses. Thus, for the Example Situation, the questions might be:
  Which bus does she usually catch?
    (The 8.15 OR The quarter past eight.)
  When is the next one?
    (At 8.40 OR At twenty to nine.)
  What time is it now?
    (8.20 OR Twenty past eight.)
  What is she doing?
    (Running out of the house.)

b) Expected responses for the situations:
 i) He won't be able to play football this evening./He'll have to go to hospital/see a doctor/stay at home.
 ii) He won't be able to put cream in his coffee./He'll have to put tinned milk in his coffee./He'll have to use tinned milk.
 iii) He won't be able to see the football match./He'll have to miss it./He'll have to do overtime./He'll have to watch it on television.
 iv) They won't be able to drive to France./They'll have to go by plane/by air./They'll have to fly to France.

2. Conversation

Key Points
1. Reinforcement of the focal points of the Unit – 'will/won't have to' and 'will/won't be able to'
2. The use of *possibly,* as in 'Do you think you could possibly . . .?' and 'I can't possibly . . .'
3. The use of *really* as in 'We really must . . .'
4. Meaning and use (+ intonation) of 'I suppose so', expressing grudging agreement

5. Practice with the pattern 'You mean you're going to . . . again?'
6. Meaning and use of 'some other time', 'It isn't my fault', and 'straight from work'
7. Meaning and use of 'that's all' in final position

Presentation Notes
1. Follow the initial presentation procedure as for previous conversations.
2. Choral repetition of parts of the conversation – male students repeat the parts of Mr. Kent and Jim, female students Julia's part.
3. *Correct my statements phase:*
    a) Mr. Kent wants Julia to leave work early.
    b) Mr. Kent can do all the work himself.
    c) They'll have to work 3 hours' overtime.
    d) Jim is glad Julia won't be able to come at 7.
    e) Julia says she'll be there at 10.
    f) The film starts at 9 o'clock.
4. *Fluency Practice*
   DO YOU THINK YOU COULD POSSIBLY WORK LATE THIS EVENING? (intonation as on tape).
   a) tomorrow evening   d) give me a lift
   b) come earlier   e) take me to work
   c) tomorrow morning   f) speak to Mr. Kent
   YOU MEAN YOU'RE GOING TO BE LATE AGAIN? (intonation as on tape).
   a) write it   d) phone her
   b) miss it   e) stay at home
   c) eat there   f) paint it

Unit 14
e/f

e Summary

1 and 2
We only practise 'Will you do . . .' when asking someone to do something, and 'I'll do . . .' when offering to do something for someone else. It is not advisable to go into the complexity and confusion of *will* and *shall* here, only to remind students again of the other way of asking someone to do something using 'Would you . . .' and 'Could you . . .', and of asking permission to do something using 'Shall I . . .' (Unit 10). Get students to practise once again in pairs this kind of dialogue:
S.1: 'I'll do that for you.'
S.2: 'Thank you. That's very kind of you.'
                        nice
                        good
                        helpful
Give prompts to replace 'do that':— carry that/open the door/fetch that book/etc. Focus students' attention on the unstressed form of *of* [əv].

3
The most important point to stress here is the use of the short forms 'Yes, I will' and 'No, I won't'.

4
To reinforce the use of the reflexive pronouns used emphatically, do another Substitution Drill:
PERHAPS WE CAN DO IT OURSELVES
a) she   d) get one
b) they   e) he
c) see it   f) buy one
(Point out that the prompt *she* gives rise to the sentence 'Perhaps *she* can do it *herself*.')

f Exercises for homework

3
Since the students might well find this Guided Composition rather difficult without preparation, it would be advisable to prepare students either by actually writing and dictating a Model note which includes the patterns, or by writing a sample note on the blackboard from suggestions made by various members of the class.
It might be pointed out that the phrases given all use contracted forms, and that in a note or short letter to a boss or teacher, we might instead use the full forms (*am, cannot, will* and *will not*).

Unit 14

e/f

e Summary

Focal points in this Unit.

1. Remember how we use *will* when asking someone to do something:
   'Will you post this for me?'/'Will you carry this for me?'
   – and how we use *I'll* when we offer to help someone do something:
   'I'll post it for you.'/'I'll carry that case for you.'

2. Remember what we say when someone offers to help:
   'Thank you. That's very kind of you.'
                       nice
                       good
                       helpful

3. Remember the Future forms of *can* and *must*:
   'I will have to see him tomorrow'/'I will be able to work late tomorrow.'
   'I won't have to take the test.'/'I won't be able to come tonight.'
   The short answers to questions like 'Will you be able to . . .?' and 'Will you have to . . .?' are *Yes, I will* and *No, I won't*.

4. Remember the emphatic pronouns:
   myself, yourself, himself, herself, itself, ourselves, yourselves, themselves. – as in 'Perhaps we can do it ourselves.'

f Exercises for homework

1. Do all the exercises on pages 81, 82 and 84.

2. **Invention Exercise**

   Write 2 sentences for each of the prompts, one sentence with 'I'll . . .' and one with 'Will you . . .?'

   Example:

   that case = a) I'll carry that case for you.
                 b) Will you carry that case for me?

   a) that letter
   b) the tickets for the concert
   c) a porter
   d) old car
   e) medicine
   f) the dog
   g) some tea
   h) a newspaper
   i) to the cinema
   j) the telephone

3. **Guided Composition**

   Write two short personal notes (only 4 or 5 lines – not long letters!):
   a) to a friend, saying that you are sorry you won't be able to go to the cinema with him or her as arranged (and give a reason).
   b) to your boss (or teacher) explaining why you won't be able to do a certain piece of work (and give a reason).

   Before you write the notes, read situations 3, 5 and 6 (on page 81) and the Conversation (on page 84) again, and notice how we use the following phrases which you will need:

   I'm afraid . . .//I can't possibly . . .//I'll have to . . .//my fault//I'll just have to . . .// some other time//I won't be able to . . ., either//I suppose . . .//

4. **Transfer Exercise**

   Write true sentences about yourself, relatives or friends, using 'will/won't have to' and 'will/won't be able to'.

   Examples:

   I won't be able to play tennis tomorrow.
   My father will have to sell his car soon; it's already fifteen years old.

Unit 15 a

Present perfect + 'Just'
(+ preview of contrast with simple past)

1
(a) What/police/ticket collector?
(b) train/yet?

2
(a) Who/Peter/with?
(b) How long/bathroom?
(c) What/Tom/want?

3
(a) Sun shining/started?
(b) rain/now?

4
(a) What/Arthur's secretary/ask?
(b) Where/Mr Tigers?
(c) catch him?

5
(a) Where/Julia?
(b) What/noticed?
(c) What/just said?
(d) boyfriend's question?
(e) Julia's answer?

6
(a) Which film/Peter?
(b) Who/noticed?
(c) Where/boyfriend?
(d) Peter's question?
(e) Julia's answer?

Main Teaching-Points
1. More practice with *has/have just done* and *Has he/Have you . . . yet?* and *He hasn't/They haven't . . . yet.*
2. Meaning and use of *I think so/I don't think so* and *I hope so.*
3. Use of *might* in *He might be on the train* (situation 1), *It might be fine this evening* (situation 3) and *She might catch him* (situation 4).

Extra Points and Activities
1. Practice with short-answer forms 'Yes, I have', 'No, I haven't', etc.
2. Use and position of *almost* with 'has/have almost done'.
3. Meaning and use of the verb *notice*.
4. Meaning and use of the verb *leave* as in 'I've left it inside'–as opposed to *forget*.

86

He (etc.) HAS ⎫ (JUST) DONE	I MIGHT
We (etc.) HAVE ⎭	I THINK/HOPE SO/DON'T THINK SO

Unit 15
a

1

The police are asking the ticket collector about a man they think might be on the London train.

"Have you seen this man?"
"No, I haven't. I mean, I don't think so."
"Has the London train left yet?"
"No, it hasn't."

1. Why are the police asking the collector about the man in the photograph?
2. Ask and answer the questions!
   a) London train/yet
   b) ticket collector/the man
3. Is the ticket collector sure?
4. What exactly does he say?

2

Peter is staying with Tom and Susan. He has been in the bathroom for half an hour. Tom wants to get in and has just asked "Have you finished yet?"

"Yes, I have. I'll be out in a second," is Peter's answer. He has had a shower and has just shaved.

1. Who is Peter staying with?
2. Where is he now? Ask "How long"!
3. What has Tom just asked?
4. Ask and answer questions about Peter!
   a) finished yet
   b) a bath or a shower
   c) shaved

3

It was raining when Arthur started the conference. He has just noticed that it has stopped and that the sun has come out.

"Look! The rain's stopped. It might be fine this evening."
"I hope so," the other man is saying.

1. What was the weather like when the conference started?
2. What two things have just happened?
3. What has Arthur just said?
4. Is he sure it is going to be fine?
5. What is the other man's answer?

4

Arthur's secretary has just stopped another secretary in the corridor.

"Have you seen Mr Tigers?" she wants to know.
"Yes, I have. I saw him only a moment ago. He's just gone down that corridor." She might catch him if she hurries.

1. What has Arthur's secretary just done?
2. What does she want to know?
3. Has the other secretary seen him?
4. Ask when (and answer)!
5. What has Arthur just done?

5

Julia has just come out of the cinema. She has just noticed she has not got her umbrella.

"I've left it inside!" she has just said.
"Are you sure you had it when we came in?" is her boyfriend's question.
"Yes, I am. At least, I think so."

1. What have Julia and her boyfriend just done?
2. Why has Julia suddenly stopped?
3. What does she think she has done with her umbrella?
4. What is her boyfriend's question?
5. What is her answer?

6

Peter has seen the same film, too. He has just noticed Julia. Her boyfriend has gone back into the cinema. Peter is sure he has seen her before. "Excuse me," he has just said, "Haven't we met somewhere before?"
"No, I don't think so," is Julia's answer.

1. Why is Peter in front of the cinema?
2. Why has he stopped?
3. What has he just said and why?
4. What is Julia's answer?

Unit 15 b
FORMATION AND MANIPULATION

1 Pronunciation
Notice that *have* and *has* are frequently pronounced either with the [ə] vowel-sound or with no vowel-sound at all. Study the examples. Practise them in class and notice the teacher's pronunciation and intonation.
Examples:
i) We've ['v] just arrived.
ii) Have [həv] you eaten?
iii) He's ['z] just arrived.
iv) Has [həz] he arrived?

2

A	B	C
I've	just	noticed it

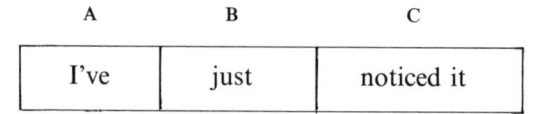

i) You know what sort of words can go into box A so look at the situations on page 87 to find words to go in box C.
ii) Make six sentences from the words you have found.
iii) Now make questions using the same words you used for exercise ii.
Example: Have you just noticed it?

3

A	B	C
Have you	finished	yet?

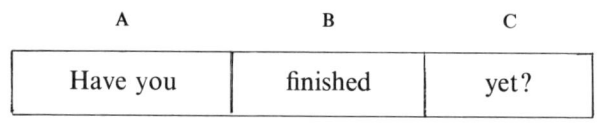

i) Find words to replace those in boxes A and B. You can find them in the situations on page 87.
ii) Now, ask two questions about each situation on page 87.
Example: Have the police found the man yet? (situation 1).

4 Use *might* for future possibilities: (See situations 3 and 4).
Make sentences from these prompts:
i) rain soon. come tomorrow. buy a new one. see the film. ask her. get one. lose it. sell them.
ii) Now think of some things you might do in the future.

5 Notice how we use the words THINK and HOPE to say *yes*.
Question: Will the weather be fine tomorrow?   Answer: I think *so*. I hope *so*.

But, be careful how we say *no* with these words.
Question: Will it rain tomorrow?   Answer: I *don't* think *so*. I hope *not*.

FORMATION AND MANIPULATION

Unit 15 b

1.

Don't get too deeply involved in explanations of stress patterns, but point out that when *have* and *has* are pronounced with the [ə] vowel sound or with no vowel sound at all, i.e. in the weak or UNSTRESSED form, the stress is transferred to another syllable, frequently the following one.
e.g. We've *JUST* seen him.
　　　Have (həv) *YOU* eaten?

2.

Don't forget the very useful technique of doing various things (opening the door, shutting it, writing a word on the board, etc. etc.) and then as soon as each action is finished, asking students to tell you what you've just done.
Then, when this first phase is finished go through the actions again, but this time pair off the students, getting one to ask and the other to answer questions about what you have just done. There are two types of questions and answers. Type one: Q: What has he/she just done? A: He/She's just opened the door. and Type two: Q: Has he/she just opened the door? A: Yes, he/she has. and No, he/she hasn't.

4.

Revise 'going to' in questions to produce *might* in answers.
First, ask students questions using these prompts, which should be written on the blackboard as each is given.
you/see new film . . . it/rain . . . he/arrive late again . . . we/stop soon . . . weather/change tomorrow . . . U.S.A./rocket to the moon . . . you/coffee after this lesson?
e.g. T: Are you going to see that new film?
　　　S: I might see it.
Now, pair off students and get them to ask and answer the same questions using the prompts which are now written on the blackboard. Teach also the very useful short answer form: I/you/he/she/it/we/they/MIGHT DO: and the negative form I (etc.) MIGHT NOT.

Fluency Practice

IT MIGHT BE FINE THIS EVENING
1. be nice
2. soon
3. rain
4. tomorrow
5. start
6. He
7. come
8. be here
9. help us

5.

Make sure that students are certain that the negative form of 'I think so' is 'I don't think so' and of 'I hope so' – 'I hope not'.
Use the same prompts as above in **4** first to get students to answer you and then in pairs to ask and answer each other.
N.B. Don't forget to get the students to change roles so that both have a chance to ask and answer questions.

Note: Have students finished learning the verb-forms yet?
　　　Don't forget to test them on recently learnt verbs and also to revise those learnt earlier on.

Unit 15 c

EXPLOITATION OF THE EPISODE

Key Structures and Vocabulary	*Suggested Explanations*
a) dyed (1)	changed the colour of.
b) dark glasses (2)	glasses with dark lenses (like sunglasses)
c) full-length mirror (4)	mirror in which Coke could see from his head to his feet.
d) odd (17)	unusual.
e) trial (23)	the police proceedings after which Coke was sent to prison.
f) Public Bar (35) Saloon Bar (36)	Different rooms in an English public house (pub). The beer is cheaper and the furniture not so comfortable in the public bar.

Section 1
1. Listening phase followed by short-answer questions.
a) What colour did she dye his hair?
b) What did she use to give him an older face?
c) What did she thrust into his hand?
d) Where did she lead him?
e) What surprised Coke about Kate?
f) And when was he even more surprised?
g) Who stared back at him?
h) How long did she spend teaching him to act like a blind man?
i) Did he learn fast?
j) Did Coke want her to come with him?
k) Why not?
l) Was her answer simple?

Section 2
1. Silent reading phase followed by completion phase (books closed).
T: 'We must look an odd . . .
Ss: couple
T: you and I,' Coke . . .
Ss: remarked. etc. etc.
2. Fluency practice. Ask students to answer *I think so* and *I don't think so* as appropriate to the following questions:
a) Were they running towards a taxi rank?
b) Were there usually several taxis there?
c) Did they look an odd couple?
d) Did Kate worry about that?
e) Would anybody guess who Coke was?
3. Now ask students to answer *I hope so* and *I hope not* as appropriate to the following questions:
a) Would anybody guess who they were?
b) Are they going to find Masters?
c) Will he be at the pub?

Section 3
1. Listening phase followed by choral reading.
2. Correct my statements phase. Here are some examples:
a) They got to Soho an hour later!
b) The streets were very dark!
c) There weren't any people there!
d) There was a woman in front of one of the clubs!
3. Ask students to read the Section again silently and to notice how these words are used: *notice, grip, marked, whisper* and *curiously*. Give more sentences with these words, then ask students to write one sentence for each themselves (in class or for homework).

THE MAN WHO ESCAPED
Episode 15

Unit **15**

c

SYNOPSIS: *Kate has come back to the flat with some clothes for Coke and other things. The Chief Inspector has told Baxter that Coke might be innocent.*

1 First Kate dyed Coke's hair grey. Then she used some theatrical make-up to give him a much older face. Finally she put a pair of dark glasses on him, thrust a white walking-stick into his hand and led him firmly to a full-length mirror. Coke was surprised at how strong her grip was. He was even more surprised when he saw himself. An old blind man stared back at him.
"And now," Kate said, "You'll have to do far more than simply look like an old blind man. You'll have to walk, talk and act like one, too!" For the next hour she taught him exactly how to do that.
"You learn fast. We can go now," she finally said.
"What do you mean 'we'? You can't come with me. It might be dangerous," he objected. Kate was already putting her coat on. Her answer was simple. "If you want my help, you'll have to take me with you. Besides, things are just beginning to get interesting!"

2 They were walking towards a taxi-rank. There were usually several taxis parked there, waiting for customers.
"We must look an odd couple, you and I," Coke remarked.
"Don't worry about that. We look so odd that nobody will guess who you are. Now just tell me where we're going!"
"To a pub in Soho called 'The Green Rider'. Masters used to go there a lot," Coke answered.
"You mean you think he's one of the spies?"
"I don't know, but he didn't tell the truth at the trial. Why else should he lie?" Coke said. Just then they got to the taxi-rank. There were not any taxis there. "We'll have to take a bus. Just remember that you're an old, blind man. I'll help you get on and get off!" Kate said.

3 They got to Soho half an hour later. The streets were brightly-lit. There were people, pubs, restaurants, cinemas and strip-tease clubs everywhere. There was a man in front of one of the clubs. Whenever someone passed by he said: "The best show in London. Twenty beautiful girls. Step right in!" He began to say that when he saw Coke but as soon as he noticed Coke's dark glasses and white walking-stick, he closed his mouth again. They walked on until Coke suddenly gripped Kate's arm very hard. "This is the place. Take me in!" he said. There were two doors. One was marked 'Public Bar' and the other 'Saloon Bar'. "Which one?" she asked.
"The Saloon Bar!" he whispered. They went into the crowded, noisy, smoke-filled room. Several people stared at them curiously when they came in.

Unit 15 d

FURTHER PRACTICE

1. Conversation
(for Paired Oral Practice)

Read this conversation, and use the prompts to make others like it.

Example:
MODEL: A: I've just been to the new Chinese restaurant.
        B: Oh! Have you? I've just been to an Indian restaurant.

Prompts:

a) A: a new French car
   B: a German car
b) A: a book by John Wyndham
   B: a book by Nevil Shute
c) A: a new job in London
   B: a new job in Bristol
d) A: lunch in the new canteen
   B: lunch in the café round the corner
e) A: the film at the Odeon
   B: the film at the Plaza
f) A: a concert on Radio 2
   B: a play on Radio 3

2. Conversation

Deborah has a car of her own. There is something wrong with it. She has just driven into a garage.

MECHANIC: Good morning, Mrs Tigers. What can we do for you?
DEBORAH: I'm afraid there's something wrong with the car. I've just noticed that it's been using a lot of petrol lately; far more than usual.
MECHANIC: Oh? Well, we'd better have a look at it, then, hadn't we? Can you leave the car with us now?
DEBORAH: I suppose I'll have to. Do you think it might be something serious?
MECHANIC: I shouldn't think so. You never know, of course. It might be the engine.
DEBORAH: I certainly hope not. I want to use the car this evening. Do you think I'll be able to? I mean, will it be ready by then?
MECHANIC: It might be. It all depends on what the trouble is. Do you think you could give us a ring around 5? We'll know by then.
DEBORAH: Around 5? All right.

AT FIVE O'CLOCK THAT EVENING

SECRETARY: Good evening. Central Garage.
DEBORAH: Good evening. This is Mrs Tigers. I'm ringing about my car.
SECRETARY: Oh, good evening, Mrs Tigers. The men have just finished your car. It's ready now.
DEBORAH: Oh, good! What was the trouble?
SECRETARY: It wasn't anything very serious. There was a leak in the petrol tank. Anyway, they've taken care of it now and you can collect your car any time.
DEBORAH: Good. When do you close this evening?
SECRETARY: At 6.
DEBORAH: I see. I'll be there by then. Good bye.
SECRETARY: Good bye.

Questions

(When Deborah takes the car to the garage in the morning)
1. Correct the statements:
   a) Deborah noticed the trouble several days ago.
   b) The mechanic says the car will definitely be ready in the evening.
   c) He thinks it is something serious.
2. Answer the questions:
   a) Why does she hope it is not anything serious?
   b) What are the two things the mechanic asks her to do?

(When Deborah rings at 5)
1. Correct the statements:
   a) The men have not finished the car yet.
   b) The garage closes at 7.
2. Answer the questions:
   a) What exactly was the trouble?
   b) What have the men done about it?

FURTHER PRACTICE

Unit 15
d

1. Conversation
(for Paired Oral Practice)

a) Unit 11 also contained an exercise of this type. Employ the presentation procedure outlined in that Unit (page 66). Try and make certain that students are not only aware of the structure 'have just done', but that they are also conscious of (and try to imitate) the intonation patterns used – especially that for 'Oh! Have you?'

b) After students have practised the conversations in pairs, provide a short writing phase by asking them to write one of the conversations. Ask them to write the rest for homework.

c) Although these conversations might well provide the beginnings for longer conversations, do *not* allow students to go on as almost any continuation would involve the use of the Simple Past tense (e.g. 'What was it like?'), and the next Unit (16) is devoted to the problem of *did* vs. '*has/have done*'. This implies that these conversations will probably take up no more than a 5-minute phase within the lesson. Whilst doing Unit 16, however, why not come back to this material and use it for Paired Practice involving 'Have done' and 'did'?

2. Conversation

Key Points
1. Meaning and use of the phrases 'have a look at something', 'give someone a ring' (= telephone), and 'take care of something' (= here, do the job)
2. Practice with the probability *might* as in 'It might be the engine'
3. Meaning and use of 'There's something wrong with . . .'
4. Practice of the tag 'hadn't we/you/I' after 'We/you/I had better' as in 'We'd better have a look at it, hadn't we.'
5. The use of 'I shouldn't think so' (= I don't think so); and 'I (certainly) hope not'
6. Meaning and use of 'You never know, of course'
7. Vocabulary item 'a *leak* in the petrol tank'

Presentation Notes
1. Follow the same presentation procedure as outlined in earlier Units.
2. An additional technique is to tell students they are about to hear a conversation between Deborah and a garage mechanic. Tell them to listen particularly for the answers to questions like the following (give them orally, dictate them or write them on the blackboard):
What has Deborah noticed about her car?
What does the mechanic think the trouble might be?
Does Deborah hope it won't be serious? Why?
When does the mechanic ask Deborah to ring?
3. Do the same with the second half of the Conversation.
4. For each of the two halves of the Conversation, use the 'Correct the statements' and 'Questions' below the Conversation orally.
5. *Fluency Practice*
WE'D BETTER HAVE A LOOK AT IT, HADN'T WE.
a) I   e) He
b) read it   f) write to them
c) You   g) She
d) give us a ring   h) tell me about it
6. As a final Recall exercise after the students have heard the Conversation right through again, give these prompts for them to give back the original sentences, using the intonation on the tape:
a) do for you?   d) taken care
b) depends   e) leave the car?
c) something wrong f) never know

Unit 15
e/f

e Summary

1 and 2
At this stage, review and actively revise the uses of the Present Perfect dealt with so far in the book (Unit 11 – 'have had', 'have been' and 'having been doing' + 'for/since': Unit 12 – 'having been doing'; and 'have done' with 'just' and 'yet': and this Unit 15 – 'have done' + 'just', and 'have done' with no time indication). Probably the best material for quick active revision are the Presentation, and the Formation and Manipulation pages.

3
For practice, ask the class questions which we could answer in English with 'I/she/he (etc.) might', said with a shrug of the shoulders:
for example:
T: Do you think it's going to rain?
Ss: It might.
T: Do you think you're going to see that film?
Ss: I might.
Tell them, too, that the negative short answer is 'I/he/she (etc.) might not'.

4
Ask some of the same questions as in the practice for **e3**, and get students to give as a response 'I think so', 'I don't think so', 'I hope so' or 'I hope not'. Ask for individual responses, but do not indicate who is to answer until you have asked the question:
for example:
T: (to whole class) Do you think it's going to rain today? (pause, then indicate student who is to answer)
S.1: No. I don't think so.
T: (indicating another student, S.6) Ask me the same question: 'rain today'.
S.6: Do you think it's going to rain today?
T: I hope not! I want to go swimming.
Focus students' attention on the formation and intonation of the two negatives 'I don't think so' and 'I hope not'.

f Exercises for homework

2
When students do this exercise, suggest that they also look back at Units 11 and 12 and revise the verbs used in the Present Perfect Simple tense there. Ask them to write 5 more sentences of their own using 'has/have done' with verbs from Units 11 and 12.

3
Once again, this Guided Composition needs careful preparation. Students need to be aware not only that they can immediately include such sentences as 'Do you think it might be something serious' and 'It all depends on what the trouble is', but also that they can add items such as 'Have you dropped it lately?', 'It might be the spring', or 'Where did you buy the watch, madam?'.
The essential thing is that at this stage students should be encouraged to draw on some of the English they might have learned much earlier and incorporate that knowledge into the use of the material in the present Unit.

Unit 15
e/f

e Summary

Focal points in this Unit.

1. Remember how we use the word *just* with 'has/have done'. Notice the position of the word *just*:

    'He has *just* gone down that corridor.'
    Remember that we use *just* with 'has/have done' when we are talking about something that happened a few seconds ago.

2. Remember that we also use 'has/have done' when we are talking about something in the past, but give no indication of the time, such as the word *When,* or 'last year' or '6 months ago':

    Example:

    'Have you seen this man?'

3. Notice the form of the verb after *might*:
    'It might *be* fine this evening.'
    Remember that *might* is the same for all persons, and that we can use it in the present and in the future. In a sentence like 'They think he *might be* on the train', *might* means 'is possibly'; in a sentence like 'She *might catch* him if she hurries', 'might catch' means 'perhaps will'.

4. Remember these phrases with *think* and *hope*. Notice the different way we form the negatives:

    'I think so.'   'I hope so.'
    'I don't think so.' 'I hope not.'

f Exercises for homework

1. Do all the exercises on pages 87, 88 and 90.

2. Change the form of these verbs and put them into the appropriate sentence.

    see; leave; come; go; meet; notice; stop; take; tell; be.

    a) Haven't I . . . that girl somewhere before?
    b) Have you . . . care of that noise in the engine yet?
    c) He's . . . in the bathroom a long time!
    d) Good! It's . . . raining. We can go out in the garden again.
    e) Has he . . . you his favourite story?
    f) Oh, dear! It's going to rain and I've . . . my umbrella at home.
    g) 'Where's Bill?' 'Oh, he's . . . to the cinema.'
    h) Have you . . . the new film of 'Hamlet'?
    i) I've just . . . from a very important meeting.
    j) I've just . . . that Mary has dyed her hair.

3. **Guided Composition**

    Read the first half of the Conversation between Deborah and the mechanic on page 90 again, and then write a conversation between a woman and an assistant in a watchmaker's shop. There is something wrong with the woman's watch and she has just taken it in for repair. Use as many of the phrases and sentence patterns as you can, and begin like this:

    WOMAN: Good morning.
    ASSISTANT: Good morning, madam. What can I do for you?
    WOMAN: Well, I'm afraid . . .

4. **Transfer Exercise**

    Write 5 sentences about things which *have just happened*. Do not write anything which is not true.

    Examples:

    We have just done exercise 2.
    I have just spoken to my girl/boyfriend on the phone.
    My parents have just gone out for the evening.

Unit 16 a Present perfect and past simple

1
(a) What/Julia/ just?
(b) What/Julia/ ask?
(c) Julia's questions?
(d) the answers?

2
(a) Who/Peter/ talk to?
(b) Peter's questions?
(c) the girl's answers?

3
(a) What George Upwell?
(b) Who/talk to?
(c) ever: cognac? factory? soldier? cowboy? prison: teacher?

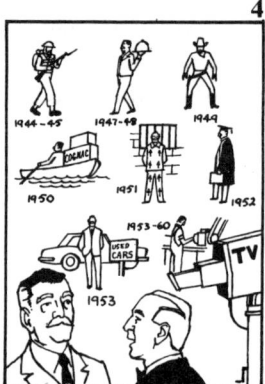

4
(a) When? cognac? prison? etc.
(b) George Upwell's answers?

5
(a) Deborah ever: Rome? etc.
(b) When/Rome? etc.
(c) Deborah's answers?

Main Teaching-Points
1. Revision of Present Perfect Simple ('has/have done') and Simple Past ('did') and contrast in use; especially 'has/have done' with *just, yet, ever* and no time; and 'did' with question word *When* and with other time phrases – 'last week', 'in 1951', etc.
2. Practice with contrasted verb forms: has come/came; have seen/saw; have been/was, were; etc.

Extra Points and Activities
1. Revision of *one* as in '*one of* the typists'/'*one of* his girlfriends'.
2. Meaning of 'What did you think of it?' – 'What was your opinion of it?'
3. Revision of 'a/an' with professions – 'a waiter', 'a teacher' etc.
4. Position of 'very much' in 'I didn't like it very much.'

Unit 16 a

HAS DONE and DID

1
Julia has just come to work. She is late again. She is asking one of the typists about her boss. He often comes in late, too.
  "Has the boss come yet?"
  "Yes, he has. He's in his office now."
  "When did he come?"
  "He came very early. He noticed you weren't here."

1. What has Julia just done?
2. Ask these questions about her boss:
   a) yet   b) early or late
   c) What/notice

2
Peter Atkins is talking to one of his girl friends.
  "Have you seen that film yet?"
  "Yes, I have. I saw it last week."
  "What did you think of it?"
  "I didn't like it very much."

1. Ask these questions about Peter's girl friend:
   a) the film yet   b) When
   c) like it

3
George Upwell is a famous writer. He has done a lot of things in his life. He is talking to a television interviewer now. "I've smuggled cognac, sold used cars and worked in a factory. I've been a soldier, a waiter and a cowboy. I've also been in prison. I've even been a teacher!"

1. What is George Upwell?
2. Ask these questions about him:
   a) many things   b) many places
   c) many jobs
3. Ask questions with "Has he ever . . .?"
   a) cognac   b) used cars   c) factory
   d) soldier   e) waiter   f) cowboy
   g) teacher   h) in prison

4
The interviewer is asking him when he did all these things. "When did you smuggle cognac? When were you in prison?" "I smuggled cognac in 1950. I was in prison in 1951."
The interviewer is going to ask him some more questions.

1. What are the interviewer's first two questions?
2. What are Upwell's first two answers?
3. Ask some more questions about his life with "When . . .?" and answer them.

5
One of Deborah's friends is asking her about all the holidays she has had and all the places she has been to.
  "Have you ever been to Rome?"
  "Yes, I have. I was there in 1967."
  "Have you ever been to Mexico City, or to Rio?"
  "Yes, I've been to all those places."
  "Oh? When were you in Mexico City . . . and when were you in Rio?"

1. What is Deborah's friend asking her about?
2. Ask questions about Deborah first with "Has she ever . . .?" and then with "When . . .?" (and answer the questions)!

Unit 16 b — FORMATION AND MANIPULATION

1 Pronunciation

i) The weak (unstressed) forms of *has* and *have* are normally used in questions starting 'Have you . . .?', 'Has she . . .?', etc.
Example: Have you ever driven a car? : [həv] you ever . . .?
Has he ever been here before? : [həz] he ever . . .?

ii) Remember: *have* and *has* at the end of a sentence are not pronounced in the weak form.
Example: Yes, I have.   No, she hasn't.

iii) When was that? is usually pronounced with the weak form of *was*–[wəz].
Example: When [wəz] that?

2 Look at these verbs: (They come from the last five units.)

	1		2		1		2
see –	saw	–	seen	come –	came	–	come
leave –	left	–	left	stop –	stopped	–	stopped
go –	went	–	gone	run –	ran	–	run
meet –	met	–	met	write –	wrote	–	written

i) Read the following conversation. Observe where verb-forms like *saw* (1) and *seen* (2) are.
A: 'Have you ever seen that film?'
B: 'Yes, I have.'
A: 'When did you see it?'
B: 'I saw it last week.'

ii) You can use other time expressions to answer: 'When did you see it?'.
Example: in 1968. last year. yesterday. two weeks ago. a minute ago. a couple of days ago.

iii) Use the verbs in columns 1 and 2 and the time expressions in exercise ii to make a dialogue like the one in exercise i. Look at the situations on page 93 to make further dialogues.

iv) Now, practise using 'When was that?' in place of 'When did you see it?', and make dialogues as in exercise iii.

FORMATION AND MANIPULATION

Unit 16 b

1. i) Remember to tell the students that the unstressed forms are used here when no particular emphasis is being placed on a structure. To change that stress by using a stressed form of *have* or *has* also changes the meaning of the sentence.
   For example: HAVE *you ever worked in a factory?* indicates that there is some doubt in the mind of the questioner.
   Similarly, *I* HAVE *worked in a factory* is intended to clear up any doubts that there might be in the listener's mind.
   N.B. The use of the stressed form of *was* in *When* WAS *that?*

   ii) Practise the short answer-forms using the stressed forms of *have* and *has*. Write these prompts on the blackboard and pair off students to practise them.
   been to London. seen the film. met her before. been here long. remembered it. listened to it. repaired the car. turned on the radio.
   e.g. S.1: Have you been to London?
   S.2: Yes, I have/No, I haven't.

2. First make sure that students understand that in English one cannot ask when a thing happened before knowing that it did happen. So the following tense sequence occurs quite frequently in conversational English:—
   A: Have you ever (been to London)?
   B: Yes, I have.
   A: Oh, really, when was that?
   B: I (went to London last year).

   Extra practice
   Pair students and give these prompts to form the sequence.
   been to Paris, gone water-skiing, driven a car, painted a picture, flown in an aeroplane, smoked a cigar, typed a letter, cooked a meal.

3. Insert a writing phase into the oral work. Get students to write five examples of a shortened version of the tense sequence practised orally above.
   A: Have you ever been to America?
   B: Yes, I went there in 1968.

Fluency Practice

HAVE YOU EVER SEEN 'HAMLET'?
1. the Tower of London
2. been to
3. Scotland
4. visited
5. my brother
6. met
7. spoken to
8. a film star
9. worked with
10. When did . . .?
11. arrive there
12. learn this language

Unit 16 c

EXPLOITATION OF THE EPISODE

Key Structures and Vocabulary	Suggested Explanations
a) Time dragged (7)	Time passed very slowly.
b) getting towards (8)	(the time was) approaching.
c) closing time (8)	the legal time-limit on the public sale and drinking of alcohol in Great Britain.
d) military type (16)	looked like a soldier.
e) casual (17)	here, not very interested.
f) went through (28)	read a large part of.
g) 'Last orders, please' (30)	'Order your last drinks, please, the pub is going to close soon.'
h) cab (36)	taxi.

Section 1
1. Listening phase followed by choral reading and general comprehension questions: e.g.
   a) Where did Kate lead Coke?
   b) What did she get then? etc. etc.
2. Fluency practice
   I'VE BEEN HERE BEFORE. I WAS HERE LAST WEEK
   Example:
   seen him = I've seen him before. I saw him last week.
   a) seen him
   b) bought one
   c) read it
   d) met her
   e) eaten some
   f) drunk it

Section 2
1. Silent reading phase followed by special questions for short answers.
   a) Did the barman think for a second? (Yes, he did.)
   b) Is Masters a military type? (Yes, he is.)
   c) Did Coke try to sound casual? (Yes, he did.)
   d) Did the barman nod? (Yes, he did.)
   e) Was Masters in that afternoon? (Yes, he was.)
   f) Did Coke know where Masters was? (No, he didn't.)
2. Now, general comprehension questions for the rest of this section.
3. Now, read the text or play the tape.
4. Completion practice for the entire section, e.g.
   T: The barman ... for a ...
   Ss: ... thought ... second.
   etc.

Section 3
1. Listening phase followed by choral reading.
2. Correct my statements. Here are some examples:
   a) The barman shouted 'First orders, please!'
   b) Kate led Coke through the empty, dark streets!
   c) Some of the pubs were opening!
   d) Kate called a taxi when they got to Oxford Circus.
3. Invention exercise based on 'They didn't notice the man. They didn't see him get into a cab and follow them, *either*.
   Example: breakfast/lunch = I didn't have breakfast. I didn't have lunch, either.
   a) the cinema/the theatre
   b) television/radio
   c) raincoat/umbrella
   d) read the book/see the film

THE MAN WHO ESCAPED
Episode 16

Unit 16

C

SYNOPSIS: *Kate has made Coke up to look like an old blind man. They have just gone to a pub in Soho. Coke thinks he might find Masters there.*

1 Kate led Coke to a table and then went to the bar to get their drinks. "I've been here before. I was here last week," she said when she came back. Coke was not listening.
"Masters isn't here," he said.
"Surely you didn't expect to walk in and find him, just like that?"
"No, I suppose not."

Time dragged. They sat there for over an hour. More people came in, but Masters was not among them. It was getting towards closing time when the barman came to their table.
"May I have your empty glasses?" he asked politely.
Coke touched him on his sleeve. "Does a man named Eric Masters ever come in here?" he asked. He did not notice the man standing at the bar who stared at him in the mirror when he mentioned Masters' name.

2 The barman thought for a second. "There's a man named Eric who comes in here a lot. He's a military type. Is that who you mean?" he asked. Coke tried to sound casual when he asked his next question. "Has he been in here today?" The barman nodded. "Yes," he answered. "He was in this afternoon." "I don't suppose you know where I can find him now?" Coke asked. "I'm afraid not. All I know about him is that he has an antique shop somewhere near Red Lion Square," he answered.

"Wasn't that a bit dangerous?" Kate asked after the barman left.
"Yes, it was. But I haven't got much time. I've got to find Masters before the police find me," he answered.
"I still don't understand why you can't simply find his address in the telephone book!"
"I've already looked. I went through the phone book in your flat. Masters might have a phone but his number isn't there."

3 The barman was shouting "Last orders, please" when Coke and Kate left. Kate led him through the crowded, bright streets. Most of the pubs were closing. It was 11.00, but the clubs and restaurants were still busy. When they got to Shaftesbury Avenue, Kate called a taxi. Neither she nor Coke noticed the man who was so close behind them in the crowd that he heard Kate say "Red Lion Square, please" to the driver. They did not see him get into a cab and follow them, either.

Unit 16 d

FURTHER PRACTICE

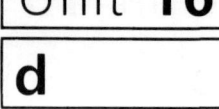

1. Invention Exercise

1) Make questions from the prompts with this model:

Example:

MODEL: Have you ever . . .?
PROMPT: spaghetti
RESPONSE: Have you ever eaten spaghetti?
　　or: Have you ever cooked spaghetti?

Prompts:

a) America
b) Danish lager
c) that book
d) a jet plane
e) a Japanese film
f) the Queen
g) that girl to the cinema
h) a Rolls-Royce
i) vodka
j) any stories by Somerset Maugham

2) Now use the questions you have made to begin conversations. Use this model:

MODEL: A: Have you ever been to America?
　　　　B: Yes I have.
　　　　A: When were you there?
　　　　B: I went there last year.

2. Conversation

Julia is in the watch department of a large store.

JULIA: Excuse me. Do you do watch-repairs?
SALESMAN: Yes, we do, madam.
JULIA: Oh, good. Would you look at mine? It's stopped.
SALESMAN: Certainly. Hmm . . . when did it stop?
JULIA: Only yesterday. Can you do anything about it?
SALESMAN: I think so. Just leave it with me.
JULIA: Good. When will it be ready?
SALESMAN: This time next week. Now, you'll need a receipt.
JULIA: Oh, yes. I mustn't forget that, must I?
SALESMAN: No. You won't be able to claim the watch without it.
JULIA: Good. Thank you. Good bye.
SALESMAN: Good bye. Wait a moment, madam! You've dropped something. Madam! You've dropped something! Madam!

ONE WEEK LATER

SALESGIRL: May I help you, madam?
JULIA: I hope so. It's my watch. I brought it in to be repaired but now I've lost the receipt.
SALESGIRL: Lost the receipt? Oh, dear. That *is* bad.
JULIA: Can't I just describe the watch to you?
SALESGIRL: I'm afraid not. Only the manager can help you and he's gone to lunch. He left only a minute ago.
JULIA: Oh, dear. I think it was the manager who served me.
SALESGIRL: Just a moment. When did you bring the watch in?
JULIA: This time last week, during my lunch hour.
SALESGIRL: And was your watch a small gold *Timamatic*?
JULIA: Yes, that's right. How did you know?
SALESGIRL: Because your receipt's still here. You dropped it when you left. The manager shouted but you didn't hear.

Questions

1. What does Julia say about her watch when she brings it in?
2. What is the manager's exact question when she says this?
3. According to the manager, why does Julia need a receipt?
4. What exactly does he shout when she leaves?
5. Why is the receipt still there when Julia comes back?

Recall

Without looking at the text, try to remember those parts of conversation between the salesgirl and Julia a week later.

SALESGIRL: help?
JULIA: hope. watch. to be repaired. the receipt.
SALESGIRL: bad. only the manager. just/lunch. a minute ago.

FURTHER PRACTICE

Unit 16 d

1. Invention Exercise

a) Follow the technique of doing this exercise as suggested in earlier Units. It is usually best to give the prompt to the whole class, only indicating which student is to answer after a short time has been given for thought.

b) This exercise is designed to make students practise questions with 'has/have done' combined with the use of *ever*.

c) The prompts call for a variety of verbs in the Present Perfect Simple. The verbs which could be used in the items are:
for a) *been to, visited* or *flown to;* for b) *had* or *drunk;* for c) *read, seen* or *looked at;* for d) *been in* or *flown in;* e) *seen* or *watched;* f) *met, seen, heard* or *visited;* for g) *taken;* for h) *had, owned, bought, driven* or *been in;* for i) *had* or *drunk;* and for j) *read* (or *heard*).

2. Conversation

Key Points
1. Meaning and use of vocabulary items '(to) claim' and 'receipt' – and pronunciation of 'receipt'
2. Use and intonation of 'Excuse me' before asking a question
3. Use and intonation of *Certainly* (= Yes, of course) after a request for help
4. Meaning and use of *drop* (vs. *fall*)
5. Use of *just* before an imperative, as in '*Just leave* it with me'
6. Meaning and use of *may* as in 'May I help you?'
7. Explanation of 'to be repaired' in 'I brought it in to be repaired'
8. Meaning and use of *describe* as in 'Can't I just *describe the watch to you?*'

Presentation Notes
1. Follow the same presentation procedure employed in previous Units.

2. Use the same *pre-question* phase as suggested for **2.** 2 page 90 for each half of the Conversation.
3. Focus students' attention on the word *just* used with an imperative, when the Salesman says – 'Just leave it with me.' Give other sentences, and ask the students to repeat them adding the word *just;* for example –
T: Put it there.   Ss: Just put it there.
T: Ask him.   Ss: Just ask him.
T: Forget it.   Ss: Just forget it. – and so on.
4. Revision and practice phase with the possessive pronouns *mine, yours, his, hers*, etc. Use articles (books, briefcases, pencils etc.) in the room; pick up articles belonging to different students and say: 'This isn't mine. Whose is it?' The owner can immediately answer 'It's mine', while the rest of the class can answer 'It's his' or 'It's hers'. Also questions like 'Is this yours?', 'Is this his?' etc.
5. *Fluency Practice*
ONLY THE MANAGER CAN HELP YOU AND HE'S JUST GONE TO LUNCH.
(Prompts to replace 'the manager' and 'to lunch'.)
a) Mr. Smith   e) chief salesman
b) out   f) to coffee
c) the manageress   g) Arthur
d) home   h) to work

Unit 16
e/f

e Summary

1 and 2
One of the greatest problems facing any students of English, whether they are Intermediate or even fairly Advanced students, is the discrimination between the use of 'has/have done' and 'did'. Students cannot have enough practice in using these two tenses. In this Unit, we have tried to give a number of situations which demonstrate how important it is to use the correct tense. Even after all the material in the Unit has been used, however, students should be taken back to some of the situations, and made to practise them again.
Take situations 3 and 4 (on page 93) for example. Give students biographical details of another famous living English person, and get them to ask each other questions like 'Has he/she ever been a teacher?' or 'Has he/she ever worked or lived in America?' Then make them ask *When*–questions about that person, such as 'When was he a teacher?' or 'When did he live in America?'

2
Many students are confused by the *been/gone* problem. Apart from the one or two examples in the Unit, it might be easiest to show these concepts:
a) by giving two short situations to illustrate them:
   for example:
   i) We saw Jane a few minutes ago. She was walking towards the church. She's there now. SHE HAS GONE TO CHURCH.
   ii) It is now 12 o'clock. Jane went to church at 11, and she has just come back. SHE HAS BEEN TO CHURCH.
b) by asking one student to leave the room for a moment (to go to the canteen). While he is out, ask the question 'Where has X gone?' When he returns, ask the question 'Where has he been?'–or even ask the student himself 'Where have you been?'

f Exercises for homework

2
With each of the sentences ask students for an example of a sentence using the other tense. For example, sentence a) is 'I sold my old car last week.' Ask for the question which might get sentence a) as an answer–'Have you sold your old car yet?' This is also the time to point out one of the spelling problems in English, namely *p* to *pp* as in 'stop–stopped', 'drop–dropped'.

3
This Guided Composition is even less controlled than any up to this point, since the student is asked not only to supply the necessary structures but is also asked to provide a considerable amount of the information himself, too. It should be prepared, of course, both referring students back to necessary items in this and previous Units, and by asking questions and allowing short writing phases within the lesson itself. The important point is that, although it is less controlled in content, there is still no reason why students should go away and make lots of errors as a result of non-preparation.

Unit 16
e/f

e Summary

Focal points in this Unit.

1. In this Unit, we have practised and contrasted two tenses, the Present Perfect 'has/have done' and the Simple Past *did*.
   a) Just look again at the types of sentences we have practised with 'has/have done':
      i) 'She has *just* come to work.'
      ii) 'Has the boss come *yet*?'
      iii) 'He has done a lot of things *in his life*.'
      iv) 'Have you *ever* been to Rome?'
      (There is no mention of a specific time)
   b) And look at the types of sentence we have practised with *did*:
      i) '*When* did he come?'
      ii) 'I saw it *last week*.'
      iii) 'What did you think of it (the film)?'
      (The speaker knows *when* the other person *saw* the film; there is a definite time element)

2. Look at these two sentences:
   a) 'He's *gone* to lunch.'
   b) 'I've *been* out to lunch.'
   Sentence a) tells us that he is not here now; he is probably eating now.
   Sentence b) tells us that the person has gone to *and come back* from lunch.

3. Remember that the question 'What did you think of it?' means 'What was your opinion of it?'

f Exercises for homework

1. Do all the exercises on pages 93 and 96.

2. Supply the correct form of the verb ('have done' or 'did') in brackets.
   a) I . . . my old car last week. (sell)
   b) . . . you . . . anything from your brother yet? (hear)
   c) We . . . John's new car. (just see)
   d) So you're back at last! Where . . . you . . . ? (be)
   e) They . . . a lot of wine last night at the party. (drink)
   f) Excuse me! I think you . . . this purse a moment ago. (drop)
   g) He . . . out of the lesson a moment ago. You can speak to him now. (come)
   h) He's still in prison because he . . . cognac last year. (smuggle)
   i) . . . it . . . raining yet? (stop)
   j) Who . . . you the last time, madam? (serve)

3. **Guided Composition**

   You are a radio reporter and you have just been sent to Hyde Park where there is some trouble. Write down what you say as you commentate on the scene, paying attention to the use of 'is/doing', 'has/have done', 'has/have been doing' and 'did'.
   Begin like this:

   'I arrived here in Hyde Park about 10 minutes ago. There is a large crowd of about 200 people here. . . .'

   Finish the short report by describing how the police came, and how all the people left without violence, using these prompts:

   an hour or more//most/standing/some/sitting/grass//at the moment/very peaceful//young man/just finish/speech//start/half an hour ago//

4. **Transfer Exercise**

   Write a number of sentences about yourself using these examples:

   I've never been to China, *but I've* been to Japan. *That was* 3 years ago.
   I've never worked in a shop, *but I've* worked in a factory. *That was* last year.

Unit 17
a
Frequent gerund constructions

1 
(a) When/phone?
(b) Who/person/ speak to?
(c) When/Arthur/ back?
(d) secretary/ saying?

2 
(a) Why/Tom/the dishes?
(b) Where/Susan?
(c) Tom/like/ dishes?
(d) Tom saying to Peter?

3 
(a) When/Fred/ army?
(b) Fred/like/ soldier?
(c) Where/Fred/ now?
(d) Fred saying to Sergeant?

4 
(a) Where/Frank?
(b) What/he/give up?
(c) Who/talk to?
(d) Frank saying to Susan?

5 
(a) Chairman shouting now?
(b) a few minutes ago?

Main Teaching-Points
1. Formation and use of the Gerund with certain verbs:
   a) *Would you mind . . . ing?* and *Would you mind not . . . ing?* and *I wonder if you'd mind . . . ing?*
   b) *hate . . . ing/like . . . ing.*
   c) *give up . . . ing/stop . . . ing.*

Extra Points and Activities
1. Intonation of the polite form 'I wonder if you'd mind . . . ing . . .?' (fluency practice through Substitution Drill).
2. Revision of *carry* vs. *wear*.
3. Meaning of 'do the dishes'.
4. Revision and practice with *has gone* (and is still there) contrasted with *has been* (and is now back). (See also page 97.)
5. Meaning and use of *at first*.

| WOULD YOU MIND ....ING? | I WONDER IF YOU'D MIND ....ING? | **Unit 17** |
| WOULD YOU MIND NOT ....ING? | STOP/GIVE UP/HATE/LIKE ....ING | **a** |

1

The phone rang a few seconds ago. Someone wants to speak to Arthur.

"I'm awfully sorry," his secretary is saying. "Mr Tigers has gone out. He'll be back at 3. Would you mind phoning then?"

1. Ask and answer the questions!
   a) When/the phone   b) Arthur there
   c) When/back
2. The person on the phone can speak to Arthur at 3; what does Arthur's secretary say to the person?

2

Tom Atkins has to do the dishes because Susan's father is in hospital and she has gone to visit him. Tom does not like washing dishes. In fact, he hates washing them.

"I wonder if you'd mind helping me?" he is saying to Peter.

1. Ask and answer the questions!
   a) Why/Tom/the dishes
   b) like . . .?
2. What is it that he hates doing?
3. What is he saying to Peter?

3

Fred Collins joined the army a few months ago. He does not like being a soldier. In fact, he hates it. He hates carrying a heavy rifle and wearing a uniform. He also hates getting up early. All the other soldiers have already got up. "I wonder if you'd mind closing that window, Sergeant?" Fred is saying.

1. Ask and answer the questions!
   a) When/the army   b) like/a soldier
2. Ask if he hates doing these things!
   a) a heavy rifle   b) a uniform
   c) up early
3. What is he saying to the sergeant?
4. Why do you think the sergeant is angry?

4

Frank Martin is in hospital. He has had to give up smoking and drinking beer, too. The doctor says these things are very bad for him. Susan is visiting him now. "Susan, I wonder if you'd mind bringing some cigarettes next time?" he is saying to her.

1. What are the two things Frank cannot do in hospital?
2. What has he had to do? Ask why!
3. What is he saying to Susan now?
4. Do you think she will?

5

This is a political meeting. It has got out of control. The chairman is telling people to stop doing certain things. At first he tried to be polite. "Would you mind not waving that red flag?" he said a few minutes ago. Now he is shouting "Stop waving that red flag!" A group of men are shouting "freedom", two others are blowing trumpets, another group is singing and a few men are fighting.

1. What sort of meeting is this and what has happened?
2. What did the chairman say to the man with the flag a few minutes ago?
3. What is he shouting now?
4. He tried to be polite with the other people, too. What do you think he said to them?
5. What do you think he is going to shout at the other people?

Unit 17 b

FORMATION AND MANIPULATION

1 Intonation
  a) Notice the secretary's intonation, situation 1, page 99 'Would you mind phoning then?' Practise saying this just as she does. Then use the same intonation pattern in the following sentences:
    i) Would you mind sitting there?
    ii) Would you mind coming in?
    iii) Would you mind going out?
    iv) Would you mind drinking tea?
    v) Would you mind asking him?
  b) Notice the very polite form 'I wonder if you'd mind . . . -ing?' Practise the intonation of this form as Tom uses it in situation 2, page 99. Notice the way *wonder* is stressed in order to make the question very polite. Use the three examples in situations 2, 3 and 4 on page 99 to practise this.

2 Make questions (with and without *not*)

Would you Would they Would she Would he	mind	(not)	waiting for me coming back later having a new one seeing him tomorrow	?

3 With someone else, practise asking and answering the questions using the following very frequent short answer forms:
  i) Yes, I (etc.) would.
  ii) No, I (etc.) wouldn't.
  iii) Not at all.
  iv) Of course not.
  v) Of course he (etc.) would ('nt).
  vi) I expect so.
  vii) I don't think so.

4 Using the table below, ask questions. Use the answers given in 3 to work with someone else.

I wonder	if	you'd they'd she'd he'd	mind	helping me opening the door asking her coming in	?

5 Using these verbs – *stop, give up, hate, like,* make sentences about these things: cigarettes, dancing, T.V., cinema, sports cars, gardens, flowers, wine, work, swimming, football, cricket.

FORMATION AND MANIPULATION

Unit 17 b

1.

Spend sufficient time on this section to give the students the practice they need in using the correct intonation pattern. The intonation is vitally important if the structures are to have their proper meaning.

2, 3 and **4.**

1. Students should be given plenty of practice in using the gerund forms *in context* by concentrating on the answers that go with the polite gerund question forms. Give students both oral and written practice. A short writing phase should be inserted in the oral practice to give variety and enable the practice to be continued over a longer period.
2. To add further variety to the activities, use the following substitution drills as a means of increasing fluency.

WOULD YOU MIND WAITING HERE?
1. helping him
2. going away
3. writing to me
4. telephoning her
5. Would he . . .
6. bringing
7. telling
8. asking her why
9. Would they . . .
10. telling me

WOULD YOU MIND NOT SINGING?
1. talking so loudly
2. smoking in here
3. making so much noise
4. waiting for me
5. us
6. them
7. Would she . . .
8. helping
9. seeing
10. telling him

I WONDER IF YOU'D MIND HELPING ME?
1. seeing her
2. asking
3. going with
4. going without
5. waiting here
6. waiting for me
7. sitting over there
8. standing
9. thinking about it
10. working on it

3. Give students the following oral prompts and ask them to respond using the forms practised in the substitution drills above.

It's cold with that window open.
It's too hot with the door shut.
The door is difficult to open.
The window is dirty.
I don't like cigarette smoke.
I've only got tea to offer you.
My car has broken down, but there's a bus stop over there.

5.

To make the situation a little more real, ask students to write five true sentences about themselves or people they know using the verbs *stop, give up, hate, like*.

N.B. How is the learning of the verb-forms going? If students are still making mistakes, begin regular testing of all the verbs. If necessary, start the students learning the forms again from the beginning.
THESE MUST BE KNOWN CORRECTLY.

Unit 17

C EXPLOITATION OF THE EPISODE

Key Structures and Vocabulary	*Suggested Explanations*
a) deserted (2)	empty of people/nobody was there.
b) obviously (4)	evidently/clearly.
c) 'Connoisseur's Corner' (7)	'A place of particular interest to the connoisseur' (an expert with good taste).
d) kept glancing (10)	glanced (looked quickly) repeatedly at.
e) bound to (14)	it must happen/it is inevitable.
f) caught his eye (17–18)	attracted his attention.
g) sabre (20)	a type of sword with a curved blade.
h) copied it down (24–25)	wrote it on a piece of paper or in a notebook.
i) watch out for (36)	be careful of.
j) hung up (37)	put the telephone back on its rest.

Section 1
1. Listening phase followed by choral reading and simple comprehension questions:
   e.g. Were they in a taxi?
   Where was the taxi?
   Who was in it? etc. etc.
2. Fluency practice
   WOULD YOU MIND DRIVING ROUND THE SQUARE?
   a) the corner
   b) waiting
   c) Would she . . . ?
   d) She wouldn't
   e) He
   f) going
   g) living in London
   h) going to
   i) Would you . . . ?

Section 2
1. Silent reading phase followed by simple comprehension questions.
2. Play the tape or read the text. Then use a completion phase.
3. Practise long and short answers to questions using the following. (Ask first for long answers.)
   a) What did Kate keep doing? (She kept glancing over her shoulder)
   b) What didn't she like?
   c) What couldn't they stop?
   Now pair the students and get them to use the three prompts (written on the blackboard) to produce long answers. Then, when students are getting quite fluent, ask them to use the short answers to the questions, i.e.
   a) Glancing over her shoulder
   b) Wandering round the dark streets
   c) Looking

Section 3
1. Play the tape or read the text.
2. Choral reading phase concentrating on the intonation of Masters when he is nervous. (I'm sorry, Hugo. But I don't know anybody like that. What did they want?)
3. Correct my statements phase. It was around 3 a.m. when . . . etc. etc. (a short practice session with the use of a.m. and p.m. could be given here).
Note: A short section of the text may be used as a dictation passage when students are thoroughly familiar with the contents.

THE MAN WHO ESCAPED.
Episode 17

Unit 17

c

SYNOPSIS: *Coke has just found out that Masters owns an antique shop somewhere near Red Lion Square. He and Kate have gone there in a taxi. They do not know they are being followed.*

1 "Would you mind driving round the Square once?" Kate asked the driver. Red Lion Square was deserted. There were a number of dark side streets around it.
"It's obviously not on the Square itself," Coke said.
They got out of the taxi, paid the driver and started exploring.

There were antique shops on several of the side streets but they all either had names like "Connoisseur's Corner" which told them nothing about who owned the shop, or other names like "Richards", and "Harvey Keen". Masters' name was not among them.

2 Half an hour later they were still looking. Kate kept glancing over her shoulder. She had the uncomfortable feeling that someone was following them but she could not see anybody.
"I don't like wandering round the dark streets at this hour," she said.
"Someone's bound to notice us!" she went on. "I don't like doing it, either, but what else can we so? We can't stop looking now. It might be our last chance," Coke answered.

Suddenly something in the window of a shop across the road caught his eye. The street was very dark but the thing gleamed. It reflected the light of a passing car. They crossed the street. The thing was an old military sabre and it was in a window marked "Antique Weapons and Military Antiques." There were old pistols, helmets and other swords in the window. Coke became excited. "This must be it!" he said. Kate lit a match so that they could see a bit better. There was no name on the window but there was a phone number on the door. Coke copied it down.

3 It was around midnight when the phone rang in Eric Masters' flat. The voice on the other end was hard and cold.
"This is Hugo," it said. "Why didn't you come to the Green Rider?"
"I'm sorry, Hugo. I . . . I don't enjoy going there any more. Not since Coke escaped. I . . . I thought it might be dangerous." Masters was nervous. He became even more so when he heard what Hugo had to say.
"There was an old blind man in the pub. He had a young woman with him. He asked about you and then went to your shop." Masters blinked in surprise. His voice cracked slightly. "But I don't know anybody like that. What did they want?"
"How do I know, you fool? Just watch out for them, that's all!" Hugo said furiously and hung up. Masters slept very badly that night.

Unit 17 d

FURTHER PRACTICE

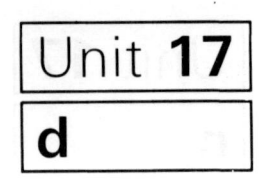

1. Invention Exercise

MODEL: Would you please STOP . . . ing . . . ?
1) Make questions with *stop* using the prompts:
Example:

   PROMPT: that terrible noise
   RESPONSE: Would you please stop making that terrible noise?

Prompts:

  a) those letters
  b) that guitar
  c) the radio
  d) those cheap cigarettes
  e) the phone so much
  f) your dictionary
  g) so many sweets
  h) that book
  i) that song

2) Now use the same prompts for examples with the verb MIND:
Example:

that terrible noise – Would you mind not making that terrible noise?
those letters – Would you mind typing those letters now, please?

2. Conversation

Julia and Jim are in a pub. They are standing at the bar. In English pubs, you always have to go to the bar to get your drink. Nobody will ask you what you want if you sit down at a table first. Jim has just paid for their drinks.

BARMAN: And here's your change, sir.
JIM: Thank you.
JULIA: Can we sit down somewhere, Jim? I don't like standing here.
JIM: All right. Look! There's a table over there. Come on.
JULIA: (sitting down) This is much more comfortable. I think women look terrible standing at the bar.
JIM: Really? I don't think so. Anyway, cheers!
JULIA: Cheers!
JIM: Would you like a cigarette?
JULIA: No thanks. I've decided to give up smoking.
JIM: Really? Why?
JULIA: Well . . . it's just that I think if you don't enjoy doing something any more you should stop doing it.
JIM: I see. You mean you don't enjoy smoking any more?
JULIA: That's right. You should give it up, too. It's bad for your health.
JIM: Stop talking like my mother. That's what she keeps saying.
JULIA: But it's true. It's a nasty habit. I can't think why I ever started. Anyway, it's obviously got you in its grip!
JIM: What do you mean? What are you talking about?
JULIA: I mean you couldn't give it up!
JIM: Who? Me? Couldn't give up smoking? Nonsense! Of course I could! I know I could!
JULIA: How do you know?
JIM: Because I've already proved it. Smoking's the easiest thing in the world to give up. I've done it hundreds of times!

Questions

1. Why does Julia want to sit down somewhere?
2. What does Jim say just before he takes his first sip from his drink?
3. What has she decided to give up?
4. Ask and answer why she has decided to give up smoking?
5. What does Jim say when Julia tells him he should give up smoking?
6. Correct these statements:
  a) Jim thinks giving up smoking is very hard.
  b) Jim has never given up smoking.

Recall

Without looking at the text, see if you can remember some of the things Jim and Julia said.
JULIA: think/women/terrible/bar.
JIM: a cigarette?
JULIA: No/decided.
JIM: You mean/don't enjoy/any more?
JULIA: right. you should/too. health.
JIM: Stop/mother. keeps.
JULIA: Nasty habit. you/grip.
JIM: nonsense. easiest thing. hundreds of times.

FURTHER PRACTICE Unit 17 d

1. Invention Exercise

a) Follow the technique of doing this exercise suggested in earlier Units.

b) As well as calling for practice with 'Would you please stop - - - ing . . .', and 'Would you mind (not) - - - ing . . .', the prompts also call for a variety of verbs. The verbs which could be used are:
for a) *typing, looking at, reading* or *writing;* for b) *playing;* for c) *listening to* or *turning on;* for d) *smoking* or *buying;* for e) *using* or *talking on;* for f) *looking at, reading, referring to* or *looking words up in;* for g) *eating* or *buying;* for h) *reading* or *studying;* and for i) *playing, singing* or *whistling*.

c) When practising 'Would you mind . . .?', make it very clear how we use both 'Would you mind . . .?' and 'Would you mind *not* . . .?' Ask students to transform the examples in situations 1, 2, 3, 4 and 5 (on page 99) using an imperative: thus—
i) Please *phone* then!
ii) Please *help* me!
iii) Please *close* the window!
iv) Please *bring* some cigarettes next time!
   - - - BUT - - -
v) Please *don't wave* that red flag!
After the pattern ('mind doing') has been practised with the prompts, get students to ask each other to do things using 'Would you mind (not) . . .?'

2. Conversation

Key Points
1. Meaning and use of 'pay for something' (vs. 'pay somebody')
2. Meaning and use of vocabulary items 'change', 'a nasty habit', and '(to) prove'
3. Use of *Cheers* in English when drinking someone's health
4. Use of the verbs 'enjoy' and 'keep (on)' + Gerund
5. Meaning and intonation of the sentence 'I can't think why I ever started'
6. Meaning and intonation of the word 'Anyway, . . .' at the beginning of a sentence
7. Meaning and use of 'It's obviously *got you in its grip*'
8. Meaning and use of *could* in the latter part of the Conversation

Presentation Notes
1. Use the same presentation as with previous Conversations.
2. Play the tape or read the Conversation, pausing for students to complete sentences.
3. Correct my statements phase (extra to those on student page), for example:
   a) Julia likes standing at the bar.
   b) She thinks women look nice standing at a bar.
   c) Jim offered Julia a cigar.
   d) Julia says smoking is good for your health.
4. *Simple Substitution (Fluency Practice) Drills:*
   a) YOU MEAN YOU DON'T ENJOY SMOKING ANY MORE?
      i) drinking
      ii) going to the cinema
      iii) watching football
   b) I CAN'T THINK WHY I EVER STARTED!
      i) began!
      ii) gave it up!
      iii) stopped going there!
      iv) bought that car!
      v) sold my bicycle!
   Note: Do both a) and b) as choral drills, and then ask students to write one or two more sentences like them.

Unit 17
e/f

e Summary

1

In this Unit we have concentrated on, and therefore focused students' attention on, the use of a small number of verbs which are followed by the Gerund.

As with other patterns and structures in English, students need continued practice with a small number of verbs taking the Gerund, adding new ones as they progress in their study and use of the language. With some classes, therefore, you may want to add other verbs for practice, for example *start, begin* and *finish*. Such new items should nevertheless still be introduced in situations and practised through Substitution Drills, Invention Exercises, and so on.

2

As this pattern 'I wonder if you'd mind (not) . . .?' is so useful, get them to work in pairs and ask each other politely to do (or not to do) certain things. Use the prompts from the Invention Exercise on page 104 again. Then give other prompts, for example:—
a) (get) me a ticket for the concert.
b) (not talk) to anyone about it.
c) (give) me a ring tomorrow.
d) (ask) John to see me.
e) (play) that violin.

f Exercises for homework

3

Remind students once again of the use of 'had better'. Then prepare this exercise orally, pausing after you have given each *situation* and allow all students to think of the advice before asking for an individual response. Give other examples of situations in which we might give advice using 'You'd better give up/stop . . .'.
for example:
a) A friend who wastes a lot of time at work.
b) A friend who smokes 40 cigarettes a day. (His health is bad.)
c) A person who has tried to learn to drive for 3 or 4 years, but who still hasn't passed his (or her) driving test.

4

The two exercises set for Guided Composition work are both types which have been set before.
a) is really a straightforward transfer exercise, asking for a re-writing of situation 3 (page 101) using different vocabulary. The result is an exact parallel of the original situation: 'John Roberts joined the bank 3 years ago. He doesn't like being a bank clerk. In fact, he hates it. He hates counting (or dealing with) money and wearing (or having to wear) a smart suit.' – and so on.
b) is similar to the exercise set in Unit 16, except that we have not given the vocabulary and sentence patterns. Indeed, these will in many cases, be the same as in situation 5 (page 101).

Unit 17
e/f

e Summary

Focal points in this Unit.

1. In this Unit, we have practised a small number of the verbs which are followed by the '-ing' form (or the Gerund) of a verb:

    mind; hate; like; give up; stop; enjoy; keep (on).

    Remember these sentences:

    a) Would you *mind helping* me? Would you *mind not waving* that red flag?
    b) Tom *hates washing* dishes.
    c) Fred *does not like being* a soldier.
    d) Frank has had to *give up smoking*.
    e) *Stop waving* that red flag!
    f) You mean *you don't enjoy smoking* any more? ⎫
    g) That's what my mother *keeps saying*. ⎭ from the Conversation, page 102.

2. Remember how we sometimes begin a sentence with 'I wonder . . .' when we want someone to do something, and we want to be very polite:

    'I wonder if you'd mind closing the window'

f Exercises for homework

1. Do all the exercises on pages 99, 100 and 102.

2. Complete these sentences:

    a) I've just given up . . .
    b) Why don't you stop . . .
    c) Do you like . . .
    d) Do you really enjoy . . .
    e) We don't mind . . .
    f) I hate . . .
    g) You really ought to give up . . .
    h) Shall I stop . . .
    i) Will you please stop . . .
    j) I wonder if you'd mind . . .

3. Give advice to these people. Use 'You'd better give up/stop . . .'

    a) A friend who spends all his money.
    b) A man who is putting on weight.
    c) A light sleeper who always drinks coffee before he goes to bed.
    d) A young girl who always drives very fast.
    e) A student who has an exam next month, but who goes out every evening.

4. **Guided Composition**

    a) Read situation 3 on page 99 again, and then, using the prompts, write about this person:

        John Roberts/bank/3 years//not like/bank clerk//In fact . . .//money/smart suit//also/to work early//other clerks/already there//'I wonder . . ./earlier?' the manager has just asked him.

    b) Read situation 5 on page 99 again, and then write a radio commentator's report of the meeting. Use the patterns and vocabulary in the situation. (Remember, you did one like this in Unit 16).

5. **Transfer Exercise**

    a) Write 5 true sentences about things you *like, enjoy* or *hate* doing.
    b) Write 5 true sentences using *stop* or *give up*.

        Examples:

        I gave up riding a motor-bike a year ago.
        I stopped studying Physics when I left school.

Unit 18 a

Future simple with 'If' or 'When' and present simple clause

1
(a) What/Fred/about to do?
(b) What/another?
(c) Why/Fred/not jump?
(d) What/if?

2
(a) What/millionaire/ask?
(b) she/make up/mind?
(c) asking him?

3
(a) What/student/ask?
(b) What/conductor/say?

4
(a) What/Julia?
(b) When/other typists?
(c) What/manager/worried?
(d) manager/angry/if?

5
(a) Which team/win?
(b) What/if/draw?
(c) How/players?

Main Teaching-Points
1. Basic distinction in meaning between *if* and *when* in English.
2. More practice with *will* in statements, questions and negatives.
3. The form of the verb (Present Simple) after the words *if* and *when* in a future sentence: 'Fred will get very wet *if he does*' (= if he *falls* into the water).

Extra Points and Activities
1. Meaning and use of *about to (do)*.
2. Meaning and use of *over* (= finished).
3. Meaning and use of 'make up one's mind'.
4. Preview of 'ask someone to do', as in 'He has just asked her to marry him'.
5. Meaning and use of *worry* and *worried* in 'Don't worry' and 'He is worried about the lights'.

| WILL DO | WHEN / IF | DOES |

Unit 18
a

1

Fred is about to jump across the stream. Another soldier has just fallen into it. Fred does not want to jump. He is afraid he will fall into it, too. He will get very wet if he does. Fred will be very happy when all this is over.

1. What is Fred about to do?
2. What has just happened?
3. Why doesn't Fred want to jump?
4. Ask and answer these questions!
   a) Fred/wet/falls
   b) happy/over

2

The old millionaire has just asked the young blonde to marry him. She can't make up her mind. Perhaps she will, perhaps she won't.
   "Will you give me all your money if I marry you?" she is asking him.

1. What has just happened?
2. Will the blonde marry him?
3. What can't she do?
4. What exactly is she asking him?

3

This foreign student does not know London at all. He has just asked the bus conductor to tell him when they get to Hyde Park. The conductor is saying, "Don't worry! I'll tell you when we get there!"

1. Where does the foreign student want to go?
2. What has he just asked the conductor to do?
3. What is the conductor saying?
4. What do you think was the student's exact question?

4

Julia is working late this evening. All the other typists left five minutes ago. The manager is leaving, too. He is worried about the lights.
   "Don't worry! I'll turn them off when I leave," Julia is saying.
He will be very angry if she forgets.

1. What is Julia doing?
2. Why aren't the other typists there?
3. What is the manager worried about?
4. What is Julia saying to him?
5. Ask and answer the question!
   a) manager angry/forgets?

5

There are only a few minutes left in this match between Liverpool and Manchester. Manchester are winning by three goals to two, but they have not won yet. Liverpool might score again, and if they do, the result will be a draw. If that happens, the Manchester fans will be very unhappy. The players are very tired. They will be very happy when the match is over.

1. What is going on here? Which team is winning?
2. What may Liverpool do? Ask and answer: Liverpool win/score?
3. Ask some more questions and answer them!
   a) Liverpool score/a draw
   b) Manchester fans happy/Liverpool
   c) players happy/over

Unit 18 b

FORMATION AND MANIPULATION

1 Pronunciation

These are short forms: *I'll, he'll, she'll, we'll, they'll* and *it'll*. Notice that short forms are not used in questions: 'Will you give me all your money, if I marry you?' (Situation 2, page 105.)

2

| I'll | turn them off | if / when | I leave. |

Notice that we use 'if' when we cannot be sure that the thing is going to happen:
He will (he'll) get wet *if* he does. (Situation 1, page 105.)
Notice that we use 'when' when we know that the thing is going to happen:
I'll tell you *when* we get there. (Situation 3, page 105.)

3 Transformations

Make sentences using *when* or *if*.
Examples: Perhaps it will (it'll) rain. He'll get wet.
HE'LL GET WET IF IT RAINS.
She knows he's arriving. She'll meet him.
SHE'LL MEET HIM WHEN HE ARRIVES.

i) I know I'll see John. I'll tell him then.
ii) Perhaps I'll see John. I'll tell him then.
iii) Perhaps I'll marry that man. He'll give me £50,000.
iv) We know it'll get dark. We'll turn on the lights then.
v) I'm going to bed. I'll turn off the lights then.

4

| Will you | give me all your money | if / when | I marry you? |

5

| Yes, I will (no short form) |
| No, I won't |

6 Make sentences, ask questions and answer them. Work with someone else. Ask and answer as many questions as you can.

| I'll do it | if / when | you | come / ask me / pay me £50 |

| Will you | come / be here / wait / stop | when / if | I | ask you / tell you / phone you / see you | ? |

FORMATION AND MANIPULATION

Unit 18 b

1.

Insist on the use of the short forms whenever possible in oral work. It is not so vital in written work, since both forms are extensively used. However, the short written forms (even *It'll*) should not be neglected because they are being used more and more frequently. Make sure that students do not try to use short forms in questions and in the 'Yes, I (etc.) will' short answer.

2.

To reinforce the IF-WHEN distinction, ask questions using the 'going to' form about the situations on page 105, e.g.
 i) Is Fred going to fall into the water? Answer: We don't know.
 ii) Is Fred going to be angry? Answer: Yes, he is.
Teacher: so we use 'IF' for i) and 'WHEN' for ii).

3.

Extra oral transformation prompts.
 i) Perhaps it will rain soon. I'll go indoors then.
 ii) The train will come soon. I'll get on it.
 iii) Perhaps the sun will shine soon. I'll sunbathe then.
 iv) Perhaps a letter will come today. I'll read it then.
 v) The phone will ring in a minute. I'll answer it then.

4. and 5.

Make students form questions using 4, and form answers using 5.

6.

Insert a writing phase in this section. Ask students to write five statements based on the first table and five questions based on the second table.

Fluency Practice

I'LL COME IN WHEN BREAKFAST IS READY
1. if
2. you call me
3. he comes
4. when
5. I'll ring you
6. Will you ring me . . .?
7. if
8. it's late
9. she's early
10. tell them
11. the parcel arrives
12. the train's late

Unit 18

c EXPLOITATION OF THE EPISODE

Key Structures and Vocabulary	*Suggested Explanations*
a) '... he had *to make* one thing *clear* to her' (7)	He had to make her understand one thing; he had to explain one thing to her.
b) 'Kate looked at him *coolly*' (9)	If you look at someone coolly, you look at him (or her) without much feeling or emotion.
c) 'We've been over this before...' (9)	We have discussed all this before. (Give more examples: e.g. Do you remember Episode 17? We *went over* it last week.)
d) '... interested in old firearms.' (23)	(Practice with 'interested in') Firearms are guns, pistols etc. – but not swords or other weapons.
e) '... difficult for him *to get about*' (28–29)	Old people who are blind or who cannot walk very well find it difficult to get about, to travel.
f) 'His hands were *trembling slightly*.' (33)	If a person is afraid of something, his (or her) hands often shake a little bit (demonstrate!): they tremble slightly.

Section 1
1. Listening phase followed by short-answer questions:
   a) Did Coke sleep very well that night?
   b) Where did he sleep? What time did he fall asleep?
   c) Where was Kate when he woke up? What was she doing?
   d) What will the police do if they learn that Kate has helped Coke?
2. Completion exercise after choral reading:
   T: Coke did not sleep very well... (pause for completion)...
   Ss: that night, either.
   T: He lay awake...
   Ss: thinking. etc.
3. Fluency practice
   I'LL WORRY ABOUT THAT IF AND WHEN IT HAPPENS
   (prompts to replace 'worry about that' and 'it happens')
   a) think about that
   b) the problem arises
   c) speak to him
   d) he comes
   e) discuss the problem
   f) it happens again

Section 2
1. Listening phase followed by questions:
   a) What is Coke going to try to get Masters to do?
   b) What was Masters doing when the phone rang in his shop?
   c) What sort of antique weapons is Masters particularly interested in?
   d) Why is it difficult for Kate's *father* to get about?
2. Fluency practice
   I'M PARTICULARLY INTERESTED IN OLD FIREARMS
   a) old paintings
   b) very
   c) antique furniture
   d) extremely
   e) old houses
   f) particularly
   g) historical buildings
   h) extremely

Section 3
1. Silent reading phase after they have first heard the Section read (or on tape) without looking at the text.
2. Get students to ask and answer these questions (working in pairs):
   a) How did Masters manage to answer?
   b) Where is Masters' assistant?
   c) When will Masters come over to see Kate and Coke?
   d) What did Masters take out of the drawer?
   e) Why do you think he took a pistol?

THE MAN WHO ESCAPED
Episode 18

Unit 18

C

SYNOPSIS: *Hugo has told Masters an old blind man and a girl have been looking for him. Coke and Kate have found what they think is Masters' antique weapon shop.*

1 Coke did not sleep very well that night, either. He lay awake thinking. He was on Kate's sofa in the sitting-room. Slowly, however, he formed a plan in his mind. He fell asleep around three in the morning.

When he woke up, Kate was already in the kitchen making breakfast. "What are we going to do now?" she asked while they were eating. Coke did not answer immediately. He stared into his coffee. He knew he had to make one thing clear to her. "Have you thought what'll happen to you if the police find me here?" he suddenly asked. Kate looked at him coolly. "We've been over this before, haven't we? Now answer my question," she answered.
"But they'll send you to prison if they learn you've helped me!"
"I'll worry about that if and when it happens."

2 "All right. I'll tell you. But I warn you, if anything goes wrong, you might get hurt, badly hurt!" he told her.
"Go on. I'm listening."
"We're going to try to get Masters to come here. That is, if the owner of that shop is Masters."
"Get him to come here? How?"
Coke began to explain the plan he had in mind.

Eric Masters was cleaning an antique pistol when the phone rang in his shop. He heard a young woman's voice at the other end. "I believe you buy and sell antique weapons," she said.
"Yes, that's right. I'm particularly interested in old firearms."
"My father is, too. He has a number of 17th-century pistols and he wants to sell some of them. Would you be interested?"
"Certainly. If you bring them to my shop, I'll look at them and give you a price."
"Well, unfortunately my father's blind. It's very difficult for him to get about. Would you mind coming to our place?" the woman answered.

3 Masters managed to answer calmly.
"Well . . . er . . . my assistant is out to lunch. I'll come over when he comes back. Is that all right?" He noted down the address she gave him and hung up. His hands were trembling slightly. "These must be the people Hugo told me about," he thought. He reached into a drawer and took out a pistol. This one was not an antique. It was a small, black, nasty-looking automatic.

Unit 18

d

FURTHER PRACTICE

1. Practice Situations

Make one sentence for each of the situations.
Use: 'I'll (do) . . . IF . . .' or: 'I'll (do) . . . WHEN . . .'

Examples:

SITUATION: a) Sally is going to arrive at 10.30. You'll be at the bus-station to meet her.
RESPONSE: I'll meet her when she arrives.
SITUATION: b) It might rain tomorrow. I'll take my umbrella then.
RESPONSE: I'll take my umbrella if it rains tomorrow.

Situations:

a) Cigars are definitely going to go up in price. You'll stop smoking then.
b) It might snow tomorrow. You'll stay at home then.
c) The weather might get better. You'll go out then.
d) You know a telegram is coming. You'll tell me the news then.
e) You are working in the garden. It might rain soon. You'll go indoors then.
f) Sir Arthur is definitely going to phone soon. You'll speak to him then.

2. Conversation

Peter Atkins has just got on a bus. He wants to go to a place where he has never been before. In most English buses, you usually pay after you have got on and sat down.

CONDUCTOR: Fares, please. Any more fares?
PETER: Hatfield Road, please.
CONDUCTOR: Hatfield Road? Four, please.
PETER: Oh, will you tell me when we get there, please?
CONDUCTOR: You'll see it yourself if you keep an eye open. It's only a few stops from here. Here's your ticket.
OLD MAN: I'll tell you when we get there, young man. It's my stop, too.
PETER: Thank you. That's very kind of you.
OLD MAN: Don't mention it. These young bus conductors won't give you any help even if you ask politely. It was different when I was young.
PETER: Yes, I'm sure it was.
OLD MAN: And these young bus drivers are even worse. This one will kill us if he doesn't slow down!
PETER: Yes. I suppose he *is* driving a bit fast.
OLD MAN: Look. Do you see those traffic lights ahead? We'll turn left when we get to them. Hatfield Road's the next stop after that. Why do you want to get off there?
PETER: I want to go to the new Technical College.
OLD MAN: Oh? You'll never find it if you go down there alone. I'll show you where it is if you carry one of my bags for me.
PETER: Well . . . er . . . thanks all the same but I'm sure I can manage. I mean, I don't want to put you to any trouble.
OLD MAN: Oh, it's no trouble at all. I have to go past there anyway. We're almost there now. Now, I'll carry this small bag if you take that big one. Hurry up or we'll miss the stop!
PETER: It's . . . it's very heavy.
OLD MAN: In fact, it'll be easier to show you the College if you take both bags. I'll have both hands free then.
PETER: I . . . I . . .
OLD MAN: Oh, don't thank me. I'm always ready to help a stranger!

Questions

1. Where does Peter want to get off? Ask why!
2. What exactly does he say to the conductor?
3. What does the conductor tell Peter?
4. What does the old man say he will do?
5. What does Peter have to do?

Practice

Explain in class exactly what these phrases mean. Then practise their pronunciation and intonation using the teacher or tape recorder as a model:

a) Don't mention it.
b) Thanks all the same.
c) I'm sure I can manage.
d) I don't want to put you to any trouble.

FURTHER PRACTICE **Unit 18 d**

1. Practice Situations

a) Follow the technique of doing this exercise suggested in earlier Units. Remember once again to *set* the situation clearly in students' minds by asking questions before eliciting the response using *if* or *when*.

b) Here are four more situations:
  i) You are definitely going to have a party soon. You'll invite Jill to it.
  ii) You have put an electric kettle on to boil. You'll make the tea then.
  iii) John might ask Alice to marry him. She'll say *yes* then.
  iv) You might have to work overtime, and you want to go to the cinema. You'll miss the film.

2. Conversation

Key Points
1. Use of 'get on'/'get off' with buses and trains
2. Meaning and use of vocabulary items: 'keep an eye open', 'fares', 'slow down', 'ahead' and 'put (someone) to . . . trouble!'
3. Revision of and practice with 'That's very kind of you'
4. Meaning, use and intonation of 'Don't mention it' (after 'Thank you')
5. Meaning and use of 'Thanks all the same, but . . .' when politely refusing an offer of help
6. More practice with the unstressed forms of certain prepositions: *from* [frəm], *to* [tə], and *of* [əv]

Presentation Notes
1. Use the same presentation procedure as with Conversations in previous Units, but this time tell students to listen particularly for any sentences with *if* or *when*. Tell them also to be ready to write down one such sentence (if they can) from the Conversation after the first time they have heard it.

2. *Correct my statements*
  a) The bus conductor was very helpful!
  b) A young man offered to tell Peter when they got there!
  c) The bus driver was driving very slowly!
  d) Peter wanted to find the New University!
3. With reference to the Practice on the student page, some students may find it difficult to explain what the phrases mean. Instead, ask them to try and describe the situation in which the phrases are used. Or if that also proves difficult, get them to supply what is often said to prompt these phrases or responses. Thus – 'Thanks very much. It was very good of you' is the stimulus to 'Don't mention it', 'Can I help you?' to 'Thanks all the same, but . . .', and so on.
4. *Simple Substitution Fluency Practice*
  THANKS ALL THE SAME, BUT I'M SURE I CAN MANAGE (prompts to replace *manage*).
  a) do it   d) carry it
  b) find it   e) mend it
  c) pay for it
5. Point out the use of 'put (someone) to . . . trouble' in positive and negative sentences:
   He *put* me *to a lot of trouble*.
   He *didn't put* me *to any trouble*.
6. Give the following prompt-words and phrases for recall of sentences from the Conversation:
  a) see/an eye open
  b) different/young
  c) kill/slow down
  d) never/down there alone

Unit 18
e/f

e Summary

1
For many students of English, the discrimination between *if* and *when* in future sentences provides a considerable problem. In summing up at the end of the Unit, it is probably advisable to ask students to read back through the various parts of the Unit (the situations, the tables on the Formation and Manipulation page, the Practice Situations, the Conversation and the Episode) and to write down a number of sentences which include *if* (in one column), and a number which include *when* (in another column). *Then* ask students if they can say what all the *if*-sentences have in common, and what all the *when*-sentences have in common.

2
To reinforce the use of the Present Simple after *if* and *when*, do once again the Substitution Drills on the Formation and Manipulation page (106).

f Exercises for homework

1 and 2
Both of these exercises could well be left purely for homework, and not prepared in class. However, exercise 2 could be prepared orally. Ask students to make sentences of their own beginning 'I'll be there if . . .', 'We'll meet you if . . .' and 'I'll be very pleased if . . .'
Then add other items which can fit into the table, such as 'the bus gets there', 'we'll be glad', 'the train is on time', and so on.

3
Although we have given the subject of the letter, the beginning and certain patterns and phrases to be used in the letter, this is now a far less controlled exercise than earlier compositions, as it is not based upon one specific piece of material in the Unit. Naturally, the subject of the letter allows for wide use of the *if/when* patterns practised in this Unit, but students are now free to recall many other items (vocabulary and structures) learned in previous Units. They should be reminded of some of the items in the previous Units, particularly *stop, enjoy, like,* 'I wonder if you'd mind', etc. + '--ing'; 'has/have done' vs. 'did'; and 'will have to' and 'will be able to'–some of which could be included in the letter. Give examples of such items as they might appear in the letter:
For example: 'I hope you'll enjoy spending a weekend with us'./'I wonder if you'd mind bringing back the books you borrowed?'/'You last spent a weekend with us about 2 years ago'/ 'We'll be able to go out in my new car'./

Unit 18

e/f

e Summary

Focal points in this Unit.

1. Remember the important difference between *if* and *when* in sentences like these:
   a) 'Fred will get very wet *if* he falls into the water.'
   b) 'Fred will be very happy *when* all this is over.'
   In a), Fred might fall into the water. It is not certain, so we use *if*.
   In b), Fred knows that all this will finish soon, so we use *when*.

2. Notice particularly the form of the verb in the *if* or *when* part of the sentence:
   a) 'Will you give me all your money *if I marry* you?'
   b) 'I'll tell you *when we get* there.'

3. The word *if* can come at the beginning or the middle of a sentence. Notice that we use a comma in the sentence only if the *if* comes at the beginning.

   The Manchester fans will be very unhappy if Liverpool scores again.
   If Liverpool scores again, the Manchester fans will be very unhappy.

f Exercises for homework

1. Put the verbs in brackets ( ) in the correct form. They are all future ideas.
   a) I (be) there when she (arrive).
   b) If you (ask) him politely, he (help) you.
   c) What (happen) to me if I (tell) them?
   d) If prices (go up) again, I (stop) smoking.
   e) Will you tell me when breakfast (be) ready?
   f) If you (catch) the 10.30 tomorrow, you'll be in Bristol at 12.00.

2. Put the phrases in this list into the right column (1 or 3):

   you come, I'll be there, you arrive on time, the weather is fine, we'll meet you, I'll be very pleased.

1	2	3
	if	

   Now write at least 5 sentences from the table you have completed.

3. **Guided Composition**

   You have just moved to a new house in a different town. Write a short letter (about 70 words) to a friend in the old town inviting him (or her) to your new home for a weekend in the near future. Suggest the bus or train he (or she) might catch, and where and what time you can meet. Begin your letter like this:

   'Dear . . .,
   You know we have just moved into our new house here in . . ., so I am writing to ask . . .'

   Use these phrases and patterns in your letter, too:

   I'll meet you . . . if you come on . . ./If you stay . . ., we'll go out . . ./We won't be able to . . ./You'll never find it if . . ./ It'll be easier to . . . if . . ./You'll be able to tell me . . . when we . . ./

4. **Transfer Exercise**

   Write a number of true sentences about yourself using 'I'll . . . if/when . . .'

   Examples:

   I'll go to the beach this afternoon if the weather is fine.
   I'll buy a new pair of shoes when I get my wages at the end of the week.

Unit 19 a

Common patterns with verb + him/her/etc. + infinitive with/without 'To'

1
(a) What/girl's father?
(b) What/he/at the moment?
(c) What/if she doesn't?

2
(a) Why/girl's mother angry?
(b) What/she/to father?

3
(a) What/Tom want?
(b) What/Susan want?
(c) Why?
(d) What/say?

4
(a) Where/Fred?
(b) ill?
(c) Sergeant/believe?
(d) What/Sergeant/do?

5
(a) When/Peter/Canada?
(b) Who else/on plane?
(c) What/at Customs?

6
(a) Where/girl?
(b) early?
(c) What/if teacher?
(d) What/before?

Main Teaching-Points
1. Formation and use of the patterns 'want someone to do', 'ask someone to do' and 'tell someone to do' in statements, positive and negative, and questions.
2. Formation and use (and discrimination) of the patterns 'make someone do' and 'let someone do' in statements, positive and negative, and questions. Notice also the use of 'will/won't' with 'let', as in 'She won't let him read . . .' (situation 3).
3. General revision of Personal Pronouns *me, you, him, her,* etc.

Extra Points and Activities
1. Revision (with more practice) of 'stop doing'.
2. Meaning and use of 'apply for'; and 'Why don't you . . .?' as suggestion in situation 3.
3. Meaning and use of *might* in 'He might not let her stay' (situation 6).
4. 'any longer' as in 'Don't let her play any longer' (situation 2).

| WANT / ASK / TELL } someone *to* do | MAKE / LET } someone do | Unit **19** a |

1

The girl's father wants her to stop playing. He wants her to wash her hands and face and eat her lunch. At the moment he is asking her to do these things. If she does not do them, he will tell her to do them.

1. What does the girl's father want her to stop doing?
2. What else does he want her to do?
3. What is he doing at the moment?
4. What will he do if she does not do these things?

2

The little girl's father told her to stop playing a few seconds ago, but she hasn't The girl's mother has just looked in. She is angry. "Make her stop! Don't let her play any longer!" she is saying to the girl's father.

1. What hasn't the little girl done?
2. What did her father do a few seconds ago?
3. What does the girl's mother think the father should do?
4. What does she think he shouldn't do?

3

Tom wants to read a book but Susan won't let him. She wants him to read something in the paper. It is an advertisement for a better job.
"Put that book down a second and look at this! Why don't you apply for this job?" she is saying.

1. What won't Susan let Tom do?
2. What are the three things she wants him to do? (book. paper. the job)
3. What does she want him to stop doing?

4

Fred is on a march. He is not really ill but he wants the Sergeant to think he is.
"Let me sit here a bit, Sergeant. I feel terrible!" he is saying.
Unfortunately the Sergeant does not believe him. He is going to make Fred get up again. He is going to make him march with the others.

1. What does Fred want the Sergeant to think?
2. Ask why (and answer)!
3. What does Fred want the Sergeant to do?
4. What exactly is Fred saying?
5. Ask three questions about the Sergeant beginning "Is he going to . . .?"
   a) Fred/up again   b) sit there
   c) march (use 'let' or 'make' with the questions)

5

Two months ago, when Peter flew back from Canada, there was a very pretty girl on the same plane. When Peter went through Customs they made him open his case. They made him take everything out. They did not make the girl do these things. They let her go through without any trouble.

1. When did this happen?
2. What did they make Peter do?
3. Ask two questions about the girl beginning "Why didn't they make her . . .?"
4. What did they let the girl do?
5. Ask why they didn't let Peter do this!

6

Here is the girl again. She is at a language institute in London. She got up late this morning. Her class has already started. She does not want the teacher to notice her. If he does, he might not let her stay. He made her go out again when she came late before.

1. Why is the girl in London?
2. Ask two questions about her!
   a) early or late this morning
   b) already started
3. What doesn't she want the teacher to do? Ask why (and answer)!
4. What happened once before?

Unit 19 b — FORMATION AND MANIPULATION

1 Pronunciation

Don't forget to use the weak (unstressed) form of *to* [tə].
Example: The girl's father wants her [tə] stop playing.

2 Notice the type of word we put in each box:

A	B	C	D	
The boss	wants	me	to work	late this evening

    A   B   C   D

i) Think of some words of your own to put in box A ('The boss'). Change 'wants' to 'want' where necessary. Make full sentences.

ii) What other words can we put in box C ('me')? Make at least 6 sentences by changing 'me' to other words, like 'him', 'us', etc.

iii) Now think of other words to go in box D ('to work'). Make sure they are infinitives. Don't use 'late this evening'. Again, make full sentences. (*Example:* He wants me to finish these letters).

iv) Finally, change box B. Make sentences with 'wanted', 'ask/asked' and 'tell/told'.

3

A	B	C	D	
People today	let	their children	do	all sorts of things that children couldn't do before.

i) What are some of these things? Make sentences of your own beginning: 'They let them . . .'

ii) Are there things you think parents shouldn't let their children do? What are they?

4 Make sentences from this table.

A	B	C		D
He She They	wanted asked 'll tell	me him them John	to	come in go away give up smoking help her
He She	made let	John them		do it wait

5 i) Now think of things that your parents wanted you to do when you were young. Make sentences beginning:
'They wanted me to . . .'

ii) Now ask someone else questions beginning 'Did your parents want you to . . .?'

iii) What were some of the things your parents *made you do*? Make at least five sentences.

FORMATION AND MANIPULATION

Unit 19 b

1.

Insist on the use of the weak form of *to* [tə]. At this stage in the course students should be doing this automatically. If they aren't, then more emphasis must be placed on the use of the most frequent weak (unstressed) forms. Remind the students of words like *to, from, of, at* etc.

2.

To help students grasp the formation of this structure, and before they do the exercises in this part, ask them to think of words to put in boxes B, C and D. Write these on the blackboard. About half a dozen words for each box will be sufficient. Now ask the students to do the exercises orally, using the words already written on the blackboard. Next, remove the words from the blackboard and ask the students to work alone on the exercises, writing out the answers. As a way of saving time, if this is important, the class can be divided into four groups (members of each group working independently) with each group working on one exercise only.

3.

It will help first of all to allow students to suggest orally some items to replace those in boxes A, B, C and D.

4. and 5.

1. It may be necessary to spend a lot of time on this section before students are able to manipulate all the different forms. To avoid monotony, alternate written and oral practice every few minutes.
2. Pair off students and write the following short dialogue on the blackboard:
   A: Why did she make him wait?
   B: Because she wanted him to help her.
   This is a natural combination of the two structures and will help the students to practise in a genuine context. They should be encouraged to work orally. Some of the items thought of by the students to fill boxes 2 D and 3 D can now be recalled and written on the blackboard again to act as prompts.
3. Don't forget the negative forms of the verbs should also be practised when the students are fluent at using the positive forms. While the students are still practising the positive forms, write the following examples on the blackboard:

         A: Why didn't she make him wait?
         B: Because she wanted him to help her.

   and   A: Why did she make him wait?
         B: Because she didn't want him to help her.

   and also A: Why didn't she make him wait?
         B: Because she didn't want him to help her.

   If you have to omit any of these dialogue practices omit the last one; it is the most complex and least frequent of the three.

N.B. How is the revision of the verb-forms going?

Unit 19

c

EXPLOITATION OF THE EPISODE

Key Structures and Vocabulary	*Suggested Explanations*
a) 'Perhaps the old man really *does* want me to look at . . .' (10)	Point out that we sometimes use 'does/do' in a positive sentence when we want to emphasise something. (Practice in the notes below, Section 1, 2.)
b) 'He patted the pistol . . .' (11)	Explain by demonstration.
c) 'Suddenly it dawned on him.' (34–35)	He suddenly had an idea; he suddenly realised something.
d) 'I hope I haven't put you to any trouble' (14–15)	I hope I haven't given you (or caused you) any trouble.
e) '. . . there was something familiar about the man's face . . .' (19)	He thought he recognised the man's face somehow.
f) 'The more he . . ., the more suspicious he became.' (33–34)	He became more and more suspicious as he looked at Coke's face.

Section 1
1. Listening phase followed by questions:
a) How did the pistol make Masters feel?
b) What did Hugo say when he rang him?
c) Was his car a black Ford? (What was it, then?)
2. Practice (with the intonation and stress on the tape) of –
PERHAPS HE REALLY *DOES* WANT ME TO LOOK AT THEM
Prompts:
a) he/give a talk
b) he/ring him
c) she/go with her
d) they/take them
e) he/get a new job
f) they/stay for a week

Section 2
1. Listening phase (with books face down) followed by a silent reading phase of lines 12–20 only.
2. Get students to ask each other questions from these prompts:
a) Who/door to Masters?
b) What/Kate say? (prompt: trouble)
c) Why/Masters/carefully at old man?
3. Read or play the second part (lines 21–30) again, and then ask questions:
a) What did the 'old, blind man' do while Kate was out of the room?
b) What sort of stick was the 'old man' holding?
c) What did Coke do when Masters asked him 'Are you a collector, too?'?
d) What did Kate bring out of the bedroom?
4. Fluency practice
WE HAVEN'T MADE YOU COME ALL THIS WAY FOR NOTHING
a) do all that work
b) study that report
c) march all this way
d) open your case
e) write all those notes
f) learn French

Section 3
1. Silent reading phase. Ask students while they are reading to write down questions to ask other students after they have finished reading it.
2. Let the students listen to the text once (read aloud or played on the tape recorder) and ask for some choral repetition, before allowing them to put their questions to other students.
3. Practice with 'The more . . ., the more . . .' Give some examples –
The more he looked at the book, the more interested he became.
The more he wrote, the more enthusiastic he became.
– and get students to repeat in chorus.

THE MAN WHO ESCAPED
Episode 19

Unit 19

C

SYNOPSIS: *Kate has asked Masters to come to her flat. She has told him that her father has some antique pistols he wants to sell. Masters is suspicious and has decided to take a small automatic pistol with him.*

1 Masters rang Hugo just before he left his shop.
"You told me about an old blind man and a woman . . . well, they've just phoned. They want me to go to their place and look at some antique pistols," he said nervously.
"Well, what do you want me to do about it?" Hugo asked sarcastically. "You have a pistol, haven't you? There isn't much an old blind man and a woman can do to you?" he added.
Masters could not understand why Hugo was so casual about it. He got into his white Jaguar and drove off.
"Perhaps the old man really does want me to look at his pistols," he thought. He patted the pistol in his pocket. It made him feel safer.

2 He felt even safer when Kate opened the door. She was slim, almost delicate-looking. "Good afternoon," he said. "I'm Eric Masters. You rang my shop earlier." She smiled. "I hope I haven't put you to any trouble. However, I'm sure you'll decide we haven't made you come all this way for nothing," she said pleasantly, and led him into the sitting-room. Masters glanced suspiciously at the old, blind man sitting on the sofa. At first he seemed harmless enough, but there was something familiar about the man's face that made Masters look more carefully at him.

"I'll go and get the pistols," Kate said. Masters stayed where he was, where he could see everything and where nobody could come in behind him. The old, blind man did not move. He simply sat there, his hands folded on his white walking-stick, his eyes behind the dark glasses staring blindly in front of him.
"Are you a collector, too?" Masters asked. The old man simply nodded. The woman came out of the bedroom with a large black case. "They're all in here," she said. "If you come over here, to the table, we can look at them. My father doesn't really want anyone else to have them, but I'm afraid we have no choice. It's a question of money."

3 Masters kept his eyes fastened on the old man's face as he walked towards the table. He was halfway there when the old man raised his face slightly. The sudden movement made Masters stop. The more he looked at that face, the more suspicious he became. Suddenly it dawned on him. He stared at both of them. They were both waiting expectantly for him to come nearer. It was the old man's nose and lips that made Masters think of Coke. He reached for his pistol.

Unit 19 d

FURTHER PRACTICE

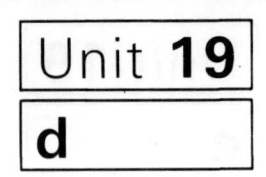

1. Invention Exercise

1. MODEL: I can't go out tonight.
   Someone wants me to do something.

Example:

PROMPT: my wife/some letters
RESPONSE: I can't go out tonight. My wife wants me to write some letters.

Prompts:

a) The boss/some extra work
b) My teacher/a composition
c) My father/his car
d) My mother/the kitchen
e) My teacher/a lecture on the radio
f) My parents/to a concert
g) My friend/a special programme on T.V.
h) My younger brother/his homework

2. MODEL: Would you please {ask/tell} someone to do something?

Example:

PROMPT: Mary/the kitchen door
RESPONSE: Would you please tell Mary to close the kitchen door?
   or: Would you please ask Mary to open the kitchen door?

Prompts:

a) Julia/the window
b) that student/the lights on
c) Julia/me before she goes
d) Mr Smith/my office
e) them/more quietly
f) that boy/here
g) him/my bicycle
h) her/the 1967 reports

2. Conversation

It's a fine spring day. Tom is sitting in his garden at home, marking some books.

SUSAN: Tom? Do you think you could come into the kitchen for a second? There's something I'd like you to look at.
TOM: What? Just let me finish these books and I'll be right there.
SUSAN: Would you mind coming right away, please? It's the washing machine. It's making a funny noise. I want you to listen to it. I'm worried.
TOM: Oh, no! Not again. (In kitchen now. Tom has to shout above a loud whirring and pumping noise) It's the pump, that's what it is.
SUSAN: I can't hear you. Let me turn the machine off!
TOM: The pump isn't working properly. What do you want me to do about it?
SUSAN: What do I want you to do about it? Repair it, of course. You don't think I made you leave your work for nothing, do you?
TOM: But I'm not a mechanic. Why don't you ring the shop where we bought the thing? Ask them to repair it!
SUSAN: Are you sure that's what you want me to do?
TOM: Of course I'm sure! Why do you ask?
SUSAN: Because the last time they came you got very angry.
TOM: Did I?
SUSAN: Yes. It was a small question of money. Don't you remember? The men were only here for half an hour but they still charged £2 for an hour's work. You didn't like that at all.
TOM: Oh? Hmm . . . yes, I remember now.

Questions

1. Why is Susan worried about the washing machine?
2. What exactly does she want Tom to do about it? Ask why!
3. What does he want her to do?
4. What happened the last time something went wrong with the machine?
5. When Susan first asks him to come in, Tom wants to finish the books he is marking; what does he say to Susan?

FURTHER PRACTICE

Unit 19
d

1. Invention Exercise

a) Follow the technique of doing these exercises suggested in earlier Units.

b) Notice that the first exercise practises 'want someone to do', and the second 'ask/tell someone to do'. At the same time, however, the first exercise reinforces once again the use of the Present Simple third person *s*; and the second exercise reinforces the use of the request form 'Would you please . . .?'

c) As in previous Invention Exercises, the prompts call for a variety of verbs. In Exercise 1, the verbs which could be used are:
for a) *to do* or *to finish*; for b) *to write* or *to prepare*; for c) *to clean, to mend, to repair, to polish* or *to wash*; for d) *to clean, to decorate* or *to help in*; for e) *to listen to* or *to make notes from*; for f) *to go with, to accompany, to take* or *to drive*; for g) *to watch* or *to see*; and for h) *to help him with* or *to do*.
In Exercise 2, the verbs which could be used are:
for a) *to open* or *to close*; for b) *to put, to switch* or *to turn*; for c) *to see, to ask, to ring* or *to telephone*; for d) *to come to, to go into, to wait in* or *to work in*; for e) *to work, to talk, to play* or *to sing*; for f) *to come, to wait, to stand* or *to sit*; for g) *to use, to ride, to take, to mend* or *to repair*; and for h) *to copy, to type, to find, to look for* or *to bring me*.

NOTE: because of the large number of possible verbs for many of the prompts, some may well be given as Simple Substitution Drills. Even the lists above are far from exhaustive!

2. Conversation

Key Points
1. Meaning and use of vocabulary items 'a spring day', 'pump', 'a funny noise' and '(to) charge (money)'
2. More practice with 'let/make someone do' and 'want/ask someone to do'. Also practice with 'I'd like you to . . .'
3. Meaning and use of 'right away' (= immediately; at once)
4. Practice (paying close attention to intonation) with these patterns:
'Do you think you could . . . for a second?'
'There's something I'd like you to . . .'
and
'You don't think I made you . . . for nothing, do you?'

Presentation Notes
1. Use the presentation procedure as with Conversations in previous Units.
2. *Correct my statements!*
   a) It is a wet winter day, and Tom is working indoors!
   b) Susan wants Tom to look at the electric kettle!
   c) Susan can't hear Tom because the cat is making a noise!
   d) Tom says: 'Why don't you ring your father about it?'
   e) The last time, the men were there for two hours and they charged £10!
3. *Fluency Practice* (All Simple Substitution Drills.)
DO YOU THINK YOU COULD COME INTO THE KITCHEN FOR A SECOND?
   a) help me   d) listen to this
   b) stop the machine e) stop talking
   c) put down that paper f) look at this
THERE'S SOMETHING I'D LIKE YOU TO LOOK AT.
   a) listen to   e) type
   b) do   f) think about
   c) buy   g) read
   d) find out   h) get for me
YOU DON'T THINK I MADE YOU LEAVE YOUR WORK FOR NOTHING, DO YOU?
   a) come in here   d) give me the money
   b) type those letters e) do all that work
   c) walk all this way f) do those exercises

Unit 19 e/f

e Summary

1
So often with a pattern like 'He wants her to wash her hands', students fail to transfer their control of the pattern because they are not given enough practice in using the pattern in different tenses. We have given examples and practice in different tenses throughout the Unit, but now is a good time to make students consciously aware of what they can do with such patterns.
Use a simple transformation exercise:
Give an example: T: 'He often asks me to help him' + the prompt word – *yesterday*.
Choral student response: Ss: 'He asked me to help him yesterday'.
Give the same example: T: 'He often asks me to help him' + the prompt word – *just*.
Choral student response: Ss: 'He's just asked me to help him'.
Do the same again, adding the prompt word *tomorrow* to elicit the student response 'He's going to ask me to help him tomorrow'.
Do the same transformations with a number of examples, and get students to write some down.

2
Focus students' attention once again on the Infinitive without *to* after *make* and *let*. Also clarify the difference in meaning between the two verbs. If some students do still seem to confuse the two, in fact, work through one or two of the situations on page 113 again – perhaps situations 5 and 6.

f Exercises for homework

2
Do this exercise quickly in class, focusing students' attention on the different forms of the pronouns we have used throughout the book: 'I/me/to me/my/mine', etc.

3
Since students have to think of ideas in order to complete the sentences here, why not make them give true sentences as well as in exercise 5?

4
Before allowing students to tackle this Guided Composition, make quite sure that they have studied the Episode, and in particular all the vocabulary and patterns in the second section which they will need to use. To help them, ask them questions which might have been put to Coke after the incident, for example:
Where were you sitting when Masters arrived?
Did you answer the door? Who did, then?
How did Masters look at you when he came in?
Did you say anything when Masters spoke to you?
The answers to many such questions, demanding as they do a 1st-person answer, will provide much of the composition for students.

e Summary

Focal points in this Unit.

1. Remember the form of the verbs which follow the verbs *want, ask* and *tell:*

   'He *wants* her *to wash* her hands.'
   'Why don't you *ask* them *to repair* it?'
   'He *told* her *to stop* playing.'

   want
   ask + Infinitive with *to*
   tell

2. Remember the form of the verbs which follow *make* and *let:*

   'They *made* him *open* his case.'
   'They *let* her *go* through without any trouble.'

   make
   let + Infinitive without *to*

3. There is an important difference in meaning between *make* and *let* as we have used them in this Unit.

   'Make someone do' means 'force or cause someone to do.'
   'Let someone do' means 'allow someone to do.'

4. Remember also the form of the personal pronouns we use in patterns 1 and 2 above: me, you, him, her, it, us, you, them.

f Exercises for homework

1. Do all the exercises on pages 111, 112 and 114.

2. Choose the correct word to put in the blanks:
   a) He wanted . . . to tell him the time. (my/mine/me)
   b) I asked . . . to clean the car yesterday. (he/him/his)
   c) Don't let . . . take the books away. (they/them/their)
   d) Don't ask . . . to make a cup of tea. (her/hers/she)
   e) She made . . . do more work. (we/us/our)

3. Complete these sentences, using the patterns we have practised in the Unit:
   a) She won't let . . .
   b) Why don't you ask . . .
   c) I hope he doesn't make . . .
   d) If you've got the time, I'd like . . .
   e) Do you really want . . .

4. **Guided Composition**

   Read the second part of the Episode (lines 12–30) again carefully, and then tell about Masters' visit as Coke might have written it down later. Begin like this:

   'When Masters arrived, I let Kate open the door. From the sitting-room, I heard Masters say 'Good afternoon' . . .'

5. **Transfer Exercise**

   Write a number of true sentences about yourself using this model:

   'I didn't want to do it myself, so I
       asked someone else to do it.
       told someone else to do it.
       made someone else do it.

   Examples:

   'I didn't want to do the shopping myself, so I made my sister do it.'
   'I didn't want to see him myself, so I asked my friend to see him.'

Unit 20
a Future in the past

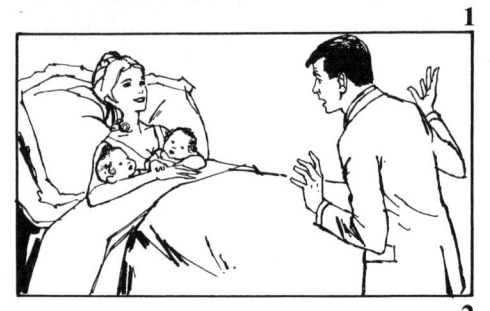

1
(a) Why/man surprised?
(b) What is the man saying?
 (sure/one baby)
 (never/twins!)

2
(a) When/Sheriff/saloon?
(b) Who/at the bar?
(c) Why/Jones/shoot?
(d) What/man really?

3
(a) When/millionaire/'a little present'?
(b) What/he/just?
(c) Why/she/surprised?

4
(a) Where/Peter/tell/girl friend/take?
(b) Peter/know/crowded?
(c) What/girl think?
(d) she/stay?

Main Teaching-Points
1. The formation and use of 'was/were going to do' as a future in the past
   a) after 'thought', 'never dreamt', 'had no idea', 'was sure', etc., as in 'I never dreamt you were going to have twins'.
   b) after *told* and *said*, as in 'He *told her* he was going to give her . . .' and 'He *said* she was going to have only . . .'.
2. Preview discrimination between *say* and *tell*.

Extra Points and Activities
1. Revision practice of 'has/have just done' vs 'did . . . ago'.
2. Use of *have* in 'have a baby/have twins'.
3. Meaning and use of *realise*, as in 'I never realised you were going to . . .'.
4. Use of *find* in 'She doesn't find it very elegant'.

| thought / had no idea / was sure / never dreamt | something | WAS GOING TO HAPPEN |

Unit 20
a

1

This man's wife has just had twins. Two months ago the doctor said she was going to have only one baby. The man is very surprised. "I was sure you were going to have only one baby. I never dreamt you were going to have twins!" he is saying.

1. What has just happened?
2. Why is the man so surprised?
3. Ask if the doctor knew!
4. What is the man saying?
5. Now correct the false statements like this:
   Prompt: The woman has just had a baby.
   Response: No, she has just had twins.
   a) The doctor told them she was going to have twins.
   b) The man knew she was going to have twins.

2

This is a scene from a cowboy film. Sheriff Wyatt Jones came into the Crazy Cactus Saloon a few seconds ago. A stranger was standing at the bar when Jones came in. He put his hand in his pocket and Jones shot him dead.
"I thought he was going to take out a revolver. I thought he was going to shoot me. That's why I shot him first!" Jones is saying. In fact, the man was only going to look at his watch.

1. What was the stranger doing when Jones came in?
2. What did the stranger do?
3. What did Jones do? Ask why!
4. What was the stranger really going to do?
5. Correct the statements as before!
   a) Jones knew the man.
   b) He shot him because he did not like him.
   c) He knew he was going to take out his watch.

3

A few weeks before Christmas the old millionaire told his young girl friend that he was going to give her "a little present". It is Christmas morning now. He has just given her the present. In fact, he has not given her "a little present" at all. He has just given her a large diamond ring. The girl is very surprised. "I never realised you were going to give me a diamond ring. I thought you were going to give me a watch, or something like that!" she is saying.

1. What did he tell her a few weeks ago?
2. What day is it now and what has he just done?
3. Why is the girl so surprised?
4. Correct the statements in full sentences!
   a) The girl thought he was going to give her a car.
   b) The girl realised two weeks ago he was going to give her the ring.

4

A few hours ago Peter told one of his girl friends he was going to take her to a "quiet, elegant restaurant". They have just come in.
"I had no idea it was going to be so crowded," Peter is saying. The girl thought it was going to be an elegant place. She does not find it very elegant, at all. She wants to go somewhere else.

1. What did Peter tell the girl earlier?
2. What is he saying now?
3. What did the girl think before she came?
4. Correct the statements as before!
   a) The girl finds the place elegant.
   b) Peter knew it was going to be like this.
   c) The girl wants to stay.

Unit 20 b FORMATION AND MANIPULATION

1 Stress

Remember to use the weak (unstressed) forms of was [wəz] and were [wə] when speaking.

2 Notice the construction

A	B	C
I didn't know	you he she they	were	going to do that

What changes must we make in box B when we use words like *he, she,* etc., instead of *you*?

A	B	C
I never dreamt	you were	going to do that

i) What other phrases can you think of to go in box A? Make complete sentences.
ii) Make more sentences by replacing 'you were' in box B.
iii) Think of some things you didn't know were going to happen. Make sentences beginning 'I had no idea/I didn't know/etc.' Then think of at least six other things to go in box C.

3 Notice the construction

A	B	C	D	E
The doctor said	she	was going to	have	only one baby

i) Think of other words to replace 'the doctor'.
ii) Think of other words to replace those in boxes B, D and E.

4 Read this. Notice the question and answer that come from it. Then, with someone else, do the same with the other sentences.

> Julia went out at 8 without an umbrella. It began to rain at 9.
> Question: DID SHE KNOW IT WAS GOING TO RAIN?
> Answer: NO, I DON'T THINK SO, BECAUSE SHE DIDN'T TAKE HER UMBRELLA

i) Julia ran to the bus stop but the bus came late.
ii) Susan put on her light summer clothes. It got very cold later.
iii) Peter's girl friend put on her best clothes. He took her to a very cheap restaurant.
iv) The stranger did not even look at Sheriff Jones. Jones shot him dead.

FORMATION AND MANIPULATION

Unit 20 b

1. As mentioned in Unit 19, the students should now be using weak (unstressed) forms automatically. Spend some time reminding them of this and practising the weak forms of *was* [wəz] and *were* [wə].

2. *Note on* THAT
   Make students practise both using and omitting THAT. Tell them that the tendency in spoken English is to omit THAT for reasons of speed in speaking. Remind students that neither using nor omitting THAT can be termed 'right' or 'wrong' in the structures being practised in this Unit.

   Invention Exercise

   Use this after students have completed Part 2. Give the following prompts orally and ask students to invent sentences using the five structures being practised. Write some of these prompts on the blackboard for a writing phase which can come during or after the oral phase:
   arrive so late/give him the book/be so angry/it was going to rain/the train was going to come early/she–marry him/the man–arrive today/the rocket–take off today/we–a picnic/the radio–so expensive/window–break/telephone–ring/my wife–twins/sheriff–shoot him/you–me–a present.
   Now, have you given the students a writing phase yet? If not, ask them to write five sentences (or more) using the prompts you wrote on the blackboard during the oral phase. (Remember to tell the students to omit *that* when speaking, but to include it occasionally for practice when writing.)

3. Give students oral and written practice (after the exercises) in forming questions and negatives with *say* and *tell*. Give the following prompts. Use the same technique as above (Invention exercise) to alternate oral and written work.
   come immediately/wait for me/phone later/do it/send one/ask them/eat it/buy one/get it/help her/make it/sell them/come in soon.
   e.g. Did he say he was going to come immediately?
   She didn't say they were going to wait for me.

Extra Fluency Practice

I HAD NO IDEA IT WAS GOING TO RAIN
1. come early
2. stop raining
3. be late
4. she was
5. I never dreamt
6. I had no idea
7. do that
8. they were
9. ask for tea
10. I thought
11. Bill was
12. ask him to come in

Unit 20 C

EXPLOITATION OF THE EPISODE

Key Structures and Vocabulary	*Suggested Explanations*
a) hysterical (2)	very excited and emotional. If a person becomes hysterical, he often starts screaming and shouting.
b) he burst out (4)	Here, he shouted.
c) he gaped at her (11)	He looked at her with eyes and mouth wide open.
d) he mumbled (22)	He spoke very unclearly in a soft voice.
e) He could not take his eyes off . . . (30)	He kept looking at (or staring at) . . .
f) in cold blood (34)	If one person shoots or kills another person in cold blood, they do it without any feeling.

Section 1
1. Listening phase followed by short-answer questions, such as
a) What did Masters pull out?
b) Where was Kate standing?
c) What part did Kate once play in a film?
d) What did she have to learn for that part?
2. Correct my statements
a) Masters put out a foot to push Kate away!
b) Kate threw Masters onto the sofa!
c) Coke left the automatic on the floor!
3. Ask students if they can use these phrases in sentences of their own:
a) stand in someone's way
b) put out a hand
c) could hardly believe (my) eyes
d) One moment . . ., the next

Section 2
1. First listening phase followed by questions:
a) What did Masters do? (He groaned.)
b) Why did he groan? (Because he could hardly believe what had happened.)
c) Why did he shake his head? (Because it all seemed incredible.)
d) He thought he was having a dream. What sort of dream? (A nightmare.)
2. Second listening phase followed by a completion exercise.
3. Fluency practice (Revision of 'mind . . . ing' from Unit 17)
PERHAPS YOU WOULDN'T MIND ANSWERING SOME QUESTIONS
a) looking at this
b) opening the door
c) coming back later
d) waiting a moment
e) getting here a bit earlier
f) having an Italian meal

Section 3
1. Silent reading phase. Ask students to note down some questions which they can ask other students after they have finished reading.
2. Then read the text (or play the tape) again and ask students to repeat in chorus the dialogue of the text, focusing their attention upon the intonation, particularly with sentences and utterances like—
'I don't know what you're talking about.'
'You can't make me tell you anything.'
and
'Couldn't I?'
3. Fluency practice
I'LL GIVE YOU FIVE SECONDS TO BEGIN ANSWERING MY QUESTIONS!
(prompts to replace 'five seconds' and 'begin answering my questions')
a) start the job
b) ten minutes
c) finish the job
d) 3 weeks
e) to do the work
f) a day
g) to find the information
h) 2 hours
i) to do the test

THE MAN WHO ESCAPED
Episode 20

Unit 20

C

SYNOPSIS: *Masters has come to Kate's flat. He has just looked at Coke carefully and realised who he is. He has pulled out an automatic pistol.*

1 When Masters pulled out the automatic, Kate was standing between him and Coke. She could see that he was almost hysterical and was probably going to shoot.
"It's you! Coke!" he burst out and came nearer. Kate was standing in his way now and he put out a hand to push her away.
Coke could hardly believe his eyes. One moment Masters was pointing a pistol at him and the next he was lying on the floor, gasping for breath. Kate had thrown him over her shoulder. "I once played a policewoman in a film and I had to learn some judo," she said rather casually and looked down at Masters. Coke did not simply stare in surprise, he gaped at her. Then he picked up the automatic that Masters had dropped and gaped again.

2 Masters groaned. He, too, could hardly believe what had happened. It all seemed incredible. He shook his head. He decided that it was probably all a nightmare, a horrible dream. He was sure that he was going to wake up at any moment, safe in his own bed. He blinked his eyes several times, hoping that Kate and Coke were somehow going to disappear. He blinked again, but when he opened his eyes, they were still there.
"And now that you're here, perhaps you wouldn't mind answering some questions," Coke said. Masters groaned again.
"Questions? What questions?" he mumbled. He was still in a daze.
"I want you to tell me everything that happened that evening you sent me to Epping Forest," Coke said in a low voice. Masters now realised that it was not a dream. For a moment he thought he was going to be sick.

3 "I don't know what you're talking about," Masters answered.
"I think you do," Coke said.
"You can't make me tell you anything!" Masters waited to see what Coke was going to do next. He could not take his eyes off the automatic in Coke's hands.
"I'll give you five seconds to begin answering my questions. Then I'll shoot," was all Coke said.
"You couldn't shoot me like that, in cold blood!"
"Couldn't I?" Coke answered, and pulled back the safety-catch. The pistol was now ready to fire. Then he began counting.

Unit 20 d

FURTHER PRACTICE

1. Invention Exercise

Make sentences with:
'I thought   he/she/it was going to . . .'
'I had no idea   we/you/they were going to . . .'

Example:
PROMPT: café/so crowded
RESPONSE: I had no idea the café was going to be so crowded.

Example:
PROMPT: work early today
RESPONSE: I thought you were going to leave work early today.
      or: I thought they were going to get to work early today.

Prompts:

a) fine yesterday
b) programme/so uninteresting
c) tests/so difficult
d) the bill himself
e) in bed yesterday
f) her a present
g) concert/so good
h) a party tomorrow night
i) film/so bad
j) a holiday in Scotland this year

2. Conversation

In the conversation in Unit 13, Tom Atkins described an accident he saw. A small white Ford shot out in front of a blue car. In this conversation we hear the two lawyers questioning the driver of the blue car.

1ST LAWYER: Please tell the court exactly what happened.
DRIVER: Certainly. I was driving home along Harbour Road. I was just going to slow down when I saw a small white Ford in a side road. I was sure he was going to wait there until I drove past. I had no idea he was going to shoot out in front of me.
1ST LAWYER: In other words, the driver of the white Ford shot out without any warning, is that right?
DRIVER: Exactly. It was completely unexpected.
1ST LAWYER: And you had no idea this was going to happen?
DRIVER: No! None whatsoever!
1ST LAWYER: Thank you.
2ND LAWYER: Hmm . . . you say you were going to slow down when the accident happened, is that right?
DRIVER: Yes, it is. I was going to slow down.
2ND LAWYER: I see. I suppose you were going very fast at the time.
DRIVER: No, not at all! I was doing 30, that's all.
2ND LAWYER: Well, why were you going to slow down, then? That suggests to me, and I'm sure to the court as well, that you were going too fast in the first place.
DRIVER: No! The reason I was going to slow down was very simple. I was going to turn into the next side road.
2ND LAWYER: Really? Why?
DRIVER: Because I live there, that's why!

Questions

1. What did the driver of the blue car think the other driver was going to do?
2. What did the other driver do? Ask if the driver of the blue car knew this!
3. What makes the 2nd lawyer think he was going very fast?
4. Ask and answer why he was going to slow down!

Recall

Without looking at the text, see if you can remember these parts of the conversation.
1ST LAWYER: any idea/happen?
DRIVER: whatsoever
2ND LAWYER: say/slow down/right?
DRIVER: Yes. down.
2ND LAWYER: very fast?
DRIVER: 30
2ND LAWYER: slow down then?
DRIVER: into the next side road. live.

FURTHER PRACTICE

Unit 20
d

1. Invention Exercise

a) Follow the technique of doing this exercise suggested in earlier Units.

b) Notice that this exercise practises not only 'was/were going to' after 'I thought' or 'I had no idea', but that it forces in particular the use of 'I had no idea' with phrases like 'so good', 'so difficult' and so on.

c) After students have given sentences according to the models here, ask them to use the same prompts to form questions with 'Did you really think . . .?' and 'Did you have any idea . . .?' + 'was/were going to'.

d) Finally, use the same prompts again for sentences with 'I was sure . . .' and 'I never dreamt . . .'

e) The verbs which could be used are:
for a) *was going to be;* for b) *was going to be;* for c) *were going to be;* for d) *was going to pay;* for e) *was/were going to stay;* for f) *was/were going to get, to buy, to give* or *to send;* for g) *was going to be;* for h) *was/were going to have, to hold, to give* or *to go to;* for i) *was going to be;* and for j) *was/were going to have, to take* or *to go on.*

2. Conversation

Key Points
1. Revision of 'was doing . . . when . . . did'
2. Practice with the pattern 'I was just going to . . . when . . .'
3. Meaning and use of *until* as in '. . . wait there until I drove past'
4. Meaning and use (and intonation) of 'No, not at all' as a strong denial
5. Meaning and use of the verb 'suggest to someone'
6. Meaning and use of 'in the first place' (= in the beginning; to start with)
7. Meaning and use of 'None whatsoever'

Presentation Notes
1. Follow the same initial presentation procedure as with previous Units. (As an optional introduction to the Conversation, you could read – or play – again the Conversation on page 78 (Unit 13), asking a number of questions and reminding them of some of the patterns and vocabulary.)
2. Choral reading phase followed by the students reading the Conversation in groups of three. Go around and listen to them, correcting errors in pronunciation and intonation. (This grouping phase might be left until the end of more detailed study and practice with pattern from the Conversation.)
3. To practise the pattern *I was just going to (do) . . . when . . .,* give three or four examples of the pattern:
   'I was just going to have lunch when the phone rang.'
   'I was just going to cross the road when a bus came along.'
   'I was just going to go out when I received a telegram.'
   – and then ask students to recall the sentences from these prompts:
   a) lunch/phone   c) out/telegram
   b) road/bus
   Then ask them to write two or three examples of their own.
4. *Fluency Practice*
   I WAS SURE HE WAS GOING TO WAIT THERE UNTIL I DROVE PAST.
   (Prompts replace 'drove past'.)
   a) arrived   d) sent for him
   b) telephoned him   e) finished talking
   c) got the tickets   f) could see him

Unit 20 e/f

e   Summary

1
Focus students' attention once again on the unstressed forms of *was* [wəz] and *were* [wə]. Also add other phrases that often precede the use of 'was/were going to', such as: 'I was absolutely convinced', 'I didn't have the faintest idea (that) . . .', 'It didn't occur to me (that) . . .' etc. If the class has enough control of the other phrases introduced and practised in the Unit, drill such new phrases in the same way as the others – and perhaps introduce them by putting them in place of others in the presentation situations.

2
As the use of 'was/were going to' with *say* and *tell* follows the pattern of the other sentences in 1, there is no need at this stage to point out the pattern as an example of Reported Speech. In the same way, the discrimination between *say* and *tell* can be left purely as preview items, although students may well notice already that *tell* must be followed by a person.

f   Exercises for homework

2
This sort of exercise allows for fairly free expression within the given framework of a pattern, and we feel it is an activity which should be cultivated by students, as they can learn to transfer this particular type of learning activity if they go on studying on their own. The first item (a) can give rise to an almost infinite number of sentences, for example:
'We didn't really know it was going to snow.
　　　　　the holidays were going
　　　　　　to be so terrible.
　　　　　the book was going to be
　　　　　　so boring.
　　　　　she was going to have a
　　　　　　baby so soon.

3
This exercise forces students to combine a pattern which they studied and practised some time ago with the new pattern. Students should be encouraged to do this type of exercise as much as possible: if they can apply such sentences to their own personal experience, so much the better.

4
The letter in Unit 18 was fairly free. The Guided Composition here is the least controlled so far. Like the letter in Unit 18, it is not based on any specific piece of material which they have studied. Rather, it is an exercise in which students can provide most of the ideas and 'story-line' themselves. They should be made aware, however, that the prompt phrases provided often force the use of a pattern which they have practised earlier in the book. For example, 'She was still waiting . . .' almost demands a completion something like '. . . when I finally arrived.'
This could be prepared in class as a 'combined effort' composition. On the other hand, students could simply be asked to write it for homework.

Unit 20
e/f

e Summary

Focal points in this Unit.

1. These are the main patterns we have learned in this Unit:

   a) I thought
   b) I had no idea
   c) I was sure   + (that)   he was going to do that.
   d) I never dreamt   they were going to come.
   e) I never realised

   Note that in everyday conversation, we nearly always leave out the word *that*.

2. Remember too how we use 'was/were going to do' after the verbs *say* and *tell*:

   a) The doctor said she was going to have only one baby.
   b) He told his young girl friend that he was going to give her a little present.

3. Remember the other pattern with 'going to' used by the driver in the Conversation on page 120:

   'I was just going to slow down when I saw a small white Ford . . .'

   Notice the position of the word *just*.

f Exercises for homework

1. Do all the exercises on pages 117, 118 and 120.

2. Complete these sentences using 'was/were going to . . .'

   a) We didn't really know . . .
   b) The doctor didn't think . . .
   c) The driver never dreamt . . .
   d) Peter never realised . . .
   e) Tom was sure . . .
   f) We all thought . . .
   g) The girl had no idea . . .

3. Do you remember the pattern 'He . . . *so (well/fast/badly* etc.) that . . .'? We practised it in Unit 7. Look at these 2 sentences. They combine 'so . . . that . . .' and 'thought, etc. . . . was going to . . .'

   He *drove so fast that I thought he was going to have* an accident.
   She *played so beautifully that I was sure she was going to win* a prize.

   Now write more sentences like this using the prompts:

   a) dangerously/job
   b) slowly/late
   c) badly/walk out
   d) carelessly/the football match
   e) fast/early

4. **Guided Composition**

   Write a short story about a day that turned out badly. Begin with this sentence:

   'When I woke up, the sun was shining and I thought it was going to be a glorious day.'

   Then use these phrases for the beginnings of some of the sentences:

   'It was the first day . . .'/'As soon as . . .'/ 'When I went into the garage . . .'/'The tyre . . .'/'I never realised . . .'/'Two hours later . . .'/'She was still waiting . . .'/'Just then it began . . .'/'It was still raining . . .'/ 'The weather was so . . .'/

5. **Transfer Exercise**

   Look at the patterns in point 1 of the *Focal points in this Unit*. Use each of them to write 2 true sentences about yourself, the weather, the lesson etc.

Unit 21
a Past perfect

1 
(a) Why/policeman/man/station?
(b) Who/corner?
(c) When/arrest?

2 
(a) How long ago/accident/happen?
(b) What/Peter/see?
(c) Why/policeman/man/station?

3 
(a) Who/Julia/bank?
(b) Why/nightsafe?
(c) What/man?
(d) Julia's answer?

4 
(a) Who/ask/questions?
(b) How long ago?
(c) What/Julia/when/man?
(d) ever before then?

5 
(a) Who/Arthur's office?
(b) What have they done to his desk? letters? money? lamp?
(c) Why/run away?

6 
(a) Who/ask/questions?
(b) Arthur/see thieves?
(c) What/Arthur/see?
(d) What sort/mess/they?

Main Teaching-Points
1. Past Perfect Simple in statements, questions and negatives, especially followed by the Past Simple, as in 'I had just put the money in the night-safe when I saw him'.
2. The use of *just, ever* and *never* with the Past Perfect: 'I'd just put . . .'/'Had you ever seen . . .?'/'No, I had never seen him . . .'.
3. Contracted forms 'I'd/he'd/we'd etc.' + past participle; and the short answers 'Yes, I had/No, I hadn't, etc.'.

Extra Points and Activities
1. Discrimination drill – *I'd done it* vs *I've done it* etc.
2. Further practice with past participles: been/run/hit/thrown/taken/made/seen etc.
3. Short revision of *did* vs *was doing* – (situation 2) 'When I got . . ., a policeman *was taking* . . .'.
4. Meaning and use of: 'run into' (situation 1); 'frightened' (situation 3); 'make a terrible mess' (situation 6).

Unit 21 a

HAD DONE SOMETHING WHEN SOMETHING ELSE HAPPENED

1

One car has run into another. A policeman is taking one of the drivers to the police station because, just after the accident, the man got out and hit the other driver. Peter has just come round the corner. The policeman arrested the man a few seconds ago.

1. What has one car done?
2. Ask what the policeman is doing!
3. Ask why!
4. What has Peter just done?
5. What did the policeman do a few seconds ago?

2

Peter is talking about what he saw a few hours ago. "I saw there had been an accident. One car had run into another. When I got there, a policeman was taking one driver to the station. The man had hit the other driver. That's why the policeman had arrested him."

1. What does Peter say that shows he did not see the accident itself?
2. What had one car done?
3. What was the policeman doing? Why?
4. What had the policeman done?

3

The office manager has sent Julia to the bank with a lot of money, but it has closed. That is why she has put it in the night-safe. A man has suddenly appeared. "I want your money!" he has just shouted.

"But I've put it in the night-safe!" Julia is saying. She is very frightened.

1. What has the office manager done?
2. What has Julia done with the money? Why?
3. What has the man just shouted?
4. Why can't Julia give him the money?

4

A policeman is asking Julia questions.
"When did all this happen?"
"Half an hour ago. I'd just put the money in the night-safe when I saw him."
"Had you ever seen the man before then?"
"No, I hadn't. He was a total stranger."

1. What is happening now?
2. Why didn't the man get the money?
3. Why didn't Julia take the money into the bank itself?
4. Correct the statements!
   a) She was going to put the money into the safe when she saw the man.
   b) She knew the man.

5

Thieves have broken into Arthur's office. They have emptied his desk, thrown all his letters on the floor and have taken most of the money from the safe. They have also smashed the lamp on his desk. They are running away because they have just heard Arthur in the office outside.

1. What have they done to his desk?
2. What else have they done?
3. What are they doing now? Why?
4. Correct the statements!
   a) They have taken all the money.
   b) They have left his letters in the desk.

6

A policeman is asking Arthur questions.
"Did you see the thieves?"
"No, they'd already run away when I came in."
"What did you see when you came in?"
"Nothing, except what they'd done. They'd made a terrible mess."

1. Why didn't Arthur see the thieves?
2. Make as many sentences as you can beginning "Arthur saw they had . . ."!
3. Ask questions beginning:
   "Had they . . . when he got there?"
   Answer "Yes, they had"/"No, they hadn't."

Unit 21 b

FORMATION AND MANIPULATION

1 Pronunciation

Remember that the word *had* has a short form *'d* [d] and a weak (unstressed) form [(h)əd].

2 Study this example:

A	B	C	D	E
She had ('d)	already just	left	when he	phoned

i) Think of some words to replace 'she' in box A. (Remember that you can use words like 'Peter' and 'the bus'.)
ii) Now, think of some words to replace 'left' in box C.
iii) Now, think of some words to replace 'phoned' in box E.
iv) Using the words you have thought of write or say ten sentences using *already* or *just*.

3 Study this table:

Julia hadn't	got up washed the dishes eaten finished her work got dressed	when Jim got there

i) Use this table for this conversation. Talk with another person.
   A: 'Why did Jim have to wait for Julia?'   B: 'Because she hadn't . . .'
ii) Use the table again to ask questions like this. Talk with someone else and tell him to take B's part.
   A: 'Had Julia . . . when Jim got there?'   B: 'No, she hadn't. That's why he had to wait.'

4 Look at this conversation
   A: 'What had happened when she got there?'   B: 'They'd already left.'
Make other conversations like this with the person sitting next to you using the following prompts:
   i) A: got there   B: left   iv) A: went in   B: started
   ii) A: arrived   B: telephoned   v) A: rain started   B: game stopped
   iii) A: saw it   B: finished   vi) A: man came   B: she gone
Now, do the same thing again using the word *just* instead of *already*.

FORMATION AND MANIPULATION

Unit 21 b

1. Discourage students from using the strong (stressed) form of *had*. Encourage them to use the unstressed and short forms, but point out that of these only the short form can be used in written English.
   Point out to students that the action described by the 'had done' form took place BEFORE the action described by the 'did' form— that is why the two different forms are used.

2. Use the exercises as a basis for the following classwork:
   Ask the students to look at the exercises for a little time, a minute or so, then ask them to give you their suggestions for replacements for the various boxes. Write these down on the blackboard so as to form a substitution table similar in form to table 3 on the student page. Put them in a framework like this:

A	B	C	D	E
	already just		when he	

   Remember only to ask for replacements to boxes A, C and E. If any of the other boxes are changed, you may produce a table which will give unrealistic sentences.

3. Use the table both for oral and written work. Work around the class (but not in any predictable order) asking students to produce sentences orally. Try to develop a lively pace, but don't turn the activity into a competition of speed. From time to time vary the activity by introducing a short writing phase. Ask students to write five sentences. As this is one of the longest structures so far practised, it may be necessary for you to insert an example of your own based on the table. Do this whenever the pace seems to be getting a little slow, or as a way of starting off the activity, to show students the sort of pace you require.

Extra Fluency Practice

I'D ALREADY GONE
1. She'd
2. arrived
3. Had she . . .?
4. just
5. She hadn't
6. seen him
7. met
8. spoken to
9. us

Unit 21

C

EXPLOITATION OF THE EPISODE

Key Structures and Vocabulary	Suggested Explanations
a) Coke had already *taken aim* (5)	He had already pointed the pistol in the direction he wanted to shoot.
b) Masters had been Coke's superior (12)	Masters had been in a position to give Coke orders.
c) Epping Forest (16)	A large forest outside London.
d) an informer (16)	An informer is a man (sometimes a criminal) who gives or sells information to the police or the secret service.
e) When he *came to*, (20)	When he regained consciousness...
f) deposited ... in his bank account (24–25)	If we put money into a bank account in order to save it, we often put it into a deposit account.
g) Masters *denied* he had ever told Coke (29–30)	Masters said that he had never told Coke...

Section 1
1. Listening phase (student books face down) followed by questions:
   a) Did Coke count to five? What number *did* he count to?
   b) Why did he stop at 4? (Because...)
   c) How much did Masters say he knew when Coke started counting?
   d) What did he say when Coke said 'Four!'?
2. Optional practice
   Using 'I'll tell you anything you want' as a Model, ask students to make more sentences from these prompts:
   For example:
   Prompts: bring/need
   Response: He'll bring you anything you need.
   a) show/want
   b) give/need
   c) cook/want
   d) make/like
   e) send/want

Section 2
1. Silent reading phase followed by questions:
   a) When had Coke and Masters been in the Army Intelligence Unit?
   b) Had they *both* been officers?
   c) Who had been the superior officer?
   d) On whose orders had Coke gone to Epping Forest?
   e) How many men had grabbed Coke while he was waiting for the informer?
2. Completion exercise.
3. Ask students to listen to the passage once again, and then ask them to reproduce a part of it orally. Give prompts: one evening/lonely place// possible informer//3 men// whisky/head//

Section 3
1. Sample questions (after listening phase):
   a) Where was Coke when he came to?
   b) Who had already arrived?
   c) Why did the police think he had got drunk?
   d) What did they find in his car?
2. Choral reading phase, focusing attention on the stress of new words:
   For example: 'ap'parently de'posited...'bank account'
3. Fluency practice based on the sentence 'Coke swore he had never seen them before'.
   I SAID I HAD NEVER SEEN HIM BEFORE
   a) her
   b) met
   c) He
   d) They
   e) spoken to
   f) I
   g) him
   h) We

THE MAN WHO ESCAPED
Episode 21

Unit **21**

c

SYNOPSIS: *Kate has thrown Masters over her shoulder. Coke has grabbed his pistol and has told Masters he will kill him if he does not answer his questions. Coke is going to count up to five before he shoots.*

1 "But I know nothing!" Masters protested. Coke had already raised the pistol and simply said, "One!" Masters said nothing.
"Two!" Coke brought the pistol nearer.
"You can't frighten me!" Masters shouted.
"Three!" Masters saw Coke had already taken aim.
"How can I tell you something I don't know?" Masters demanded.
"Four!" Masters watched Coke's finger beginning to press the trigger.
"All right, all right, I'll tell you anything you want, but for God's sake, put that pistol down!" Masters gasped.

2 Coke's mind went back to the time, five years earlier, when both he and Masters had been officers in the same Army Intelligence unit. Masters had been Coke's superior. Several important military secrets had disappeared and they were both trying to find out who had taken them.

One evening, Coke had gone, on Masters' orders, to a lonely place in Epping Forest. Masters had told him he would meet a possible informer there. While he was waiting, three men had grabbed him from behind. They had poured whisky all over him and down his throat and then hit him over the head.

3 When he came to, he was back in his car, but it had crashed into a tree. The police had already arrived. It appeared that Coke had got drunk and lost control of his car. The police had found several files marked 'Top Secret' in his car. Coke swore he had never seen them before. The police also found Coke had apparently deposited more than £2,000 in his bank account a few weeks before. Coke had known nothing of the money. The bank said the cheques had arrived by post, drawn on a Swiss bank, with Coke's countersignature. Nobody believed Coke's story. It appeared he had sold secrets for money and was going to do so again the night he had crashed. Masters denied he had ever told Coke to go to Epping Forest. This is what Coke wanted to ask questions about now.

Unit 21 d

FURTHER PRACTICE

1. For Comprehension

Read this newspaper report and then answer the questions:

LIVERPOOL UNITED VS. REAL VALENCIA
by our Football Correspondent, Hugh MacTully.

This was a wonderful match. The two teams had been playing for only 3 minutes when Gomez scored the first goal. Jimenez had almost scored a minute before.

Liverpool came back with a fine attack. Unfortunately Tarleston, their centre forward, left the field in the 35th minute. He had hurt his ankle badly earlier, but had been playing despite the injury.

Bobby Good scored for Liverpool in the 40th minute. He had taken a pass from Biles, had run 40 yards and had beaten at least 3 Valencia defenders when Torez almost brought him down with a hard tackle. Good got past him somehow, shot over the head of the goalkeeper and scored.

Final Score: Liverpool United 1   Real Valencia 1

a) How long had they been playing when Gomez scored?
b) Did Jimenez score a goal in this match?
c) Did Tarleston leave the field the moment he hurt his ankle?
d) Cover the text and write down what Good had done when he scored the equalising goal for Liverpool. (Prompts: a pass from Biles/ 40 yards/3 Valencia defenders)

2. Conversation

Arthur is at dinner with an old friend, George Tetley. George has just told Arthur a joke.

ARTHUR: (laughing loudly) That was very good. I'd never heard that one before.
GEORGE: Hadn't you? Well, here's another one like it. This one's about a travelling salesman named Phil, who was quite a whisky-drinker. Phil had gone to a strange town one day and had spent the evening in a pub. He'd drunk quite a lot and had just come out of the pub when he saw another man in the middle of the road. The other man had been in the pub, too, and had drunk even more than Phil had. He'd obviously seen something strange in the sky because he was pointing upwards. 'Excuse me,' the man asked Phil, 'is that the sun or the moon?' Phil looked at it for a second and then said, 'I'm afraid I can't help you. I'm a stranger here myself'.
ARTHUR: (laughing again) Very good. Now let me tell you one. A doctor was examining a lady who was no longer very young. She'd fallen down and had hurt her knee. The doctor wanted to be sure that that was all she'd hurt. 'Tell me,' he asked her casually, 'how old are you?'. 'Twenty-five' was the answer. The doctor wrote 'Loss of Memory' down on his notes.

Questions

1. Where had Phil spent the evening and what had he done there?
2. When did he notice the man and why?
3. What did the other man ask and what was Phil's answer?
4. Why was the doctor examining the lady?
5. What did he ask her and what did he do afterwards? Ask why!

Recall

Tell someone else both jokes without looking at the text.
Use these prompt words to help you.
Phil/strange town and/evening/pub. quite a lot/ just out when/man/road. something strange/sky. upwards. 'Excuse me'

doctor/lady/very young. fallen down/knee. doctor/sure that was all. 'How old . . .?' 'Twenty-five'. memory.

FURTHER PRACTICE

Unit 21
d

1. For Comprehension

a) Ask students to read this report silently for two or three minutes. Tell them not to worry if they do not understand one or two words, as you will explain these in a moment.

b) Now ask a number of simple factual short-answer questions, for example:
   Who were the two teams in the match?
   Did Liverpool win?
   Did Real Valencia win?
   What was the score, then?

c) Now explain, and use in sentences for choral repetition, some of the vocabulary items which you think are causing difficulty:
   (to) score a goal; a fine attack; ankle; despite (the injury);
   (to) take a pass; he brought him down with a hard tackle.

d) Now read the report aloud, followed by choral repetition.

e) Use a text completion technique to aid comprehension.

f) Ask the questions on the student page and get oral responses. (Optional: To provide a different activity before studying the Conversation, ask students quickly to write down the answers to the same questions.)

2. Conversation

Key Points
1. Meaning and use of vocabulary items: 'tell someone a joke'; 'travelling salesman'; 'obviously'; 'knee'; 'casually'; 'loss of memory'
2. Meaning and use of *spend* as in 'had spent the evening in a pub'
3. Use of *just* with *had done* as in 'He had just come out of the pub when . . .'
4. Revision and practice with Past Continuous 'was doing'
5. Revision of the use of 'Excuse me' before asking or telling someone something

6. Practice with 'I'm afraid I can't help you. I'm a stranger here myself'

Presentation Notes
1. Follow the same presentation procedure used with previous Conversations.
2. Ask a number of general questions, for example:
   a) Who is Arthur having dinner with?
   b) Why is Arthur laughing at the beginning of the conversation?
   c) What was the name of the travelling salesman in the first joke?
   d) In the second joke, how old did the lady say she was?
3. *Optional Practice*
   Ask students to repeat in chorus (using the intonation on the tape)–
   'I'm afraid I can't help you. I'm a stranger here myself.'
   Then ask questions (to the whole class and then to individuals) with–
   'Excuse me. Could you tell me the way to . . .?'
   –and get students to give the response they have just repeated above in chorus. Finally pair students and get them to ask each other the way to places. Use the names of streets, buildings, villages etc. they know.
4. *Fluency Practice* with *spend (time) (somewhere)*
   HE SPENT THE EVENING IN THE PUB.
   a) We   f) 3 weeks
   b) at the cinema   g) She
   c) at a dance   h) 6 months
   d) They   i) in Paris
   e) in London   j) a weekend

Unit 21
e/f

e Summary

1
One of the greatest problems for students with regard to 'had done' is knowing when they must use the tense in English, and when they need not use it. Give examples showing that if we describe a number of consecutive actions in the past in a chronological order, there is no need to use the Past Perfect. Thus:
'Yesterday morning I *woke up* at 7 o'clock. I *got* out of bed and *went* straight to the bathroom. I *washed*, *shaved* and *cleaned* my teeth, and then *went* back to my bedroom to get dressed. I *put* on my best suit and *went* downstairs to breakfast.'
If the starting point (and therefore the point of original interest) is 'went downstairs to breakfast', however, then when we start looking back from that point of interest, we begin to use the Past Perfect:
'By the time I went downstairs to breakfast, I *had already been* to the bathroom. I *had washed*, *shaved* and *cleaned* my teeth; and I *had put* on my best suit, because my boss *had phoned* the evening before and *had asked* me . . .'

2
Focus students' attention once again on the stressed and unstressed forms of *had*–
a) [(h)əd] as in 'They had run away'
b) [(h)æd] as in 'He hadn't drunk very much.' ['hæ(d)nt]
'Had you ever seen him before?' [hæd] and 'Yes, I had' ['hæd]/'No, I hadn't' ['hæ(d)nt]

f Exercises for homework

2
Although it is possible to make more of this type of exercise in the classroom by making Substitution Drills from the various sentences, it is probably best left as a pure homework exercise and marked rather as a short test.

3
This exercise is designed to make students use different forms of the verb in one sentence. For example:
'I *had never eaten* Chinese food before I *ate* some last night.'
As with the Transfer Exercise, students could be asked to make true sentences using the pattern.

4
Since Composition (a) is in effect a transformation exercise involving the use of structures and vocabulary in the two situations 5 and 6, it can usefully be prepared orally in the classroom and then set as a written homework exercise. Composition (b) asks for a re-telling of the events in situations 1 and 2, but in the form of a courtroom cross-examination. Whilst still bearing in mind that the main point to be practised is the use of 'had done', students should read the previous two conversations in court (pages 78 and 120) so that they can once again use patterns and vocabulary which they have already studied intensively once, but which they might not as yet have had to use again. This Composition, then, provides a means of practice with the focal point of the Unit together with active revision of earlier focal points.

Unit 21

e/f

e Summary

Focal points in this Unit.

1. In this Unit we have studied and practised the Past Perfect Tense 'had done' in sentences like—"When I got there, I saw there *had been* an accident.'
and 'They *had run* away when I came in.'
When we use 'had done' in English, we are concerned with what someone *had already done* or what *had already happened before* 'I got there' or 'I came in' etc.
We often make this more obvious by using a phrase like 'By then' or 'By the time . . .'
    Example:
    '*By the time* I got there, the thieves *had already escaped.*'

2. Remember the negative form—
    'He *hadn't drunk* very much.'
    and the question form—
    '*Had you ever seen* the man before then?'
    and the short answers—
    'Yes, I had'/'No, I hadn't', etc.

f Exercises for homework

1. Do all the exercises on pages 123, 124 and 126.

2. Supply the correct 'had done' form of the verb in brackets:
    a) When I went back to the shop, they (sell) the book I wanted.
    b) She (visit) England only twice before she came this year.
    c) As soon as they (go), I went straight to bed.
    d) When we got to the station, we found that the 8 o'clock train (already leave).
    e) When the police got to the bank, the thief (already escape).
    f) I spoke to the woman because I thought I (meet) her somewhere before.
    g) Deborah woke up with a terrible headache because she and Arthur (hold) a party the night before.

3. Look at these two sentences:
    I had never been to America before I went there last year.
    She had never seen the Eiffel Tower before she visited Paris last month.
Now write 5 sentences like this yourself. Use these verbs in the place of *been* and *seen* in the sentences above: eat, stay, drink, fly, visit.

4. **Guided Composition**
    a) Read situations 5 and 6 on page 123 again, and then write a short newspaper article (about 60 words) about the theft.
    Here is the headline:
    THIEVES BROKE INTO DIRECTOR'S OFFICE
    And begin your article:
    'At about 7.20 yesterday morning, thieves broke into the office of Arthur Tigers, director of the British Car Company. When Mr Tigers arrived at about 7.30, he found . . .'
    b) Read situations 1 and 2 on page 123 again, and then write the conversation in court one or two days later between a lawyer and Peter. The policeman had taken Peter's name and address as a witness, and Peter had to go to the court case.
    (Remember you read two Conversations like this before, one on page 78 and the other on page 120.)
    Begin like this:
    LAWYER: Now Mr Atkins, would you please tell the court what you saw when you arrived on the scene of the accident?

5. **Transfer Exercise**
Write true sentences about things that happened to you or another member of your family or a friend yesterday. Include a 'had done' idea at the same time. Here are two examples: When I got home yesterday evening, the rest of the family had already had dinner.
I had just gone out in the garden to sunbathe yesterday afternoon when it started to rain.

Unit 22
a Conditional sentences

1
(a) What/in tree?
(b) Why/not run?
(c) What/they/if?

2
(a) What/attendant/say?
(b) Tom's question?
(c) more expensive?

3
(a) What/Peter/say?
(b) Why/Tom/use it?

4
(a) What/ 2 men?
(b) Why/difficult?
(c) What/both men/say?
(the job?)
(these axes?)

5
(a) What/not understand?
(b) Why/not/job?

6
(a) Who/live/house?
(b) home/better/if:
grass?
gate?
flowers?

Main Teaching-Points
1. Formation and use of conditional sentences 'If they knew . . ., they would do . . .' and 'It would do . . . if it did/had/were . . .' in statements, negatives and questions.
2. Concentration on the unstressed form of *would* [d] as in 'I'd/he'd/we'd' etc. and [əd] in other sentences such as 'The job would . . .' pronounced 'The job'd . . .'
3. The forms *were* and *weren't* after *if*; and *could* after *if*.
4. Short answers *Yes, it would/No, it wouldn't* etc.: and short questions *Wouldn't it? Would it really?* etc.
5. The pattern *Would it be all right if I (did) . . .?*

Extra Points and Activities
1. Meaning of vocabulary items 'axe', 'sharp', 'electric saw' and 'petrol attendant'.
2. Meaning and use of *definitely* in 'Yes, it would! Definitely!'
3. Meaning and use of 'try to do'.
4. Revision of emphatic pronouns as in 'I need it *myself* . . .' and '. . . if he didn't need it *himself*'.
5. Meaning and use of *borrow* (vs. *lend*).
6. Meaning and use of *otherwise* (initial or final position) as in 'I'd let you have it otherwise'.

	WOULD COULD	DO IF	DID HAD WERE

Unit 22
a

1

These people do not know there is a snake in the tree. If they knew, they would probably start screaming and the man would drop his sandwich. If the man had a gun, he could shoot the snake.

1. Why don't the people get up and run now?
2. What would they all do if they knew?
3. Ask and answer the same type of question about
   a) the man   b) the woman
4. Why can't the man shoot the snake?
5. Now make a sentence: if/a gun/shoot.

2

"If I were you, I'd use Super Petrol. Your car would go faster if you did," the petrol attendant said a moment ago.
   "Would it really?" was Tom's question.
   "Yes, it would! Definitely!"
   "But wouldn't it be more expensive?"
   "No, it wouldn't!" is the answer.

1. What did the attendant say he would do if he were Tom? Ask why! (answer)
2. What was Tom's first question?
3. What was the answer and what did Tom ask then?
4. What is the attendant's answer?

3

Peter has just said "Would it be all right if I borrowed your car this evening? It'd help me a lot if I could use it." Tom would let him use it if he did not need it himself. He is saying: "Unfortunately, I need it myself this evening. I'd let you have it otherwise."

1. Ask and answer why Peter wants to borrow Tom's car!
2. What are the exact words of his question?
3. What is Tom's answer?
4. Ask and answer a question beginning "Would Tom . . . if . . . ?"

4

These two men are trying to cut down a very large tree. Their electric saw is broken. Their axes are not very sharp. "The job would be easy if that saw weren't broken!" one man has just said.
   "These axes would be all right if they were a bit sharper!" the other is saying.

1. What are these men doing?
2. Why is it so difficult?
3. Ask and answer the questions!
   a) easy/saw
   b) easy/axes sharper

5

"I can't understand why I can't find a job!" this man is saying. He would probably find one if he got a haircut, shaved off his beard, bought a new suit, put on a clean shirt and polished his shoes.

1. What is the man saying?
2. What do you think he should do?
3. Ask and answer questions beginning "Would he find a job if . . . ?"

6

Two very old, poor people live here. The house would look much better if they painted it, cut the grass, mended the gate and planted a few flowers. They would probably do this if they weren't so old and had a bit more money.

1. What sort of people live here?
2. Ask questions beginning: "Do you think the house would . . . if . . . ?"
3. Now ask and answer two questions beginning: "What would they do if . . . ?" (money/old)

Unit 22 b

FORMATION AND MANIPULATION

1 Pronunciation
  i) The word *would* has a short form [d] and a weak form [wəd].
     Example: If I could come, I'd [d] tell you.
                If I could come, I would [wəd] tell you.
  ii) The word *were* has a weak (unstressed) form [wə] which is very frequently used.
     Example: If I were [wə] you, I'd do it.

2 Look at and repeat these sentences:
  i) If they knew, they would start screaming.
  ii) Your car would go faster if you bought some.
  iii) Would it be all right if I borrowed your car?
  iv) If the man had a gun, he could shoot the snake.

Questions:
  i) What do you notice about sentences that begin with *If*?
  ii) Now, what about sentences that don't begin with *If*?
  iii) Does it make any difference if the sentence is a question?
  iv) So, what can you say about 'IF' and the comma?

3

A	B	C	D	E	F	G
If	the man	had a gun	,	he	could shoot	the snake

  i) Look at the situations on page 129 and find words to replace those in boxes B, C, E, F and G.
  ii) Now, make at least ten sentences from the new words you have found in exercise i.
  iii) Now, practise starting sentences with boxes E, F and G and finishing with A, B and C.

4

a)
| What could | he | do | if | he | had a gun? |

b)
| He | could | shoot | the snake |

Look at the answers you found for exercise 3 ii and use them to make questions and answers like those above. *Example:*
  a) What would you do if it rained?   b) I would (I'd) go home.

5

A	B	C
If I were you,	I'd	use super petrol

NOTE: We use this form to give advice.
Look at the situations on page 129. Give advice to all of the people.

6

A	B	C
Would it be all right if	I	borrowed your car . . .?

  i) Change the words in boxes B and C. Use words like these in box C: used the phone, got up late, had a bath, came in now, saw her, etc.
  ii) Think of other phrases to put in box C. (Look at the situations on page 129; you may find some help there.)

FORMATION AND MANIPULATION

Unit 22 b

1. This is a fine opportunity to teach the stressed (stong) forms of *could* and *would*. It is easily understood and not difficult to use. Use a short dialogue like this as an example:
   A: Why won't you help me?
   B: I *would* help you if I *could*.
   Give students oral prompts to create dialogues like this. Use these prompts (and any others you can think of): tell me, ask him, see him, marry her, buy it, get one, give up smoking, listen to it.

2. Students should be able to deduce the rule about the use of the comma from the exercise. However, if they can't, here it is.
   i) Sentences starting with 'IF' have a comma after the first part.
   ii) It makes no difference if the sentence is positive, negative or interrogative.

3. Make part of the exercises written, perhaps as the end of an oral phase. Get students to write a few examples both starting with and without 'IF'. Don't forget to insist on the correct use of the comma.
   Tell students why we choose to start the sentence with or without 'IF'. Quick definition: We start the sentence with the element which is most important to the speaker at the time of speaking. So, we emphasise the element that comes first.

4. Pair students for the short dialogue practice here.
   Practise first as indicated in the exercises, then, when students have reached a reasonable degree of fluency, get them to practise the shorter and very frequent dialogue form:
   A: What could he do if he had a gun?
   B: Shoot the snake. (i.e. omitting the first two boxes from the second sentence.)

5. A very frequent form in everyday use in English for giving advice.
   Invention Exercise Give these prompts for a quick oral invention exercise:
   I feel ill. I smoke too much. My car won't go. It's my wife's birthday tomorrow. I've lost my purse. The rain is coming in through the window. I can't see in this room. I'm tired.
   Tell students to look at situations **2** and **4** on page 129. Note that the word *were* is the same for all persons – 'if I were'/'if you were'/'if he were'/'if it were' etc.

6. After doing the exercises, spend a short time practising the 'Would it be all right if I . . .?' form orally. Get students to ask for permission to do various things connected with life in the classroom. They should at first ask the teacher for permission. Now, when students ask for permission, answer using various forms, for example: *Yes, that would be all right. Yes, all right. Yes, O.K. Yes, I think so. No, it wouldn't. No, I'm afraid not. No, that isn't allowed. Of course not!* etc. Each time you use a new form, write it on the blackboard. Then pair off the students to use the question and answer forms together. At sometime during the practice, remove the answer prompts from the board and get students to continue oral work. You can also ask them to write out two or three examples of dialogues.

Unit 22 c

EXPLOITATION OF THE EPISODE

Key Structures and Vocabulary	*Suggested Explanations*
a) Coke got a grip on himself (4)	He managed to control his strong feelings.
b) ...*ruin* any man... (19)	The sort of things that would put a stop to a man's career; he wouldn't be able to get a job again.
c) 'Why did you *involve* me...?' (21–22)	Why did you make me get mixed up in it; or make me get into this difficult situation?
d) 'The police suspected someone.' (23)	The police thought someone had done it.
e) microfilms (34)	Very small films which can be hidden inside pens, cigarettes, books etc.
f) '...*pose as* foreign collectors' (35)	They make people believe they are collectors of antiques, but they are really spies.

Section 1
1. Sample questions after listening phase:
a) Why did Coke hate Masters so much?
b) Why was it important for Coke to control himself and not kill Masters?
2. Correct my statements:
a) For a moment Coke wanted to sit down!
b) He had often killed people in cold blood!
c) Because of Masters, Coke had lost fourteen years of his freedom!
d) Coke couldn't control himself!
3. Focus students' attention on line 2: '... he found it difficult not to hate Masters.'
Write this on the blackboard.

I find it	difficult easy	not to do to do

Ask students to tell you about things they find easy or difficult to do. Give some examples first:
'I often find it difficult to get up early in the morning.'
'I find it quite easy to understand English people.'

Section 2
1. Listening phase, followed by choral repetition of parts of the dialogue, focusing attention on the intonation and rhythm.
2. Short-answer questions:
a) How did Coke speak?
b) What does Hugo sell to any foreign country?
c) How long did Masters stare at the floor before he answered Coke's question 'How did he make you?'?
3. Fluency practice to revise the focal points from Unit 19:
HE MADE ME GIVE HIM INFORMATION
(prompts to replace 'He made' and 'information')
a) some money
b) He asked me
c) a glass of water
d) She told me
e) the report
f) He made

Section 3
1. Silent reading phase, followed by comprehension questions:
a) Why did Masters involve Coke?
b) What did Hugo think would happen to Coke?
c) Why isn't Masters still in the army?
d) How do they send microfilms of secret documents abroad?
2. Listening phase, followed by some choral reading, correct my statements or a completion exercise.
3. Give more examples of sentences using the words *involve, suspect, swallow, stare at* and *pose as*. Ask students to repeat your examples. Then ask them to write a sentence of their own for each of the words.

THE MAN WHO ESCAPED
Episode 22

Unit 22

c

SYNOPSIS: *Masters has agreed to tell Coke everything.*

1 For a moment Coke wanted to pull the trigger. He had never killed anyone in cold blood, but he found it difficult not to hate Masters. Because of him, he had lost four years of his freedom. Because of him everybody thought he was a spy. Somehow, Coke got a grip on himself. Perhaps it was because he knew Masters was his only chance to prove he was innocent, and he knew if he killed him, he would lose that chance.

2 "Let's start at the beginning . . . when you sent me to Epping Forest that night," Coke said in a flat, cold voice.
"That was Hugo's idea. I had nothing to do with it."
"And who is Hugo?" Coke demanded.
"He sells government secrets to any foreign country that's interested. He made me give him information. I didn't want to!"
"Made you? How did he make you?" Coke asked.
Masters stared down at the floor for several seconds before he answered. "He knew things about me. He said he would tell the police about them if I didn't help him."
"What sort of things?" Again, Masters hesitated before answering. "What does it matter? The sort of things that would ruin any man if the police or anyone else found out about them."

3 There were only a few more things Coke wanted to know now. "Why did you involve me in all this?"
"The police suspected someone. We wanted to make them think you were the spy. We knew they would if they found your dead body in a car after a crash with all sorts of secrets in it."
"My dead body?"
"Hugo thought the crash would kill you," Masters said.
"A pity it didn't. You'd still be safe if I were dead!"
Masters swallowed and stared at the floor.
"And why aren't you still in the army? You'd be a lot more useful to Hugo if you were," Coke went on.
"It became too dangerous. Anyway, he still uses me."
"How?" Coke asked.
"We hide microfilms of secret documents in the antique weapons I send abroad. The people we send them to pose as foreign collectors."
Coke had one last question. It was the most important. "Where's Hugo now? Take me to him!"

Unit 22 d

FURTHER PRACTICE

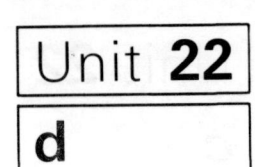

1. Invention Exercise

Write sentences with 'If . . . (did) . . . would (do) . . .':

Example:

PROMPT: that film/it
RESPONSE: If you saw that film, you'd enjoy it.
or: If they went to see that film, they'd enjoy it.

Prompts:

a) by bus/to work earlier
b) that house/some flowers and trees
c) my car/on time
d) a haircut/a job
e) super petrol/much better
f) less/more money
g) better meals/healthier
h) a car/you to London
i) more carefully/fewer mistakes
j) enough money/theatre this evening

2. Conversation

Arthur's secretary has told him she would like to see him about something personal. She has just come into his office.

ARTHUR: Sit down, Miss Bradley. It's something personal, you say?
MISS BRADLEY: Yes. You see, I'm going to get married next month and . . .
ARTHUR: Get married? I didn't know that. Congratulations!
MISS BRADLEY: Thank you, but I'm afraid it means I've got to give in my notice. I'd like to leave at the end of the month.
ARTHUR: Really? I'm very sorry to hear that. Do you intend to stop working altogether, then?
MISS BRADLEY: Oh, no! My fiancé and I want to save up enough for a house and we wouldn't be able to do that if I stopped working right away. And it isn't that I don't like my job here, either. I'd stay if Terry, that's my fiancé, weren't a Canadian.
ARTHUR: A Canadian? I'm sorry, I don't understand. What's that got to do with it?
MISS BRADLEY: Well, we're both going to live in Canada as soon as we get married.
ARTHUR: Oh, I see. What does your fiancé do for a living, by the way?
MISS BRADLEY: He's an engineer. He often says he'd earn far more if he were back in Canada. That's why he wants to go back.
ARTHUR: But engineers are quite well paid here in England. How much does he earn here, then, if I may ask?
MISS BRADLEY: £20 a week.
ARTHUR: Is that all? That's very poor for a qualified engineer. You ought to tell him he'd get far more if he came and worked for us.
MISS BRADLEY: Well . . . er . . . you see . . .
ARTHUR: I mean, I'm sure that if I were a young engineer and if my salary were that low, I'd want to go to Canada, too. Where does he work, by the way?
MISS BRADLEY: Er . . . as a matter of fact, he works here in your factory, Mr Tigers. He's in your motor-design department.

Questions

1. Ask and answer these questions
   a) Why/her notice?
   b) stop working altogether?
   c) fiancé come from?
   d) earn?
   e) Why/back to Canada?
2. What does Arthur say Miss Bradley ought to tell her fiancé?
3. Where does he work?

Practice and Recall

Without looking at the text, see if you can remember how these phrases were used. Then try to make other sentences of your own with the same words.

a) I'm afraid it means
b) my notice
c) It isn't that I . . .
d) for a living
e) by the way
f) as a matter of fact

FURTHER PRACTICE

Unit 22
d

1. Invention Exercise

a) Follow the technique of doing this exercise suggested in earlier Units.

b) As well as calling for the use of 'If . . . did . . ., . . . would do . . .', the exercise also calls for a variety of different verbs. The verbs which could be used are:
for a) *came, went* or *travelled/would get;* for b) *had, owned* or *bought/would plant;* for c) *had, used, went in* or *came in/would get there* or *would arrive;* for d) *had* or *got/would get* or *would find;* for e) *used, had* or *bought/would go* or *would run;* for f) *smoked* or *drank/would save;* for g) *ate* or *had/would be;* for h) *had* or *owned/would drive* or *would take;* for i) *worked, typed, wrote* or *spoke/would make;* and for j) *had/would go to the.*

c) Ask students now to make questions from the same prompts. Note from the examples that this will involve using the prompts the other way round. So, from the prompt 'by bus/to work earlier', we can form the question—
  'Would you get to work earlier if you came by bus?'
Or from the prompt 'that house/some flowers and trees', we can form the question—
  'Would you plant some flowers and trees in the garden if you bought that house?'

2. Conversation

Key Points
1. Meaning, use and intonation of 'Congratulations!' and 'I'm very sorry to hear that'
2. Meaning and use of 'to give in one's notice', '(to) intend to do', 'altogether' (= completely) and 'to save up' (= to save money for a special purpose)
3. Meaning and use and intonation of 'What's that got to do with it?'
4. Use of 'by the way' and 'as a matter of fact'
5. Meaning and use of 'for a living' in 'What does he do for a living?'
6. Revision and practice with the modifier *that* as in 'If my salary were that low, . . .'

Presentation Notes
1. Follow the initial presentation procedure as used with earlier Conversations.
2. *Extra comprehension questions*
   a) When is Miss Bradley going to get married?
   b) What does Arthur say when she tells him?
   c) What does he say when she tells him she'd like to leave?
   d) What is the name of her fiancé and where does he come from?
   e) What does Terry do for a living? How much does he earn?
   f) Does Arthur think Terry gets a high or a low salary?
3. Both Arthur and Miss Bradley use sentences with *if* in the pattern we are practising in this Unit. Ask students if they can remember some of these sentences. Give prompts to help them. For example: able/stop working
   Response: We wouldn't be able to do that if I stopped working right away.
   Prompts:
   a) stay/Canadian
   b) earn/back in Canada
   c) far more/worked for us
   d) young engineer; and salary that low/Canada, too.
4. Ask students to listen once again very carefully to the way in which we say 'Congratulations!' and 'I'm very sorry to hear that.' Ask them to repeat in chorus. Then ask them to use one or the other appropriately to things you say, such as:
   'I've just won £50!'/'My brother's just had a rather nasty accident.'/'I've got that job I applied for!'/'I've got to go into hospital for an operation.'

Unit 22
e/f

e   Summary

1

In order to finalise the reason why, and the types of situation in which, we use this particular kind of Conditional sentence, give more examples of the pattern, ask questions, and then get students to give back the same examples with *if*.

For example:

T: Listen! If I had a lot of money, I wouldn't work.

Questions:

'What do I do?' (Ss: You work.)

'Have I got a lot of money?' (Ss: No, you haven't.)

'Do you think I like working for my living?' (Ss: No, you don't.)

'Why don't you think I like working for my living?' (Pause) and then prompt the response –'Because *if* . . .' (Gesture for response)

Ss: Because if you had a lot of money, you wouldn't work.'

Give a number of sentences of this type to reinforce the use of the pattern. If necessary, also do one or two Simple Substitution Drills here, too, concentrating mainly on the use of the Past form of verbs after *if*.

For example:

HE'D PROBABLY GET A JOB IF HE BOUGHT A NEW SUIT.

a) had a haircut
b) cleaned his shoes
c) stopped smoking so much
d) took more care of his personal appearance
e) shaved off his beard

3

As a final reinforcement phase with *were* and *weren't*, do this transformation exercise:

Example:

T: I say –'I'm busy, so I can't help you.'

You say –'If I weren't busy, I would help you.'

T: I say –'John isn't rich, so he goes to work.'

You say –'If John were rich, he wouldn't go to work.'

a) They aren't here, so you can't speak to them.
b) She is in a hurry, so she can't stay.
c) I'm not very young, so I don't go to pop concerts.
d) He's away on business, so he can't see you.

f   Exercises for homework

3

If you have used the transformation exercise above, go straight on to practise the use of *were* in the common advice situation as given in this exercise. Students should do this completely orally in the classroom. Add others to those in the exercise:

j) A friend who often has bad headaches.
k) A woman who is bored because she stays at home all the time.
l) A man who doesn't earn much money, and who doesn't ask for a rise because he is afraid of his boss.
m) A friend whose car doesn't go very well because he buys cheap petrol.

4

Although this Composition is only *guided* in so far as it sets the situation and the subject, there are nevertheless two things which the students are forced to do:

a) The Composition has to be in the form of a letter, so that students will have to be reminded of the format of a personal English letter – no name of sender (except the signature at the end), the address (commas in the right places, and no underlining of towns etc.), the form of the date, and so on.
b) Because of the situation, they will have to use a considerable number of sentences using *if*, such as –'If I were you, I'd think seriously about . . .'

Unit 22
e/f

e Summary

Focal points in this Unit.

1. a) In this Unit we have practised another kind of Conditional sentence with the word *if:* 'If ... did ..., ... would do'. This is sometimes called the unreal Conditional, because, in a sentence like –
'The job would be easy if that saw weren't broken'
– the fact is that the saw *is* broken, and the job *isn't* easy.
   b) The verb in the *if* half of the sentence is in the Simple Past form of the verb:
'If they *knew*, ...'/'If he *had* a gun, ...'/
'If he *bought* a new suit, ...'
   c) The form of the verb in the other half of the sentence is 'would (do)':
'... they *would start* screaming.'/'... it *would go* faster.'

2. Remember that we only use a comma in the sentence if it begins with *if:*
'If they painted the house, it would look a lot better'.

3. Remember the form of the verb 'to be' in this kind of sentence:
'If I *were* you, I would stay at home.'
We use *were* with all persons: 'If *I were* rich, ...'/'If *he were* in your position, ...'/
'If *they were* here, ...' etc.

f Exercises for homework

1. Do all the exercises on pages 129, 130 and 132.

2. Supply the correct form of the verb in brackets in these sentences.
   a) If you (work) harder, you would earn more money.
   b) She (get) a much better job if she learnt to type.
   c) If I (drink) a bottle of wine, I would be ill.
   d) That house (probably look) very nice if they painted it.
   e) I'd drink a cup of tea if you (make) some.

3. Give advice to the following people. Use: 'If I were you, I'd ...'
   Example:
   A student who doesn't work very hard.
   Advice: If I were you, I'd work a bit harder.
   a) A woman who always goes to bed very late.
   b) A friend who smokes more than 50 cigarettes a day.
   c) A man who is very thin and unhealthy.
   d) A friend with a bicycle that often goes wrong.
   e) A man who is very unhappy in his job.
   f) Someone with very bad toothache.
   g) A person who is trying to open a tin with a hammer.
   h) A friend who has just bought a new car, and the car has just broken down.
   i) A man who wants a job in Sweden, but can't speak Swedish.

4. **Guided Composition**

   A friend of yours has written to you recently to ask your advice about a problem. The problem is that the friend wants to brush up his (or her) English, but doesn't know whether to go to a school in England for an intensive course or to go to evening classes in his (or her) home town. Write a letter advising the friend what you would do.

5. **Transfer Exercise**

   Write down a number of things you would do right away if you won a lot of money.

Unit 23
a
Passive voice in present perfect and past

1
(a) Why/house look better?
(b) Why/window?
(c) Why/gate?
(d) Why/garden?
(e) Who?
(f) When?

2
(a) When/these 3 cowboys?
(b) know who?
(c) How/Tom? How/Dick? How/Harry?

3
(a) Who/Tom's favourite record?
(b) When?
(c) Susan/record?
(d) What/Tom say?

4
(a) What/Tom/policeman?
(b) What/happen? (bumper. headlight.)
(c) policeman's question?
(d) Tom's answer?

5
(a) When/storm?
(b) How much damage? (trees. telephone wires. windows. a roof. a car.)
(c) When/all this?

6
(a) When/Arthur's office?
(b) money?
(c) damage?

Main Teaching-Points
1. Formation and use of the Passive in Present Perfect and Past – *has/have been done* and *was/were done* in statements, positive and negative and questions.
2. Intensive revision of the 'has done' vs. 'did' concepts. (Unit 16.)
3. Concentration on contracted forms '*It's* been broken' and '*They've* been stolen'.
4. Intensive revision and practice of regular and irregular past participle forms in this and earlier Units.

Extra Points and Activities
1. Lexical items *bumper, bent, headlight, favourite* and *damaged* vs. *smashed*.
2. Revision of 'some/any' and 'How much' – especially with Mass noun *damage*.
3. Meaning, use and intonation of 'Well, don't look at me' (situation 3).
4. Meaning and use of *all* in
   a) 'They were all killed' and 'They have all been done' and
   b) 'All we can say is . . .' (situation 2).

Unit 23 a

HAS BEEN DONE/WAS DONE

1

This is the same house we saw in Unit 22. It has been painted. The window has been mended. So has the gate. The garden looks better because some flowers have been planted. We do not know who did these things or even when they were done. All we can say is that they have been done.

1. What has happened to the house?
2. Ask and answer the same question for
   a) the window   b) the gate
3. Why does the garden look better?
4. There are two things we do not know; what are they?

3

Tom's favourite record has been broken. "It's been broken" he said a moment ago.
   "Well, don't look at me. I didn't break it," Susan said.
   "I didn't say you did. All I said was 'It's been broken,'" Tom is saying now.

1. What has happened to Tom's record?
2. What are Tom's exact words when he notices this?
3. What is Susan's answer?
4. What is Tom saying now?
5. Why do you think he does not say "It was broken"?

5

There was a terrible storm during the night. A lot of damage was done. Trees and telephone wires were blown down, windows were smashed and a roof was blown off. A car was even overturned. All this happened last night.

1. Ask and answer questions beginning "What happened to that/those . . . last night?"
2. Ask a question beginning "How much damage . . .?"
3. Suppose you have *just* seen all these things for the first time and perhaps do not know when they happened; what would you say?

2

These three cowboys were all killed a long time ago in Cactus City. We know how they died but not who killed them. All we can say is that Tom was hanged, Dick was shot dead and Harry was stabbed, all in 1877.

1. Correct the statements!
   a) We see the houses of three cowboys.
   b) They were killed a short time ago.
2. What do we know? What do we not know?
3. Ask and answer questions beginning "How was . . . killed?" and "When was . . . killed?"

4

Tom's car has been damaged. He is telling a policeman about it.
   "Look! The bumper's been bent and a headlight's been smashed!"
   "Do you know when this was done, sir?"
   "No. All I know is the car was all right when I parked it here three hours ago!"

1. Ask and answer three questions beginning "Does he know when . . .?"
   a) the headlight   b) the car
   c) the bumper
2. What exactly is he saying about these three things?
3. What is the policeman's question?
4. What is the only thing Tom knows?

6

Arthur's office was broken into this morning. Two typists are talking.
   "Have you heard? Mr Tiger's office has been broken into!"
   "I know. It was broken into this morning."
   "Was any money stolen?"
   "I think so. I know some damage was done."

1. How does the first typist begin the conversation?
2. What does the other one say?
3. What exactly is the question with the words "any money"?
4. Ask and answer questions with these words:
   a) When/the office   b) How much money
   c) A lot of damage

Unit 23 b — FORMATION AND MANIPULATION

1 Pronunciation

BE VERY CAREFUL WITH THE PRONUNCIATION OF THE SHORT FORM OF 'HAS' [z].

i) After words ending like CAT, CAP, BOOK, WIFE, PATH (where the last sounds are unvoiced) 's is pronounced [s].
Example: The cat's [kæts] been found.

ii) After words ending like HEAD, THING, WAVE, TREE, BOY (where the last sounds are voiced, vowels or diphthongs) 's is pronounced [z].
Example: The boy's [bɔiz] been seen.

iii) After words ending like HOUse, GAze, FIsh, CHURch, JUDge the short form *cannot* be used. Instead the full or weak forms must be used.
Example: The house has [hæz] or [həz] or [əz] been painted.

iv) Don't forget to use the weak (unstressed) forms of: was–[wəz] and were–[wə].

2

A	B	C
The window	has ('s) been	mended

i) Look at the situations on page 135 and find words to replace those in boxes A and C. (Of course, you'll have to change box B sometimes.)

ii) Now say or write at least ten sentences.

iii) Now, try to think of five *new* things to replace those in boxes A and C.

iv) Look at this simple dialogue
    A: 'What's happened?'
    B: 'The window's been broken.'

v) Using the words you have found in exercises i and iii, make these short dialogues with the person sitting next to you.
Example: 'What's happened?'
    'My car's been stolen.'

3

A	B	C
Some damage	was	done

i) Make at least five sentences of your own by putting new words in boxes A and C. (Change 'was' to 'were' when necessary.)

ii) Now make those sentences into questions beginning 'When . . .?'

iii) How many questions can you ask with 'When . . .?' about the pictures on page 134?

4

It hasn't	been done	yet

Make sentences using these words:
my watch/repair. the house/sell. window/mend. flowers/plant. radio/switch on. car/clean.

FORMATION AND MANIPULATION

Unit 23 b

1. It will probably take you quite a time to get these points about *'s* across to students, and even longer to make sure that they are all using them properly. For this reason do not be afraid of returning to this section several times until the skill has become automatic. There may well be too much for a student to absorb and use all at once. Break the practice up into two- or three-minute phases during the study of the Formation and Manipulation pages.
A useful oral test of handling the difficulty is to use this sentence as a base form for practice.

   THE [ ] 'S/HAS BEEN SEEN

   Write this sentence on the board using one of the following prompts to fill in the box AFTER you have written the sentence:
   boy, box, car, man, book, fish, train, bird, table, ship, etc. etc.
   Then give the prompts orally and rapidly, getting the students to repeat the complete sentence with the appropriate form of *has* in it.
   If students want to know what the difference is between the '*'s*' form and the weak form [həz], tell them that it is largely a matter of taste when there is a direct choice between the two, as for example: 'The car's been seen' and 'The car has [həz] been seen.' The use may vary from speaker to speaker.

2. Insert a writing phase in the oral practice, but don't make it too long, a minute or two, or two or three sentences is sufficient.
   Exercise i:
   Ask first for oral answers from the situations, then allow students to write down any words they want to, but make sure that their books are closed when they are writing down the words – otherwise it will simply be a matter of copying and will not be of great value.
   Transfer:
   Look around the place you are now teaching in. Get students to make comments on features of that place i.e. The window's been opened/closed, the table's been moved, the blackboard's been cleaned/written on. (Don't practise the negative form yet, that is dealt with in Part 4.)

3. It may help the pacing of this particular part if the students are asked at first to close their books and you give them the questions and prompts orally so that they can become proficient before practising in pairs. Also give the students a chance to ask you questions which you can answer before starting paired work.

4. *Variation:*
   Use the prompts, but to create a simple dialogue like this:
   What's the matter with your watch?
   My watch? Oh, it hasn't been repaired yet.
   or *Oh, it hasn't been repaired yet.*
   or *Well, it hasn't been repaired yet.*
   or *It hasn't been repaired yet.*

Unit 23
C
EXPLOITATION OF THE EPISODE

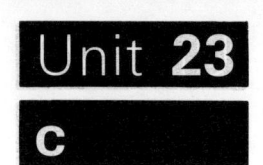

Key Structures and Vocabulary	Suggested Explanations
a) ... was *surrounded* by ... (7)	There were shops and small houses all around Hugo's garage.
b) *At first* Masters did not answer. (15)	See practice below, Section **2**, 2.
c) Masters *went pale* ... (20)	His face lost its colour and went almost white.
d) 'Perhaps I can find *proof* ... (33)	Documents, information, evidence which might show (or prove) that Hugo is a spy.

Special Note:
Although the rest of the material in this Unit practises the Passive only in the Present Perfect ('has/have been done') and the Past ('was/were done'), this Episode includes examples of the Passive in other tenses and forms. They are:
  'He thought Coke *would be killed* ...' (Synopsis)
  'Cars that *had been damaged* were taken there *to be repaired*.' (2)
  'When the last one *had been turned* off ...' (10–11)
  '... where the documents *are kept* before they're sent off.' (13–14)
  '... waiting *to be sent off*?' (26)
  'What if *you're seen* and *caught* ...' (35)

These forms are for recognition, however, and we feel that students' attention should only be focused on them if you think that they could actively practise one or two of them.

Section 1
1. Listening phase followed by short-answer questions:
a) Where was Hugo's garage? (In the North of London.)
b) Why were cars often taken there? (To be repaired.)
c) What documents were also kept there? (Secret documents.)
d) What colour was Masters' Jaguar? (White.) etc.
2. Let students listen to the Section again, asking them to repeat certain parts in chorus.
3. Then ask for information about the text to make them give full-sentence answers:
For example:
a) *Tell me* where Coke, Masters and Kate sat in the car.
b) Tell me what they did when they got to the street.
c) Was the garage already closed or did they have to wait?

Section 2
1. Listening phase, followed by mixed questions:
a) What things have happened to Coke because of Masters?
b) Where are the documents kept? And what about the micro-films?
c) Have any been sent off recently?
d) What did Coke do to *make* Masters answer his questions?
2. To teach and practise 'at first' (line 15), focus students' attention on the sentence, and then ask: 'Did Masters answer later?' The answer is 'Yes, he did', so—'*At first* Masters didn't answer, *but later he did*'. Give other examples like this with 'At [ət] first ...', but later ...'
a) At first I didn't want to go out, but later I did.
b) At first I didn't pay much attention, but later I listened very carefully.
c) At first my father didn't want me to be a teacher, but later he agreed.

Get them to repeat the examples, and then write one or two sentences of their own beginning 'At first ...'

Section 3
1. Silent reading phase. As suggested before, ask students to write some questions to ask other students about the passage.
2. Read the text (or play the tape) for students to listen.
3. Students ask each other the questions they have written.
4. Fluency Practice
KEEP HIM HERE UNTIL I GET BACK
(Prompts to replace 'keep him here' and 'until I get back')
a) until I phone
b) Stay here
c) Wait there
d) until she arrives
e) until lunch is ready
f) Sit in the garden
g) Listen to the radio
h) until it's bed time.

THE MAN WHO ESCAPED
Episode 23

Unit 23

C

SYNOPSIS: *Masters has told Coke that Hugo had planned what had happened to Coke in Epping Forest. He thought Coke would be killed in the crash and that the police would think he was the spy when they found the documents in his car. Coke wants Masters to take him to Hugo.*

1 Masters told Coke that Hugo owned a large garage in the North of London. Cars that had been damaged were taken there to be repaired. It was also where the secret documents Hugo sold were kept before they were micro-filmed and sent abroad.
  They got into Masters' white Jaguar and drove there. Coke sat in front with Masters. Kate sat behind. It was almost evening when they got to the garage. It was at the end of a street and was surrounded by shops and small houses. They parked at the end of the street. People were beginning to close their shops and go home. The garage stayed open until six. Coke sat and watched the lights go off. When the last one had been turned off and the garage was completely dark, Coke turned to Masters again.
  "Now tell me exactly where the documents are kept before they're sent off," he said.

2 At first Masters did not answer. He had become a little braver again. Coke pressed the pistol into his stomach.
  "Because of you, I've been kept in prison for four years. Because of you, my life has been ruined. I'll kill you here and now if you don't answer!"
  Masters looked at the pistol and went pale.
  "They're kept in Hugo's office, in an ordinary file in his desk," he answered. "And the microfilms?" Coke demanded. "They're kept there, too."
  "Do you know if any documents have been sent off recently?"
  "Some were sent last week. I know. I sent them myself," Masters said. "And will there be any there now, waiting to be sent off?" Again Masters hesitated. Coke pressed the pistol even harder into his stomach. "I don't know. There might be. Hugo told me he was going to give me some soon," he said.

3 Coke gave Kate the pistol. She was still sitting behind Masters. "Keep him here until I get back," he said.
  "But what are you going to do?" she asked.
  "Break into that garage if I can. Perhaps I can find proof that Hugo sells these things. If I do, I'll phone the police."
  "But what if you don't? What if you're seen and caught before you can find anything at all?" Kate asked. But Coke had already started walking towards the dark garage. In the dark winter evening, it looked very much like a prison.

Unit 23
d
FURTHER PRACTICE

1. For Comprehension

1) There has been another rail crash in Scotland. The crash occurred last night in freezing fog outside Glasgow. Four people were killed and at least ten people were injured. The railway lines have not yet been cleared and a number of trains have been delayed.

2) Heavy snow has fallen in the North of England. Many roads have been blocked and traffic has been brought to a standstill. One town, Castlepool in Yorkshire, has been completely cut off. Supplies will be dropped into the town by air this afternoon.

3) The office of Mr Arthur Tigers, the prominent industrialist, was broken into during the weekend. A small amount of money was taken and the office itself was left in what the cleaning woman described as 'a terrible mess'. The burglary was discovered by cleaners early this morning. Mr Tigers is away on holiday in South America and has not yet been located.

Questions:

1 a) Where did the rail crash occur?
  b) Were there any casualties in the crash? (killed/injured)
  c) Have the lines been cleared yet?
  d) Are the trains still running normally? (trains/delayed)

2 a) Where has heavy snow fallen?
  b) What are conditions like? (many roads/traffic)
  c) What has happened to Castlepool?

3 a) What happened to Mr Tiger's office during the week-end?
  b) Was any money taken?
  c) How was the office left?
  d) Who was the burglary discovered by? When was the burglary discovered?

2. Conversation

Joe Burns is a famous racing-driver. He is being interviewed on a sports programme.

REPORTER: You've had a very dangerous life, haven't you, Joe? I mean, you've almost been killed several times, haven't you?

JOE: Yes. I suppose that's right.

REPORTER: When was your worst accident?

JOE: I'd say last year. It was during the British Grand Prix. I smashed into a wall. The car was completely ruined and my left leg was broken. Luckily, nobody was killed.

REPORTER: Is that the only time you've been . . . er . . . close to death?

JOE: No. Once, during the Mexican Grand Prix, two cars in front of me had a bad accident. One of them ran into the other. I swerved to avoid them and hit a fence. My car was badly damaged but luckily I wasn't even hurt.

REPORTER: You must enjoy danger. I mean, you wouldn't be a racing-driver if you didn't, would you?

JOE: I don't know about that. I had a very frightening experience quite recently. I was frightened to death! I thought I was going to be killed at any moment.

REPORTER: Really? When was that? During your last race?

JOE: No. It was on my way to this studio. I had to drive through London during the lunch hour.

Questions

1. What has almost happened to Joe several times?
2. When was his worst accident? Describe it! (wall. car. leg.)
3. What happened during the Mexican Grand Prix? (two cars. swerved. his car.)
4. What did Joe think was going to happen to him very recently?
5. When did this last experience take place?

FURTHER PRACTICE

Unit 23
d

1. For Comprehension

a) Ask students to turn their books face down.

b) Read aloud (or play the tape of) all three news items. After students have heard the three items once, just ask them what each was about (i) a rail crash/ii) heavy snow in the North of England/iii) a burglary.) At this point, do not ask any more questions!

c) Read (or play) each item again separately, preparing vocabulary, doing choral reading and asking comprehension questions:
For Item 1: Vocabulary: occur/freezing fog/
  injured/to clear (railway lines)/delayed
For Item 2: Vocabulary: blocked/brought to a
  standstill/cut off/supplies
For Item 3: Vocabulary: a small amount of
  money/cleaning woman/a terrible mess/
  burglary/hasn't been located

d) Get students to work in pairs asking and answering the questions under the text on the student page.

e) Optional completion exercise for consolidation.

f) Optional recall of text from prompts. See if students can give back the complete sentences from these words:
a) four people/ten people
b) railway lines/number of trains
c) Many roads/traffic
d) Castlepool
e) small amount/office itself
f) burglary

2. Conversation

  Key Points
1. Revision of 'has/have done' vs. 'did' concepts together with 'has/have been done' vs. 'was/were done'
2. Use and intonation of 'I suppose . . .' as in 'I suppose that's right'
3. Meaning and use of 'I'd say . . .' as in 'I'd say last year'

4. Vocabulary items 'smash into', 'run into', 'swerve (to avoid something)' and 'fence'
5. Meaning and use of *luckily*
6. Discrimination between *damaged* and *smashed*
7. Use and meaning (and intonation pattern) of 'I was frightened to death!'
8. Discrimination between adjectives of the *frightened/frightening* type (and practice with others like it)

Presentation Notes
1. Follow the same initial presentation procedure as with previous Conversations.
2. *Correct my statements*
   a) Joe Burns is a famous cyclist!
   b) Joe has had a very ordinary life!
   c) His worst accident was three years ago!
   d) His leg was broken in the Mexican Grand Prix!
   e) His most recent frightening experience was driving through Paris!
3. Use these two sentences as a Model to practise *interesting* vs. *interested* etc: 'It was *a frightening experience. I was very frightened.*'
   For example: interesting/interested
   It was an interesting lecture. I was very interested.
   a) interesting/interested
   b) boring/bored
   c) amusing/amused
   d) horrifying/horrified
   e) embarrassing/embarrassed

Unit 23
e/f

e Summary

1 and 2

The important points upon which to focus students' attention in the Summary stage of the lesson are:

a) The formation of the Passive with any tense of 'to be' + *done*. Students will have been reminded of a number of past participle forms throughout the Unit – *broken, hurt, stolen, damaged* etc.
b) The conversational forms of 'It has been'.
c) The unstressed forms:
   [həz] and [əz]   as in 'It has been broken';
   [həv] and [əv]   as in 'They have been stolen';
         [wəz] as in 'It was broken into this morning';
   and [wər] as in 'They were all killed in 1877'.
d) The reinforcement here of the 'has/have done' vs. 'did' concepts, as exactly the same concepts apply when using 'has/have been done' or 'was/were done'.

3

Although we have not focused students' attention on the preposition *by* used with the Passive until now, you might ask students to go back to the presentation situations and ask them to tell you who or what various things have been or were done by; for example, in situation 6, 'Mr Tiger's office was broken into by burglars.'

f Exercises for homework

2

As in some earlier Units, this exercise is really the sort of exercise to be done at home rather in the way of a test, but useful classroom activity can still be done by using some of the sentences for the beginnings of Simple or Progressive Substitution Exercises. For example, with sentence (d):
OUR HOUSE WAS BROKEN INTO LAST WEEK.
a) last Saturday   d) That shop   g) sold
b) The bank   e) last month   h) That cinema
c) last night   f) repainted

3

Once again we have returned to a more controlled type of Composition. Students may well be able now, however, to write short news items of their own, not only based on the items they have read on page 138, but also based more on actual news they have heard on the radio at the time of studying this Unit. Thus it may be possible to combine this exercise with the Transfer Exercise.

Unit 23
e/f

e Summary

Focal points in this Unit.

1. Remember that we form the Passive in English with 'to be + done'. In this Unit we have practised two tenses – 'has/have been done' and 'was/were done'.

2. Remember that we use these two Passive tenses in the same way as we use the Active forms:

   a) *'has/have been done'* + *just, yet, ever, since, for* or no time.
      'The house *has been painted* (since we last saw it).'
   b) *'was/were done'* + *'last night'*, *'yesterday'*, *'3 weeks ago'*, etc.
      'Mr Tiger's office *was broken* into this morning.'

3. We usually use the Passive when we don't know or don't want to say who has done, or who did something. If we use the Passive and still mention the person, however, we use the preposition *by*, as in the third news item on page 138 – 'The burglary *was discovered by cleaners* early this morning.' In this sentence, the burglary is the most important piece of information.

f Exercises for homework

1. Do all the exercises on pages 135, 136 and 138.

2. Supply the correct form of the verb in brackets (has/have been done or was/were done) in these sentences:

   a) The President (be shot) late last night.
   b) There isn't any food left. All of it (be eaten)!
   c) I can't find my car anywhere. I think it (be stolen)!
   d) Our house (be broken into) last week.
   e) Those paintings (be sold) last month for £500 each.
   f) His car (be damaged) in an accident last month.
   g) 'Have you heard? The old police station (be repainted).'
   h) That's a good book. It (be written) by George Orwell.
   i) Because of bad weather yesterday, the traffic on the motorway (be brought) to a standstill.
   j) I (be frightened) to death when I drove through Paris last month.

3. **Guided Composition**

   a) Read the first news item on page 138 again. Use that as a model and write about a bad car crash. Use these prompt words:

      car crash/Bristol//yesterday afternoon/snow storm/near the centre//one old lady/4 other people/2 cars/completely wrecked//not cleared/traffic/held up.

   b) Now read the second news item on page 138, and write a similar article beginning:

      'Heavy rain has fallen . . .

4. **Transfer Exercise**

   Write six sentences about the news today, using the Passive.

   Examples:

   'The President of . . . arrived in . . . today, and was met by the Prime Minister.'

   '. . . was beaten by . . . in the international football match at . . . today.'

Unit 24
a Reported speech

1 
(a) Where/Julia and Jim?
(b) What/she/know?
(c) Julia's question?
(d) How/Jim/know/good restaurant?

2 
(a) How long/restaurant?
(b) Why/Julia/angry?
(c) What/Jim/the place?

3 
(a) Why/Julia/conductor?
(b) Where/money?
(c) Who/next stop?

4 
(a) When/inspector?
(b) What/see?
(c) What/conductor say?

5 
(a) Where/Tom?
(b) What/Susan?
(c) Susan's question: flowers?
(d) Tom's answer? (worry. forget.)

6 
(a) Why/Susan/upset?
(b) What/tell Tom?

Main Teaching-Points
1. Discrimination between *say* and *tell* when reporting what people say, as in 'I *told you* it was . . .' and 'You *said* you would . . .'.
2. Formation of the verb form in reported statements, positive and negative, after 'said' or 'told someone': is → was; know → knew; loves → loved; doesn't (matter) → didn't (matter); has/have done → had done; can → could; will → would.
3. Note the two following points:
   i) Most of the practice here is without the conjunction *that,* since it is often unnecessary in everyday speech;
   ii) We have not practised Reported questions.

Extra Points and Activities
1. Meaning and use of 'upset', 'bus conductor/inspector' and 'it doesn't matter'.
2. Meaning and use of *service* (situations 1 and 2)– Mass noun, no *a*.
3. Revision of '*leave something somewhere*' (vs. *forget*).

| told someone | it was/did
could/would do
had been/had done | / | said | it was/did
could/would do
had been/had done |

Unit 24
a

1

Julia and Jim, her boyfriend, are outside a restaurant. Julia wants to know something before they go in.

"Are you sure it's a good restaurant?"

"Oh, yes!" Jim is saying, "I've been here before. It's very good. I know the owner and I always get good service."

1. Where are Julia and Jim?
2. Correct the statements!
   a) Jim says it is a bad place.
   b) He says he has never been here before.
   c) He says he does not know anyone.
   d) He says he never gets good service.

2

Jim and Julia have been in the restaurant for an hour and they still have not been served. Julia is angry. "You said this was a good place!" she is saying. "You said you had been here before! You said you knew the owner and always got good service!"

1. Where are Julia and Jim?
2. Ask "How long . . .?" and answer.
3. Why is Julia angry?
4. What did Jim say before they came?
   a) good place   b) before
   c) the owner   d) good service

3

It is lucky Julia takes the same bus every morning and knows the conductor. This is their conversation this morning:

"I'm sorry. I've left my money at home."

"It doesn't matter. You can pay tomorrow."

Unfortunately an inspector is going to get on the bus at the next stop.

1. Why is it lucky she knows the conductor?
2. What are her exact words?
3. What are the conductor's exact words?
4. What is going to happen at the next stop?
5. Ask if the conductor knows! (and answer)

4

The inspector got on a minute ago and he wants to see everyone's ticket. Julia is explaining why she has not got one.

"I told the conductor I had left my money at home. He told me it did not matter and that I could pay tomorrow."

1. What does the inspector want to do?
2. What is Julia doing?
3. What did she tell the conductor?
4. What did he tell her?

5

Tom is going into town and Susan wants him to do something for her there.

"It's my mother's birthday tomorrow. Will you get her some flowers in town? She loves roses."

Tom is saying "Don't worry. I'll get her some! I won't forget!"

1. What does Susan want Tom to do?
2. Ask why! (and answer)
3. Ask and answer these questions!
   a) When/birthday
   b) What sort of flowers
4. What is Tom saying?

6

Tom has come back from town but he has forgotten to get the roses. Susan is very upset.

"I told you it was my mother's birthday tomorrow and that she loved roses. You said you would get her some! You said you wouldn't forget!"

1. Ask why Susan is upset! (and answer)
2. What did she tell him?
3. What did he say?
4. Correct the statements:
   a) He said he'd get them tomorrow.
   b) She said her mother's birthday was next week.

Unit 24 b

FORMATION AND MANIPULATION

1 Notice the change:
IS/ARE/DOES

> Jim says 'This *is* a good restaurant'   Jim said it *was* a good restaurant
> Jim says 'I *know* the owner'   He said he *knew* the owner

Now make the same change yourself for these sentences that Jim says. Change them to 'Jim said . . .'
i) 'The food is good.'
ii) 'The waiter speaks five languages.'
iii) 'My boss often goes there.'
iv) 'A lot of famous people eat there.'
v) 'The vegetables aren't fresh.'
vi) 'The meat tastes strange.'
vii) 'The soup has a fly in it.'
viii) 'I don't like this place.'

2 HAS/DONE/DID

> Julia says *either* 'I've left my money at home'   Julia said she *had left* her money at home
> *or* 'I left my money at home'

Now change these statements to sentences beginning 'Julia said . . .'
i) 'I've lost my purse.'
ii) 'I've broken my watch.'
iii) 'I ate earlier.'
iv) 'I knew Susan at school.'
v) 'The manager has already come.'
vi) 'The bus has just left.'
vii) 'The bus left 5 minutes early.'
viii) 'My alarm clock didn't go off.'

3 WILL DO/CAN DO

> Tom says 'I'*ll* get some in town'   Tom said he *would* get some in town
> Tom says 'I *can* do it later'   He said he *could* do it later

Now change these statements to sentences beginning 'Tom said . . .'
i) 'We can buy them later.'
ii) 'I'll remember.'
iii) 'I won't come home without them.'
iv) 'Peter can get them.'
v) 'He'll be home soon.'
vi) 'He won't mind.'
vii) 'Susan will be very angry.'
viii) 'I can't go home without them.'

4 SAY/TELL

Notice that when we want to mention the person we said something to, we use the word *tell*.

> I said I was coming
> I told you I was coming

Now look at pictures 2, 4 and 6 on page 140. Ask questions like 'What did . . . tell . . . earlier?' Answer these questions with: 'He/She told her/him that . . .'

FORMATION AND MANIPULATION

Unit 24 b

Note: You will see from the situations on page 140 that the word *that* after *said* and *told me* has been omitted except in situations 4 and 6 where it is inserted to clarify that the second part is still being reported. However even in these two cases *that* could be omitted without changing the meaning or emphasis of the sentence. Tell students that it is almost entirely a matter of taste and that the word may be included or omitted as they wish. In spoken English *that* is usually (although not always) omitted.

Pronunciation:

Don't forget to remind students to use the weak (unstressed) forms of *was, were, to, have, had*. Introduce the weak (unstressed) forms of the following:
- i) *and* [ənd] if followed by a vowel sound (situation 1 last line) [n] if followed by a consonant sound (situation 1 first line).
- ii) *at* [ət] (situation 3 'I've left my money at home.').
- iii) *can* [kən] (situation 3 'You can pay tomorrow.').
- iv) *could* [kəd] (situation 4 last line).
- v) *that* [ðət] after words like *said, told, thought*.

1. Make part of the exercise work written. First allow all the students to do the exercises orally, then ask them to write down five answers. Check these answers immediately before going on to the next section. If there are any serious errors, do the exercise orally again, then ask students to write out the other five answers.

Fluency Practice:

(FIRST DO WITHOUT 'THAT', THEN WITH 'THAT' [ðət].)

JIM SAID THE FOOD WAS BAD
1. good
2. expensive
3. She said
4. the car
5. fast
6. dangerous
7. new
8. the restaurant

2. Make quite sure that students understand that when 'have done' and 'did' are put into reported speech they both become 'had done'. (Try this one with *that* [ðət].)

JULIA SAID THAT SHE HAD GOT TIRED
1. left home
2. gone home
3. gone by bus
4. eaten it
5. seen him
6. been there
7. first met him in London
8. in Paris

3. (Don't forget *would* [wəd] and *could* [kəd].)
HE SAID HE WOULD DO IT
1. see me
2. tell him
3. ask her
4. could
5. get one
6. buy one
7. would
8. phone me

4. (Don't forget *was* [wəz].)
I TOLD HIM I WAS TIRED
1. hungry
2. she was
3. She told him
4. them
5. going to bed
6. said
7. sleepy
8. unhappy

Unit 24

c

EXPLOITATION OF THE EPISODE

Key Structures and Vocabulary	Suggested Explanations
a) a drainpipe (3)	Pipe down the side of a building for carrying off water from the roof.
b) a sky-light (6)	Window set in a roof to let smells out and light in.
c) peer (7)	Look carefully and narrowly. If you have to look at or for something in the dark, and you haven't got a light, you have to peer.
d) lost consciousness (17)	Everything went black, he became unconscious and fell to the floor.
e) ... *tied* to a chair ... (21)	They had made Kate sit on a chair, and had tied her to it with rope so that she couldn't move.
f) slap (27)	Hit someone with the palm of your hand.
g) stammer (29)	Tell students to notice *how* Masters said the sentence: 'But ... but ... Pl ... please.' If a person is frightened, and repeats small words or parts of words, he stammers.
h) ... do the job properly ... (38)	*Properly* here means *correctly*; without any mistakes.

Section 1
1. Listening phase followed by short-answer questions:
a) What sort of training had someone told him was useful in many ways? (An Army training.)
b) What did Coke climb up to get to the roof? (A drainpipe.)
c) How did he get down into the garage from the roof? (Through a sky-light.)
d) What was parked directly underneath the sky-light? (A lorry.) etc.
2. After students have heard or read the text a second time, either a) get them to complete sentences: For example:
T: 'Once, a long time ago, someone had ...'
Ss: 'told him that an Army training was useful in many ways'
or b) ask questions to get full-sentence answers: For example: 'How did Coke manage to get onto the roof of the garage?'

3. Ask students to think of more sentences with 'manage to'. For example: 'I missed the bus, *but I managed to get to work on time*. I took a taxi.'

Section 2
1. Give students 2 or 3 minutes to read this Section silently.
2. Tell them to turn their books face down, and then give a number of statements, some correct, some incorrect, to which students simply respond 'That's right' or 'That's wrong'. Here are some examples:
a) Someone grabbed Coke from behind.
b) The same person shone a powerful light into his eyes.
c) He had a pain in his leg.
d) He lost consciousness. etc. etc.
3. Revision practice with 'did/was doing' based on line 19. Invention exercise:
Example: station/train = when I got to the station, the train was leaving.
a) home/telephone
b) work at 5/others/leave
c) bus-stop/bus
d) concert/first piece on the programme

Section 3
1. Listening phase. Just before they hear this Section, tell students to listen carefully and to notice how these words are used: *stammer, worry, interrupt* and *properly*. Immediately after they hear the Section, ask if they can remember the sentences these words were used in. If they cannot, read the sentences and get the class to repeat them in chorus.
2. Finally, ask students to read back through the whole page, finding all the examples they can of Reported Speech. Then ask them to say exactly what the person said in each case.

THE MAN WHO ESCAPED
Episode 24

Unit 24

C

SYNOPSIS: *Coke has gone to Hugo's garage. He has told Kate he is going to try to find proof that Hugo is a spy.*

1   Once, a long time ago, someone had told him that an Army training was useful in many ways. Coke knew now that that was true. There was a drainpipe at the back of the garage that led to the roof, and Coke managed to climb up it. He had often done such things in the army.
   There was a window in the roof, or a sky-light, as it is called. It was closed but not locked. Coke managed to get it open and then peered down into the dark garage below. There was a lorry parked almost directly underneath. He jumped down onto it. It was completely dark inside the garage itself.
   "Masters told me the secrets were kept in the office, but where's the office?" he wondered. Suddenly he heard a sound behind him, and realised he was not alone in the garage.

2   Before he could turn around, someone grabbed him from behind and someone else shone a powerful light into his eyes. He was blinded. Then, there was an explosion of pain in his head. He realised, just before he lost consciousness, that what had happened in Epping Forest was happening to him all over again.
   When he came to again, he was lying on the floor of the garage. It was at least an hour later. He heard loud voices. When he opened his eyes, he saw Kate tied to a chair. Four men were standing above him. One of them was Masters, looking pale and frightened. He was listening to a short blond man. Coke knew it must be Hugo himself. Hugo was shouting.
   "I told you you were a fool . . . and idiot! Do you believe me now?" he demanded. Masters tried to say something but could not.
   Hugo slapped him across the face.
   "I asked you if you believed me now?" he shouted.

3   "But . . . but Hugo. Pl . . . please listen to me!" Masters stammered.
   "I told you someone had phoned me and had asked me to look at some pistols! I told you it was an old, blind man but you said there was nothing to worry about!" Masters said.
   "No, I didn't. I asked you what you wanted me to do about it, you idiot!" Hugo roared. Suddenly, one of the other men interrupted.
   "What did you say we were going to do with the girl and Coke?" he asked.
   "I said we were going to kill them! And I said we were going to do the job properly this time!" Hugo answered.

Unit 24 d

FURTHER PRACTICE

1. For Comprehension

Read this newspaper article and answer the questions.

When Mr Long, the Minister of Education, was asked about the school-leaving age again at a press conference yesterday, he said that there were still a large number of problems to be considered. One reporter asked what the Government was going to do about children who wanted to go out and earn money at the age of 16. Mr Long said that he realised a lot of young people wanted to stand on their own two feet early in life, and he thought this was very good. But he added that he felt young people needed as much education as we could give them: so the Government was seriously considering raising the school-leaving age some-time in the future.

Questions:

a) Where was Mr Long yesterday?
b) What was he asked about?
c) What did he say about 'a large number of problems'?
d) Write down the exact words which one reporter used when he asked Mr Long about the school-leaving age.
e) What did Mr Long say a lot of young people wanted to do?
f) What did he think about this?
g) What did he say about young people and education?
h) What is the Government doing now?

2. Conversation

Most of Tom's students at the Technical College are between 15 and 18. Most of them are serious students, too. A few are not. Tom is talking with one of the few now. She has just told him she can't come to school tomorrow because her grandmother is ill.

TOM: You've already missed far too many lessons this term, Miss Grey.

MISS GREY: Yes, I know I have. I'm very sorry. You see, I have these terrible headaches and . . .

TOM: Headaches? Only last week you said you had trouble with your stomach!

MISS GREY: Er . . . well . . . I have headaches *and* trouble with my stomach, you see. That's why I've been absent so often.

TOM: And you often come to college late as well. Yesterday, for instance, you . . .

MISS GREY: Yes. I'm very sorry about that. You see, my alarm clock didn't go off and . . .

TOM: Your alarm clock? But you told me yesterday that the bus had broken down!

MISS GREY: Oh, did I? Well . . . er . . . I suppose I just forgot to say that my alarm clock hadn't gone off, either.

TOM: It's a very complicated story, if you'll forgive me saying so, Miss Grey. Now, tell me again why you want tomorrow off.

MISS GREY: Well . . . er . . . you see . . . my grandfather's ill. He's in hospital and . . . and he's going to have an operation. I want to visit him.

TOM: Oh, I see. So your grandfather's ill as well.

MISS GREY: As well? I . . . I don't understand.

TOM: Neither do I, Miss Grey. When we began this conversation, you said your *grandmother* was ill. And you didn't say she was going to have an operation! You said she'd already had one! And by the way, you also said she was in an old people's home, not in a hospital!

Questions

1. Miss Grey has been absent a lot. What reason did she give for this last week?
2. What reason did she give for being late yesterday?
3. What did she say about her grandmother earlier?

Practice

Go through the conversation again. Find all the examples you can that begin with 'you said' or 'you told me'. Then say what the *exact* words were at the time Miss Grey first said these things.

FURTHER PRACTICE Unit 24 d

1. For Comprehension

a) Preview and explain any necessary vocabulary items. The following might be new items: 'the school-leaving age'/'a press conference'/'to go out and earn'/'to stand on their own two feet'/'he added'/'(to) consider'/'(to) raise the school-leaving age'
When previewing such items, don't simply give an explanation of the word or phrase. Ask the students to repeat the item once or twice. Give an example: 'All children in England must stay at school until they are 16. After that, they can leave and start work. The school-leaving age is 16.' Then give another sentence or two for completion using the item: 'In (name a country) children must stay at school until they are 17, because 17 is . . . (pause for response – and gesture for response) . . . Ss: the school-leaving age'.

b) Read the article aloud; student books are face down.

c) Optional choral reading phase.

d) Comprehension questions – use those on the student page.

e) Optional silent reading phase.

f) Get students to work in pairs and to ask each other the questions under the article.

2. Conversation

Key Points

1. Use of *most* (with no *the*) as in 'Most of Tom's students' and 'Most of them'
2. Meaning and use of *far* as a modifier with *too* as in 'far too many lessons'
3. Use of 'as well' at the end of a positive sentence: 'You often come to college late as well.' Use of *either* at the end of a negative sentence: '. . . my alarm clock hadn't gone off either'
4. Meaning and use of 'for instance' and 'by the way'
5. Use of the introductory 'I suppose I . . .'
6. Meaning and use of the expression '. . . if you'll forgive me saying so' when making a remark which could be offensive
7. More practice with 'Neither do I' after a negative statement
8. Reinforcement of Reported Speech

Presentation Notes

1. Follow the initial presentation procedure as for previous conversations.
2. Choral repetition of parts of the Conversation – male students take Tom's part, female students Miss Grey's part. (Later, if the composition of the class allows, get students to work in pairs doing the same thing.)
3. Ask the questions on the student page, and add others; for example:
    a) How many lessons has the girl missed? (Far too many.)
    b) What sort of story does Tom think it is? (A complicated story.)
    c) Who did the girl say was ill just before the conversation? (Her grandmother.)
4. Discrimination exercise for 'far too many' and 'far too much'.
    Give a number of words and ask students to add 'far too many' or 'far too much'.
    Example: T: I say *work*. You say 'far too much work'.
    I say *jobs*. You say 'far too many jobs'.
    chairs/furniture/cheese/sandwiches/students/homework/milk/tea etc.
5. Give some remarks of a slightly offensive nature and ask students to repeat them adding the expression '. . . if you'll forgive me saying so.' For example:
    T: 'That colour doesn't really suit you.'
    Ss: 'That colour doesn't really suit you, if you'll forgive me saying so.'
    a) That doesn't sound very logical.
    b) That's not quite right.
    c) Your hair's a bit long.
    d) You smoke too much.

Unit 24
e/f

e Summary

1
To give final revision and summary activity at this stage, why not give this simple transformation exercise orally:
T: I say – 'He said he would be late' – *me*
You say – 'He *told me* he would be late.'
a) She said she was ill. (him)
b) I said I couldn't go. (them)
c) They said they were tired. (me)
d) You said you would be there. (her)
e) He said he had done it. (us)

2
Perhaps the best way to summarise the concept governing the form of the verb which follows *said* or *told me* is in fact to look once again at the many examples throughout the Unit, turning sentences from or into Reported Speech. In fact, Exercise 2 in the Exercises for Homework asks for just this activity, and might well be done orally in class as part of this summary.

f Exercises for homework

3
Before students are asked to do this exercise at home, it might be advisable to clear up any problems which students might have with vocabulary items, such as 'weather forecast', 'announcer', 'changeable' and 'stable'. First of all, ask if they can use these words in a sentence of their own. Then give examples. Here is one which asks for immediate feedback:—
T: I wanted to know what the weather was going to be like today, so I listened to the radio this morning. I listened to the *weather forecast*. What will you listen to this evening if you want to know what the weather is going to be like tomorrow?
Ss: The weather forecast.

4
Once again, this Composition is far less controlled than were the Compositions in earlier Units. If you feel that the particular class you are teaching will find this too demanding as it is, give them ideas and more prompts for them to use, for example:
   missed the bus/very sorry/alarm clock, either/ late breakfast/no change for bus/had to walk/ bus-strike.

Unit 24

e/f

e Summary

Focal points in this Unit.

1. Remember how we use the two verbs *say* and *tell*–
   a) 'I said' is simply followed by the reported information.
   b) We add a person ('him/her/us/John', etc.) after 'I told'.
   Compare these two sentences:
   '*He said* he would be late.'
   '*He told me* he would be late.'

2. Remember that the verbs in the past of the sentence after *said* or 'told him' goes back one tense from what was said originally:

   'am/is' become 'was', and 'are' becomes 'were'; 'knows/know' become 'knew', and 'doesn't/don't know' become 'didn't know'; 'did' and 'has/have done' become 'had done'; 'can' becomes 'could', and 'will' becomes 'would'.

   Example:
   Original statement: 'I don't know.'
   Reported statement: He said he didn't know.

f Exercises for homework

1. Do all the exercises on pages 141, 142 and 144.

2. Change these sentences into Reported Speech.
   Example:
   'I'm French,' she said.
   You write: She said she was French.

   a) 'I like tea,' she said.
   b) 'I hate it,' he told me.
   c) 'John never wears a dark suit,' she said.
   d) 'I think that is a very good idea,' he said.
   e) 'You can't get very far,' Baxter told him.
   f) 'You are a free man,' Baxter told Coke.
   g) 'I'll buy a new suit if I get the job,' the young man said.
   h) 'My car has broken down,' he told the mechanic.
   i) 'I'm going to give up smoking!' he told the doctor.
   j) 'I've just been to the optician's,' he told me when I saw him a minute ago.
   (Begin: When I saw him a minute ago, . . .)

3. Read this passage and write down exactly what they said:

   When I woke up, I asked my wife what the weather was like. She looked out of the window and said it was raining very heavily, but she thought it was going to get brighter. Later, when we were having breakfast, I listened to the weather forecast. The announcer said that the weather in the south would probably be very changeable. He added that the Meteorological Office couldn't say when the weather would become more stable. My wife said that was fine because she had decided to stay at home and do some cooking.

4. **Guided Composition**

   Read the Conversation between Tom and Miss Grey on page 144 again. Think of an excuse for being late for school, college or work. Write down how you told a friend what happened when you used the excuse to your teacher, lecturer or boss. Report what you said and what he or she said. Begin like this:

   'I was late for school (or college or work) again last . . . When I went in, . . .'

5. **Transfer Exercise**

   Report a number of things that different people have said to you in the past couple of days. For example, if a friend said to you yesterday: 'I'm going to a party tonight.' – you write:

   'My friend told me he was going to a party last night.'

Unit 25
a Past conditional

1
(a) time now?
(b) Tom/play?
(c) Why not?

2
(a) When/Fred?
(b) other soldier's questions?
(c) Fred's answer?

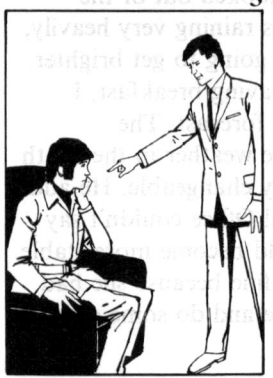

3
(a) When/Peter/from Canada?
(b) job yet?
(c) What/Tom/say?
(d) What/Peter/think?

4
(a) Why/Jones/dead?
(b) Jones' explanation?

5
(a) When/old lady/road?
(b) What/if/driver?
(c) What/2nd and 3rd cars?
(d) What/if/old lady/careful?

Main Teaching-Points
1. Formation and use of Past Conditional sentences
    a) positive: 'He *would have watched* it *if he had had* the time'.
    b) questions: '*Would you have joined if* you *had known*?'
    c) negative: '*If he hadn't been* a stranger, I *wouldn't have been* so suspicious'.
2. Concentration on the weak forms normally used in the structure, [əv] in 'would *have* done', and [(h)əd] in '(If I) *had* done.'
3. Short answers 'Yes, I would/No, I wouldn't' etc. in reply to a 'Would you have done?' question.
4. Contraction '*d* in both '*I'd* (= would) *have done*' and '*I'd* (= had) *done*'.

Extra Points and Activities
1. Revision of 'would do . . . if did' (situation 1).
2. Practice with the pattern 'have a lot of work to do'.
3. Meaning and use of 'swerve' and 'lose one's temper' (situation 5).
4. Revision of *ago* and *yet* (situation 3).

146

Unit 25a

WOULD HAVE DONE IF HAD DONE

1
It is 9 o'clock. Susan has just asked "Aren't you going to watch the play?" Unfortunately Tom has a lot of work to do. "I would if I had the time" is his answer.

It is 11 o'clock. The play is over. Tom did not watch it. He would have watched it if he had had the time.

1. What is Susan's question at 9?
2. What is Tom's answer?
3. What can we say about Tom at 11?

2
Fred joined the army 6 months ago. At that time he did not know how hard life was going to be for him. Another soldier has just asked him a question.

"Would you have joined if you had known?"
"No, I wouldn't" is Fred's answer.

1. What happened 6 months ago?
2. What was it that Fred did not know then?
3. What is the other soldier's question and what is Fred's answer?
4. Correct the statements:
   a) He would still have joined if he had known.
   b) He knew how hard life was going to be.

3
Peter came back from Canada six months ago. He has not found a job yet. His brother Tom often tells him:

"You would have found a job long ago if you had looked harder!"

Peter often says: "Perhaps it would have been better if I'd stayed in Canada!"

1. Ask and answer the questions!
   a) When/from Canada?
   b) a job yet?
2. What does Tom often tell Peter?
3. What does Peter often say?

4
We saw this scene earlier. When Sherriff Jones came into the bar, a stranger made a sudden move. Jones shot him dead. The man only wanted to look at his watch. Jones is explaining

"I'd never have shot him if he hadn't made a sudden move. If he hadn't been a stranger, I wouldn't have been so suspicious."

1. Why was Jones so suspicious?
2. Ask and answer a question with 'if'! (suspicious/a stranger?)
3. What did the stranger do when Jones came in?
4. Ask another question with 'if' and answer! (shot him/sudden move)

5
A few seconds ago, that old lady suddenly stepped into the road. The first car would have killed her if the driver had not stopped just in time. Unfortunately, the second car crashed into him and the third car swerved and hit the curb. The first driver has lost his temper, the second driver has damaged both cars and the third has knocked down a lamp-post. None of this would have happened if the old lady had been careful. Unfortunately the damage has been done now.

1. What happened a few seconds ago?
2. Make as many sentences as you can beginning "If the old lady had been careful . . ."
3. Ask as many questions as you can like this: "Would the first driver have stopped so suddenly if the old lady hadn't stepped into the road?" (and answer)

Unit 25 b

FORMATION AND MANIPULATION

1 Pronunciation

i) Notice the pronunciation of *have* in the last sentence of situation 1, page 147 'He would have [(h)əv] (sometimes written *would've*) watched it if . . .'

ii) Notice the pronunciation of *had* in the last line of situation 1, page 147, where the word *had* occurs twice.
The first *had* may be pronounced in its short form ('d) or weak form [(h)əd]. BUT THE SECOND 'HAD' MUST BE STRESSED (i.e. in its full form).
Example: '. . . if he had had ['d hæd] or [əd hæd] or [həd hæd] the time.'

2

A	B	C	D	E
He would have	watched it	if	he'd	had the time.

i) Think of words to replace those in boxes B and E. You'll find some in the situations on page 147 and also in the other conditional situations on page 129.

ii) Look at this simple dialogue:
'Did he watch it?'
'No, he didn't, but he would have watched it if he'd had the time.'

iii) Now, using the words you have found in exercise i, make at least ten examples of the dialogue in exercise ii. You should do this orally with the person sitting next to you and also write down a few examples (two or three).

3

A	B	C	D
Would you have	joined	if you had	known?

i) By using pages 147 and 129 again, find words to replace those in boxes B and D. (You can, of course, change 'you' in A and C.)

ii) With the words you have found in exercise i, write or ask at least ten questions like the example above.

iii) Now practise asking the same ten questions starting with *if*.
Example: If you had known, would you have joined?

4

A	B	C	D
If he hadn't	been a stranger	I wouldn't have	been so suspicious.

i) Think of other words to go in boxes B and D.

ii) Change 'he' and 'I' in boxes A and D as necessary.

iii) First write or say at least ten sentences using the words you have found in exercises i and ii.

iv) Now, write the same sentences, or some new ones starting with box D.
Example: I wouldn't have been so suspicious if he hadn't been a stranger.

FORMATION AND MANIPULATION

Unit 25 b

1. To get the students really proficient at producing the correct sounds, it is necessary to drill them thoroughly. Simple repetition is sufficient. Say the following sentences one at a time and get students to repeat both in chorus and individually.
   He would *have* come. Pronounced both [əv] and [həv].
   If he *had had* the time. Pronounced ['d hæd], [həd hæd] and [əd hæd].

2. After the exercises.
   Further rapid oral invention exercise. Give the following prompts:
   Did he come?/interested.
   Did she wait?/want to.
   Did they phone?/any news.
   Did you get the letter?/Postman come.
   Did it snow?/colder.
   Did you see him?/go there.
   to elicit the following conditional sentence form:
   He would have come if he had been interested.

3. To extend the use of this section, the following prompts can be given either orally or written on the blackboard:
   begin work/tired.
   bring friend/ill.
   build new house/very expensive.
   buy that car/£1,000.
   catch train/arrive late.
   choose diamond/cheap.
   do that/know.
   drink beer/ill.
   drive to London/sleepy.
   fly to Paris/enough money.
   learn Spanish/enough time.
   Write this short dialogue on the blackboard.
   A: I didn't begin work after all.
   B: Yes, but *would* you have begun work if you'd had the time?
   Keep the second part 'if you'd had time' as a constant part of the response and give the first part of the dialogue based on the prompts above.

   e.g. *I didn't bring my friend after all.*
   Expected response: *Yes, but would you have brought him if you'd had time?*

4. Make some of the exercise work oral. Ask students to give you prompts which you can write up on the blackboard. (Write them in columns corresponding to the position of the words in the structure, i.e. words for box A should be on the left of the blackboard etc.) When sufficient words have been collected, ask students to form sentences orally, either individually choosing their own prompts or in chorus using prompts indicated by you. Now, remove or cover the prompts on the blackboard and allow students to write down some of the sentences. The challenge provided is very low if students merely have to copy down from the blackboard because the urgent pace of the oral formation of sentences is lacking. Use oral work for sentences both starting with box A and with box D. Substitution drills (fluency practice) are not really suitable here because of the length of utterance.

Unit 25

c

EXPLOITATION OF THE EPISODE

Key Structures and Vocabulary	Suggested Explanations
a) seize (Synopsis)	grab or catch hold of.
b) knock out (Synopsis)	hit someone so hard he becomes unconscious.
c) a shark (2)	large, very dangerous fish (often man-killers).
d) 'I'd never have *got you into all this* (10)	I'd never have involved you . . .
e) trapped (11)	In a trap, with apparently no escape.
f) 'You'd never have *bothered* us . . .' (13)	You wouldn't have worried us again, or been a cause of trouble to us.
g) *protect (one's) property* (24)	If a person tries to damage my house (my property), I will try to stop him, because I want to *protect* my property.
h) . . . the others were led away. (35)	Focus attention on this past form of *lead*.

Note: Focus students' attention on the examples of the Past Conditional in the episode – lines 4, 8, 10, 13 and 33. Get them to repeat these examples, and after the episode has been studied in detail, ask them to make more sentences with the Past Conditional about this and previous incidents throughout the story (see also Guided Composition, page e/f).

Section 1

1. Listening phase followed by questions:
   a) Why couldn't Coke get up?
   b) Do you think Coke had a headache?
   c) Why did Hugo become suspicious?
   d) Why did Coke make 'such a stupid mistake'? etc.
2. Invention exercise based on 'Coke tried to get up but his hands were tied'.
   Example: out/door locked = He tried to get out but the door was locked.
   a) in/all the windows shut
   b) in/hall crowded
   c) a ticket/all sold out
   d) car/tyres flat
   e) money/bank closed
   f) a letter/typewriter broken
3. Give lines 8–15 as a short dictation, remembering to use natural stress and intonation, as on the tape.

Section 2

1. Silent reading phase, during which students write down some questions to ask other students later.
2. Listening phase, stopping occasionally to let students complete a sentence:
   For example: 'No, Hugo. Look up here!' a voice roared from . . . (pause) . . .
   Ss: . . . 'the sky-light above'.
3. Comprehension questions
   a) How many policemen came in through the door?
   b) What did Hugo do when he saw them?
   c) How did Baxter get into the garage?
   d) How many more policemen came in the same way? etc.
4. Now let students ask each other questions they wrote down while reading.

Section 3

1. Listening phase followed by questions:
   a) Why are the police there now?
   b) How long has Baxter been on the roof?
   c) Why doesn't Baxter believe that Hugo only wanted to 'protect his property'?
   d) Did Hugo have time to protest?
2. Fluency practice (Revision)
   I'VE BEEN UP THERE FOR HALF AN HOUR
   a) ten minutes
   b) down here
   c) an hour
   d) We
   e) ages
   f) at this college
   g) He
   h) there

THE MAN WHO ESCAPED
Episode 25

Unit 25

c

SYNOPSIS: *When Coke broke in, Hugo and two other men seized him and knocked him out. That was at least an hour ago.*

1 Hugo saw that Coke had come to. Coke tried to get up but his hands were tied. His head hurt terribly. Hugo looked at him like a shark inspecting his dinner.
"We would never have become suspicious if you hadn't used Masters' white Jaguar," he said. "When we saw it parked halfway up the road, we decided to wait and see what would happen. Then, after we got you, we went out and got your girl friend," he continued.

Coke knew he would never have made such a stupid mistake if he had not been so tired. He had not slept properly for days. He looked at Kate. "I'd never have got you into all this if I hadn't asked you for help," he said to her. He was trapped. It seemed there was nothing he could do and nobody who could help him. Hugo took out a revolver. "You'd never have bothered us again if I'd used this four years ago," he said. He came closer to Coke and aimed the revolver carefully at his head.

2 Suddenly there was a terrific crash as three policemen broke down the side door of the garage. Hugo turned round and gaped. "No, Hugo. Look up here!" a voice roared from the sky-light above. Suddenly, everybody stopped. Nobody made a move. Then Baxter dropped through the sky-light, which was still open, and onto the lorry and finally to the ground. Three more policemen followed him. Baxter walked over to Hugo.
"Your revolver, please," he said simply.

"I was only protecting my property," Hugo answered. "This man broke in. That girl helped him. Send him back to prison!" Baxter listened and smiled. "Certainly, but only after you've given me that revolver," he replied. Hugo handed it to him silently.

3 The policemen around Baxter and at the door suddenly moved forward and seized Hugo, Masters and the three men.
"We've followed you everywhere for days; that's why we're here now," Baxter told Masters. Then he turned to Hugo and said "And I've been up there for half an hour. I've heard everything you've said. Also, I think you'd have phoned us an hour ago, when Coke first broke in, if you'd only wanted to protect your property!"

Before Hugo could protest, he and the others were led away. Baxter helped Coke to his feet. "What we know now already proves you were innocent," he said. Then he untied Coke's hands. Coke was a free man again.

THE END

Unit 25 d

FURTHER PRACTICE

1. Invention Exercise

Make sentences with '... would/wouldn't have done ... if ... had/hadn't done.'

Examples:

1) PROMPT: that film/time
   RESPONSE: I would have seen that film if I had had the time.
   or: We would have gone to see that film if we had found the time.
2) PROMPT: accident/asleep
   RESPONSE: He wouldn't have had an accident if he hadn't been asleep.
   or: I would have had an accident if I had fallen asleep.

Prompts:

a) that job/a haircut
b) so suspicious/a stranger
c) some flowers/enough money
d) football/leg
e) the book/the film
f) married/the right man
g) train/bus/so slow
h) money/cleverer
i) university/intelligent
j) job/carefully

2. Conversation

Peter, Tom and Susan have all gone to a very expensive restaurant. They've just finished eating.

SUSAN: I must say your roast beef looked even better than my steak. I think I would have ordered that if I'd known.
TOM: Do you mean you didn't like the steak?
SUSAN: Oh, no. Just the opposite. I enjoyed my meal very much.
PETER: Well, I'm glad you both did because I'm going to pay. Waiter!
TOM: Don't be silly, Peter! We can't let you do that.
SUSAN: No, we can't. I mean, we'd never have come to such an expensive place if you'd told us that earlier.
PETER: No, let me pay. I insist.
WAITER: Yes, sir. Did you call?
PETER: Yes, the bill please.
WAITER: Er ... do you want the bill separate or all together?
PETER: All together, of course.
WAITER: Very well, sir. I'll be right back.
PETER: What a strange question. It's my long hair. He'd never have asked me that otherwise.
TOM: What do you mean?
PETER: Oh, it's just that all these snobbish waiters think people like me never have any money.
SUSAN: He's coming back now.
PETER: Oh, good Lord!
TOM: What's wrong?
PETER: I ... I'm terribly sorry. I've just noticed ... I haven't got any money. I must have left it at home. I ... er ... I'd never have offered to pay if I'd known. Do you think you could lend me a few pounds, Tom?

Questions

1. What would Susan have done if she had known about the roast beef?
2. What does Susan say when Peter tells them he is going to pay?
3. What does the waiter ask when Peter asks for the bill?
4. What is Peter's comment?
5. What does Peter notice just before the waiter comes back?
6. What does he ask Tom to do?

FURTHER PRACTICE

Unit 25 d

1. Invention Exercise

a) Follow the same technique of doing this drill as in previous Units.

b) The prompts once again call for a variety of verbs (and other linguistic items which collocate with the prompts). It is impossible to list all the collocations which could be used, or all the combinations of 'would/wouldn't have done . . . if . . . had/hadn't done' which students might think of. Therefore we have given three or four possible sentences for a), and for the rest of the prompts, a number of possible collocating verbs:

for a) *He would have got that job if he had had a haircut.*
I wouldn't have got that job if I hadn't had a haircut.
He wouldn't have found that job if he hadn't gone to the hairdresser's for a haircut.

for b) *been* or *become/been, seen* or *met;* for c) *sent, bought* or *given (her)/had;* for d) *played/broken;* for e) *read* or *bought/seen* or *watched;* for f) *got/met;* for g) *caught* or *missed/been;* for h) *saved, won, kept* or *made/been;* for i) *gone to/been;* and for j) *got* or *found/looked*.

c) With all responses, make certain students use the unstressed forms [(h)əv] in 'would *have* done' and [(h)əd] in 'if I *had* known'.

d) With all responses, too, ask students to say what *really* happened. For example, 'I would have seen that film if I had had the time – But I didn't see the film because I didn't have the time.'

2. Conversation

Key Points
1. Meaning and use of *must* in the introductory phrase 'I must say . . .'
2. Reinforcement of 'would have done if . . . had done'
3. Revision of *let* as in 'We can't let you do that', and 'Let me pay'
4. Meaning and use of 'I insist' when offering to pay for a drink or a meal
5. Meaning and use of 'separate' and 'all together' in the restaurant situation
6. Revision of *otherwise*
7. Meaning and use of past supposition *must* as in 'I must have left it at home'
8. Revision of 'Do you think you could . . .' and 'Could you lend me a few pounds?'

Presentation Notes
1. Use the presentation procedure outlined in earlier Units; but this time, before you read the conversation or play the tape, ask students to listen carefully for the three sentences with *if.* Then, as soon as they have heard the conversation, ask them for the sentences. Give these prompts if they find it difficult to remember:
   a) ordered b) expensive place c) offered to pay
2. Read (or play the tape) again for choral repetition and completion exercise alternating.
3. *Paired Practice phase* with this part of the conversation:
   Tom: 'Do you mean you didn't like the steak?'
   Susan: 'Oh, no. Just the opposite. I enjoyed my meal very much'.
   Prompts: (to replace 'the steak' and 'my meal')
   a) 'From Russia With Love'/the book
   b) the Beaujolais/the wine
   c) the singing/the opera
   d) the orchestra/the concert
4. Recall exercise for whole sentences (intonation important) from these prompts:
   a) silly!   c) strange question
   b) pay. insist.   d) sorry. money. at home.

Unit 25
e/f

e Summary

1

As a final revision and summary stage, do the following transformation exercise with the class. This is to remind them not only of the positive statements with this Conditional pattern, but also of negative statements and questions.

T: I say – 'I would have gone there if I had known that.'

You say – *I wouldn't have gone there if I had known that.*

and – *Would you have gone there if you had known that?*

a) He would have met her if he had gone to the dance.
b) They would have seen it if they had stayed at home.
c) You would have enjoyed it if you had seen it.
d) She would have found a job if she had waited.
e) He would have joined if he had known.

N.B. Whilst revising the focal point, focus students' attention once again on the unstressed forms [(h)əd] in 'If I *had* stayed . . .' and [(h)əv] in '. . . would *have* watched', and [d] in 'I'd never have done . . .' and 'if I'd known.'

4

Do the following final aural discrimination exercise. Write up on the blackboard –

1		2
I'd have done	and	(if) I'd done

– and then give the following (and other) phrases and ask the class to say whether they are like 1 or 2:

we'd have seen/we'd seen/they'd been/I'd have gone/she'd have noticed/you'd have read/I'd read/he'd stayed/he'd have stayed

Make certain that in phrases like 'we'd have seen', you use the unstressed [(h)əv]. Also ask students to add the word *if* when they hear a phrase like 'I'd done'.

f Exercises for homework

2

As suggested in an earlier Unit with an exercise of this type, students can already be encouraged to make these sentences *real* and *true*, as well as the sentences in the Transfer Exercise.

3

Here are some further items for purely aural/oral work:
f) A friend who bought a very large house, and who only has a small family.
g) A girl who married a travelling salesman and who is now very unhappy because he is away so often.
h) A friend who took the first job he found, and now doesn't like it.
i) A person who tried to read a very long English novel, and who is now very bored with it.

4

Since we have set very little work on the episode in the student pages of the book, this particular exercise should encourage students to go back over some of the story and thus revise many of the patterns and vocabulary items which have been used in it. If you have set reading homework at various times on the Episode, this will be the time to ask students to try to re-read the whole story and make a short summary, including as many sentences of the 'If he hadn't done . . .' type as they can.

Unit 25 e/f

e Summary

Focal points in this Unit.

1. In this Unit we have practised another kind of Conditional sentence with the word *if*:
   'If . . . had done, . . . would have done.'
   This is sometimes called the Past Conditional because when we use it, we are always talking about the past. Like the other Conditional sentence we practised in Unit 22, however, this is also *unreal*. In a sentence like 'I'd never have shot him if he hadn't made a sudden move', the fact is that the stranger actually made a sudden move, and the sheriff shot him!

2. Remember that the verb in the *if* half of the sentence is in the Past Perfect tense:
   'If I *had stayed* at home, . . .

3. Remember that the verb in the other half of the sentence is 'would have done':
   'If I had stayed at home, I *would have watched* that programme on television.'

4. Remember that the shortened form of both *would* and *had* is *'d*. Look at this sentence:
   '*I'd* never have done that if *I'd* known.'
   (I would)   (I had)

f Exercises for homework

1. Do all the exercises on pages 147, 148 and 150.

2. Complete these sentences:
   a) If I had known, . . .
   b) We wouldn't have gone there . . .
   c) If we hadn't been in such a hurry, . . .
   d) I wouldn't have asked them . . .
   e) If the prices hadn't gone up so much, . . .

3. Make comments to the following people. Use 'I wouldn't have . . . if I had been you.'
   Example:
   A friend who failed an exam because he wasted time.
   Comment: *I wouldn't have wasted so much time if I had been you.*

   a) A person who paid £500 for a car that was only really worth £250.
   b) A friend who went on a 3-week holiday, but who spent all his (or her) money in the first week.
   c) A man who has a bad headache this morning because he drank too much at a party last night.
   d) A friend who went for an interview for a job and wore an old sweater and jeans and not a smart suit. (The interview was for an office job.)
   e) A friend who was arrested by the police because he was involved in a violent political demonstration.

4. **Guided Composition**
   Look at these two sentences:
   'Coke went to Epping Forest. If he hadn't gone to Epping Forest, the three men wouldn't have attacked him.'
   Now write about other incidents from 'The Man Who Escaped' and say what the consequences would or wouldn't have been if . . . Here are some reminders:
   a) the old lady's cottage
   b) the motor-bike incident
   c) Kate's flat
   d) 'The Green Rider'

5. **Transfer Exercise**
   a) Do you remember sentences like 'I had no idea it was going to be so crowded'? We practised a lot of sentences like this in Unit 20. Write some true sentences using 'would/wouldn't have done . . . if . . . had done' + 'was/were going to'.
   Examples:
   I wouldn't have gone to the football match if I had known it was going to be so boring./We wouldn't have booked a table at that restaurant last night if we had realised how bad the service was going to be.
   b) Write a number of true sentences about yourself, friends or relatives, like this:
   'I watched a film on television last night, and it was terrible! I wouldn't have watched it if I had known.'

Irregular verbs

INFINITIVE	PAST TENSE	PAST PARTICIPLE	INFINITIVE	PAST TENSE	PAST PARTICIPLE
be	was	been	lend	lent	lent
beat	beat	beaten	let	let	let
become	became	become	lie	lay	lain
begin	began	begun	light	lit	lit
bend	bent	bent	lose	lost	lost
bite	bit	bitten	make	made	made
blow	blew	blown	mean	meant	meant
break	broke	broken	meet	met	met
bring	brought	brought	put	put	put
build	built	built	read	read	read
burn	burnt	burnt	ride	rode	ridden
buy	bought	bought	ring	rang	rung
catch	caught	caught	rise	rose	risen
choose	chose	chosen	run	ran	run
come	came	come	say	said	said
cost	cost	cost	see	saw	seen
cut	cut	cut	sell	sold	sold
dig	dug	dug	send	sent	sent
do	did	done	set	set	set
draw	drew	drawn	shake	shook	shaken
dream	dreamt	dreamt	shine	shone	shone
drink	drank	drunk	shoot	shot	shot
drive	drove	driven	shut	shut	shut
eat	ate	eaten	sing	sang	sung
fall	fell	fallen	sink	sank	sunk
feed	fed	fed	sit	sat	sat
feel	felt	felt	sleep	slept	slept
fight	fought	fought	slide	slid	slid
find	found	found	smell	smelt	smelt
fly	flew	flown	speak	spoke	spoken
forget	forgot	forgotten	spend	spent	spent
freeze	froze	frozen	stand	stood	stood
get	got	got	steal	stole	stolen
give	gave	given	stick	stuck	stuck
go	went	gone	strike	struck	struck
hang	hung	hung	swear	swore	sworn
have	had	had	swim	swam	swum
hear	heard	heard	take	took	taken
hide	hid	hidden	teach	taught	taught
hit	hit	hit	tear	tore	torn
hold	held	held	tell	told	told
hurt	hurt	hurt	think	thought	thought
keep	kept	kept	throw	threw	thrown
know	knew	known	understand	understood	understood
lay	laid	laid	wake	woke	woke/woken
lead	led	led	wear	wore	worn
lean	leant	leant	win	won	won
learn	learnt	learnt	write	wrote	written
leave	left	left			